Reconnoitring Russia

Reconnoitring Russia

Mapping, exploring and describing early modern Russia, 1613–1825

Denis J. B. Shaw

First published in 2024 by
UCL Press
University College London
Gower Street
London WC1E 6BT

Available to download free: www.uclpress.co.uk

Text © Author, 2024
Images © Author and copyright holders named in captions, 2024

The author has asserted his right under the Copyright, Designs and Patents Act 1988 to be identified as the author of this work.

A CIP catalogue record for this book is available from The British Library.

Any third-party material in this book is not covered by the book's Creative Commons licence. Details of the copyright ownership and permitted use of third-party material is given in the image (or extract) credit lines. If you would like to reuse any third-party material not covered by the book's Creative Commons licence, you will need to obtain permission directly from the copyright owner.

This book is published under a Creative Commons Attribution-Non-Commercial 4.0 International licence (CC BY-NC 4.0), https://creativecommons.org/licenses/by-nc/4.0/. This licence allows you to share and adapt the work for non-commercial use providing attribution is made to the author and publisher (but not in any way that suggests that they endorse you or your use of the work) and any changes are indicated. Attribution should include the following information:

Shaw, D. J. B. 2024. *Reconnoitring Russia: Mapping, exploring and describing early modern Russia, 1613–1825*. London: UCL Press.
https://doi.org/10.14324/111.9781800085909

Further details about Creative Commons licences are available at
https://creativecommons.org/licenses/

ISBN: 978-1-80008-592-3 (Hbk)
ISBN: 978-1-80008-591-6 (Pbk)
ISBN: 978-1-80008-590-9 (PDF)
ISBN: 978-1-80008-593-0 (epub)
DOI: https://doi.org/10.14324/111.9781800085909

Reconnoitring Russia

Mapping, exploring and describing early modern Russia, 1613–1825

Denis J. B. Shaw

First published in 2024 by
UCL Press
University College London
Gower Street
London WC1E 6BT

Available to download free: www.uclpress.co.uk

Text © Author, 2024
Images © Author and copyright holders named in captions, 2024

The author has asserted his right under the Copyright, Designs and Patents Act 1988 to be identified as the author of this work.

A CIP catalogue record for this book is available from The British Library.

Any third-party material in this book is not covered by the book's Creative Commons licence. Details of the copyright ownership and permitted use of third-party material is given in the image (or extract) credit lines. If you would like to reuse any third-party material not covered by the book's Creative Commons licence, you will need to obtain permission directly from the copyright owner.

This book is published under a Creative Commons Attribution-Non-Commercial 4.0 International licence (CC BY-NC 4.0), https://creativecommons.org/licenses/by-nc/4.0/. This licence allows you to share and adapt the work for non-commercial use providing attribution is made to the author and publisher (but not in any way that suggests that they endorse you or your use of the work) and any changes are indicated. Attribution should include the following information:

Shaw, D. J. B. 2024. *Reconnoitring Russia: Mapping, exploring and describing early modern Russia, 1613–1825*. London: UCL Press. https://doi.org/10.14324/111.9781800085909

Further details about Creative Commons licences are available at https://creativecommons.org/licenses/

ISBN: 978-1-80008-592-3 (Hbk)
ISBN: 978-1-80008-591-6 (Pbk)
ISBN: 978-1-80008-590-9 (PDF)
ISBN: 978-1-80008-593-0 (epub)
DOI: https://doi.org/10.14324/111.9781800085909

For Andrea, our children and grandchildren

Contents

List of figures	ix
List of text boxes	x
Preface	xi
Acknowledgements	xiii
Publisher's note	xvi
Note on translation, transliteration and place names	xvi
About the author, by Jonathan Oldfield	xvii

1	Introduction: geographical endeavour in early modern Russia	1
2	Russian geographical endeavour before Peter the Great (sixteenth and seventeenth centuries)	29
3	'The Great Designs of the Tsar': the era of Peter the Great (c. 1694–1725)	57
4	The post-Petrine period: the Academy of Sciences, the 1745 atlas and the Great Northern Expedition (1725–62)	87
5	The era of Catherine the Great (1762–96): a new age of imperial expansion	117
6	Widening horizons: geographical endeavour at the end of the 'long eighteenth century' (1796–1825)	147
7	Conclusion	175

Glossary	183
References	185
Index	197

List of figures

1.1 Russia in the late-eighteenth century showing natural features. 9
1.2 Isaac Massa's map of European Russia in the mid-seventeenth century. 10
1.3 Russian and Soviet territorial expansion from the late-fifteenth century to 1991. 12
1.4 Russia in the late-eighteenth century showing natural vegetation. 15
1.5 D. W. Meinig's scheme of European imperial expansion applied to Russia and the USSR. 17
2.1 Larger towns in mid-seventeenth century European Russia. 36
2.2 Russia's southern frontier in the late-sixteenth century showing principal towns, defensive lines and Tatar tracks. 38
2.3 Voronezh district in the early-seventeenth century. 44
3.1 A simplified version of the Mengden-Bruce map of south European Russia (1699). 63
5.1 Late-eighteenth and early-nineteenth century Russian expansion into Ukraine and the southern European steppe. 118
5.2 The province of Voronezh in the late-eighteenth century. 123
6.1 Introductory page of volume three of Afanasii Shchekatov's 'Geographical Dictionary of the Russian State', Moscow, 1804. 165

List of text boxes

2.1 Extract from the *Verst-Book* indicating towns, routes and distances in the neighbourhood of Moscow, probably dating from the 1680s.   47
2.2 Extract from the *Description* (c. 1667) indicating the capitals of principal states, their distances from Moscow and the routes to access them.   48
2.3 Title and Source – see Text Box 2.2 above.   48

List of figures

1.1 Russia in the late-eighteenth century showing natural features. 9
1.2 Isaac Massa's map of European Russia in the mid-seventeenth century. 10
1.3 Russian and Soviet territorial expansion from the late-fifteenth century to 1991. 12
1.4 Russia in the late-eighteenth century showing natural vegetation. 15
1.5 D. W. Meinig's scheme of European imperial expansion applied to Russia and the USSR. 17
2.1 Larger towns in mid-seventeenth century European Russia. 36
2.2 Russia's southern frontier in the late-sixteenth century showing principal towns, defensive lines and Tatar tracks. 38
2.3 Voronezh district in the early-seventeenth century. 44
3.1 A simplified version of the Mengden-Bruce map of south European Russia (1699). 63
5.1 Late-eighteenth and early-nineteenth century Russian expansion into Ukraine and the southern European steppe. 118
5.2 The province of Voronezh in the late-eighteenth century. 123
6.1 Introductory page of volume three of Afanasii Shchekatov's 'Geographical Dictionary of the Russian State', Moscow, 1804. 165

List of text boxes

2.1 Extract from the *Verst-Book* indicating towns, routes and distances in the neighbourhood of Moscow, probably dating from the 1680s.   47
2.2 Extract from the *Description* (c. 1667) indicating the capitals of principal states, their distances from Moscow and the routes to access them.   48
2.3 Title and Source – see Text Box 2.2 above.   48

Preface

Early in the morning of a grey November day in 1969 I arrived by train at Voronezh railway station in what was then the USSR to be greeted by a small group of fellow British exchange students, who guided me to the student hostel which was to be my base for the next twelve months. My purpose in coming to Voronezh was to gather library and archival materials for a doctoral thesis on the Russian settlement of the southern steppe in the early modern period. The Soviet authorities who administered the academic exchange, however, had seemingly overlooked the fact that Voronezh had been on the front line for a period in the Second World War and, partly because of that, its university library and archival holdings were sparse. In the event, the authorities fortunately proved generous in allowing me to spend as much time as possible in Moscow, making use of the capital's rich historical sources. And so the eventual thesis was saved.

The events of that November day (which as I recall culminated in a boozy party with some Russian students to celebrate my arrival) proved to be the start of an academic journey that has occupied the whole of my subsequent career. My focus on the historical geography of Russia soon broadened into a series of studies of other geographical and environmental problems in that country, but historical geography has remained my first love or, as one celebrated American geographer called it, 'the apple of my eye'. And the early modern period, when Europeans set out to discover the world, proved to be especially attractive.

This book, which reflects my longstanding interests in Russian colonization, empire and state-building, focuses on how the Russians set out to discover Russia. Its significance lies not only in the fact that its attention centres upon the building and scientific study of what became one of the world's greatest empires, but also the fact that that empire was built overland and not, as was the case with most European empires, overseas.

Several Russian scholars, and most notably Dmitrii Lebedev in the 1940s and 1950s, and Olga Aleksandrovskaya in the 1980s, have written comprehensive studies of the growth of geographical knowledge and understanding of Russia's expanding empire in the early modern period. Lacking the opportunity to spend extensive periods of time in Russian libraries and archives, my study is inevitably less all-encompassing than theirs. I have, however, emphasized three points which are underemphasized or even ignored in their work. First, I have attempted to place the development of geographical understanding or science into its political, social and economic context in keeping with a modern view of the history of science. This contrasts with a traditional view, which regards science as a purely objective and autonomous activity. Second, I have stressed the interconnectedness of the different facets of geographical practice, such as mapping and exploration, as responses to problems posed by space, all part of what I have termed 'geographical endeavour'. And third, I have introduced a comparative dimension whereby Russian geographical endeavour is compared with what was going on elsewhere in Europe at the same time. Again this contrasts with scholars like Lebedev and Aleksandrovskaya, whose studies tell us little or nothing about the outside world.

I regard this book as a contribution to the history of geographical thought and practice in the early modern period, a field which has so far attracted relatively few devotees. I also see it as a contribution to Russian history, approached perhaps from a rather unusual angle. Until now I had no idea that this would be the ultimate fruit of something which began so long ago on a Russian railway platform on a grey day in November.

Acknowledgements

I owe a huge debt of gratitude to the many friends, colleagues and institutions who have made this book possible. First and foremost I wish to thank Janet Hartley, who heroically read through the entire book at what proved to be a difficult time for her. Janet provided much advice, help and encouragement, and kept me on the straight and narrow when I was tempted to get lost in an esoteric world of spells and amulets (Janet will know what I mean). Thank you, Janet. You are a star!

I also thank other friends who kindly read and commented on individual chapters: Roger Bartlett, Simon Dixon, David Moon and Charles Withers. Many others have also contributed in different ways. The late Will Ryan gave much advice on sources and Russian terminology while the book was being written. Of the many Russian scholars to whom I am indebted for their help and advice in recent years I should like to thank Olga Aleksandrovskaya, Alexandra Bekasova, Nikolai Dronin, Alexei Kraikovskii, Julia Lajus, and Alexei Postnikov. Others who have sadly passed away include Alexei Karimov and Natalya Sukhova. Of Western scholars I should like to mention Tony Cross, Jim Gibson, Paul Keenan, Jon Oldfield, Maureen Perrie, Andreas Renner, Margret Schuchard, Erki Tammiksaar and Barbara Wiley. The passing of Lindsey Hughes, talented specialist on Peter the Great and so much else, came as a great shock to many of us. From the more distant past I particularly wish to mention the late Tony French (R. A. French) of UCL, Bob Smith (R. E. F. Smith) of Birmingham University, and Vladimir Zagorovskii (V. P. Zagorovskii) of Voronezh State University for their advice, correction and encouragement. Although they are no longer with us, their scholarship continues to inspire.

More generally I am most grateful for the stimulation and friendship provided by members of the Study Group on Eighteenth-Century Russia at their annual conferences and international meetings over many years. Without the encouragement provided by the Group this book might never have seen the light of day.

None of the above scholars is responsible for any mistakes or misapprehensions to be found in this book. For these I thank only myself.

Librarians and archivists at many institutions have guided me through the wealth of sources available for this study. In the United

Kingdom I have benefited from the help provided by the British Library (especially to Daniel Wilkinson), the Bodleian Library Oxford, the University of Birmingham library (especially Nigel Hardware) and the Royal Geographical Society. In Russia, the Russian National Library and the Library of the Russian Academy of Sciences in St Petersburg have provided much help and advice, as has the Russian State Library in Moscow. Elsewhere I am indebted to the National Library of Finland in Helsinki (especially to Irina Lukka) and, in the United States, to the Library of Congress and the New York Public Library. With regard to archives I should particularly thank the archivists of the Russian State Archive of Ancient Acts and the Russian State Historical Archive.

The final writing of this book was greatly hindered by events surrounding the COVID-19 pandemic and by Putin's unconscionable war on Ukraine. I was therefore forced to rely heavily on online sources at that point. I found those of the British Library, the Boris El'tsin Presidential Library in St Petersburg and the Russian State Library especially valuable, and wish to thank those libraries and their personnel for making such materials available. At the same time I must apologize to readers for the fact that these distressing events made it impossible to consult other important materials which are not available online.

Over the years my research has been underpinned by funding from numerous agencies. My gratitude goes to the UK Arts and Humanities Research Council, the University of Birmingham, the British Academy, the British Council, the Royal Geographical Society and the Leverhulme Trust.

Since the research for this book has extended over many years, parts of it have inevitably involved reusing some of the materials I have published earlier, albeit modified in various ways. I wish to thank the following publishers for their permission to do this:

Elsevier for permission to reuse parts of the following:
Shaw, D. J. B. 1983. 'Southern frontiers of Muscovy, 1550–1700'. In *Studies in Russian Historical Geography*, edited by J. H. Bater and R. A. French, vol. 1: 118–42. London: Academic Press.
Shaw, D. J. B. 1996. 'Geographical practice and its significance in Peter the Great's Russia', *Journal of Historical Geography* 22: 160–76.
Shaw, D. J. B. 1999b. '"A strong and prosperous condition": The geography of state building and social reform in Peter the Great's Russia', *Political Geography* 18: 991–1015.

Shaw, D. J. B. 2005. 'Mapmaking, science and state building in Russia before Peter the Great', *Journal of Historical Geography* 31: 409–29.

Taylor and Francis for the use of a modified version of Figure 4 from:
Shaw, D. J. B. 1989. 'The settlement of European Russia during the Romanov period (1613–1917)', *Soviet Geography* 30/3: 207–28.

The publishers of *Studies in the History of Biology* kindly granted permission to reuse some of the following:
Shaw, D. J. B. 2010. 'Utility in natural history: Some eighteenth-century Russian perceptions of the living environment', *Istoriko-Biologicheskie Issledovaniya* [Studies in the History of Biology] 2/4: 35–50.

Similarly, the publishers of *Slavonic and East European Review* kindly allowed me to use a modified version of:
Shaw, D. J. B. 1991. 'Settlement and landholding on Russia's southern frontier in the early seventeenth century', *Slavonic and East European Review* 69/2: 232–56.

The Study Group on Eighteenth-Century Russia is to be thanked for permission to reuse portions of the following essay:
Shaw, D. J. B. 2021. 'The transition to "Enlightenment exploration": Russian expeditions to Siberia and the Far East in the late seventeenth and early eighteenth centuries'. In *Magic, Texts and Travel: Homage to a scholar, Will Ryan*, edited by J. M. Hartley and D. J. B. Shaw, 227–44. London: Study Group on Eighteenth-Century Russia.

Finally, I am grateful to Indiana University Press for permission to use material from:
Steller, G. W. 2020. *Eastbound through Siberia: Observations from the Great Northern Expedition by Georg Wilhelm Steller*, translated and annotated by M. A. Engel and K. E. Willmore. Bloomington: Indiana University Press.

Some publishers requested that specific wording be used in connection with their granting of permission to use copyright material. This will be found in footnotes or captions at the appropriate place in the book.

Isaac Massa's map of European Russia (Figure 1.2) is reproduced by permission of the British Library board.

I am indebted to Martin Brown, who drew many of the maps with skill and efficiency.

I owe a special debt of gratitude to Pat Gordon-Smith at UCL Press whose ever-cheerful and encouraging comments and directions made finishing the final stages of the book a pleasure rather than a burden. I also thank Elliot Beck and other staff members at UCL Press for their assistance, and also the anonymous readers for their correction and advice.

For their constant love and support I thank my wife and family, to whom I dedicate this book.

Publisher's note

Very sadly Denis Shaw died on 5 March 2024 just as this book was entering the production process. UCL Press is very grateful to Professor Janet Hartley for subsequently acting as the author's proxy during production in resolving editorial queries and checking proofs.

Note on translation, transliteration and place names

All translations from Russian-language sources are by the author unless otherwise noted. Transliteration is based on the British Standard system, without diacritical marks. Apart from the names of places which have long been anglicized in the English-language literature (for example, Moscow, St Petersburg, Siberia), place names are rendered in the form in which they generally appeared in the early modern period. In quotations from seventeenth- to nineteenth-century English translations, some spellings have been updated.

About the author

Until his death in March 2024 Denis J. B. Shaw was an Honorary Senior Research Fellow at the University of Birmingham, where he had formerly been Reader in Russian Geography.

Denis gained his BA (Hons) and PhD degrees from UCL before joining the University of Birmingham in 1971. His early research, funded by Hayter and British Council Academic Exchange Studentships, explored the development of Russia's frontier region during the seventeenth and eighteenth centuries. This interest in Russia's historical geography broadened during subsequent decades to embrace developments during later centuries.

He published numerous articles on the historical and cultural geography of Russia and the Soviet Union. His books include: *Planning in the Soviet Union* (with Judith Pallot, 1981), *Landscape and Settlement in Romanov Russia, 1613–1917* (with Judith Pallot, 1990), *Russia in the Modern World* (1999) and *The Development of Russian Environmental Thought* (with Jonathan Oldfield, 2015).

Following retirement in 2010, he was an Honorary Senior Research Fellow at the School of Geography, Earth and Environmental Sciences, University of Birmingham. His activities were underpinned by grants from the British Academy and the Arts and Humanities Research Council (AHRC), with a focus on the history of the geographical sciences in Russia and the former Soviet Union. This work has included significant collaborations with environmental historians from the UK, Russia and the United States.

Jonathan Oldfield

1
Introduction: geographical endeavour in early modern Russia

> *I love my country in the way that Peter the Great taught me to love it.*
> Petr Chaadaev, 1837

This book is about how the Russians came to know Russia. It focuses on 'those practices – observing, mapping, collecting, comparing, writing, sketching, classifying, reading, and so on – through which people came to know the world' (Withers 2007, 12). More precisely, it concerns those geographical practices through which the territory of the Russian state and empire, and to a lesser degree the rest of the globe, became known to the country's rulers and its educated public.

As intimated by the epigraph to this chapter, a key moment for this book is the reign of Peter the Great (1682–1725). The noted Russian writer and philosopher Petr Chaadaev regarded Peter's reign as a turning point in the history of his country, a time when Russia threw off the shackles of its medieval past and adopted a new, more progressive role, one open to the influences of the outside world, and of Europe and the West in particular (Kohn 1962, 50–1). Writing in 1837, Chaadaev declaimed:

> One hundred and fifty years ago the greatest of our kings – the one who supposedly began a new era, and to whom, it is said, we owe our greatness, our glory, and all the goods which we own today – disavowed the old Russia in the face of the whole world. He swept away all our institutions with his powerful breath; he dug an abyss between our past and our present, and into it he threw pell-mell all our traditions. He himself went to the Occidental countries and made himself the smallest of men, and he came back to us so much

the greater; he prostrated himself before the Occident, and he arose as our master and our ruler. He introduced Occidental idioms into our language; he called his new capital by an Occidental name; he rejected his hereditary title and took an Occidental title; finally, he almost gave up his own name, and more than once he signed his sovereign decrees with an Occidental name.

Chaadaev's contemporaries and subsequent writers engaged in heated debates about whether Peter's policies had had positive or negative consequences for Russia's long-term development. In the present book I shall adopt a more nuanced stance on Peter's reign than that taken by Chaadaev, but I do agree with him that the reign represented a significant break with the past. The book will focus on geographical practices, or what I shall call geographical endeavour, over the period between 1613, when the Romanov dynasty assumed power (but with some attention paid to the preceding era) and 1825, the conclusion of Alexander I's reign, or what is often termed the end of Russia's 'long eighteenth century'. Hence it will focus on the period between the inauguration of the dynasty to which Peter belonged and end at the point immediately before the onset of the precipitate changes that characterized the nineteenth century – the building of the railways, the Emancipation of the Serfs (1861) and the initial industrialization and urbanization of Russia. Chronologically, Peter's reign is thus the period around which the book pivots.[1]

Chaadaev's emphasis on the significance of Peter the Great's reign points to a central feature of the book – the comparative dimension. Peter's reforms derived from his admiration of a series of Western developments, and these he strove to emulate in Russia, adapting them to the very different circumstances prevailing in his homeland. We cannot understand Russian geographical endeavour from Peter's time (and even to a limited extent before Peter) without placing it in a broader European context. Throughout the book, therefore, explicit reference is made to this broader context.

The principal question to be addressed in this book is: by what means did Russian geographical endeavour reveal and explain to Russians the variable character of the territories which formed their expanding realm? Related questions include: how far did Russian geographical endeavour inform Russians of the character of the globe as a whole, and to what extent was Russian geographical endeavour distinctive? Finally: how far did Russian geographical endeavour inform Europeans of the nature of Russian territory and of Russia's place in the world? Of course, I am aware that these questions are far too broad to tackle in a single volume, but I do at least hope to build on earlier work relating to such themes and to open up new questions for future research.

Whilst the book will consider many different types of geographical endeavour over the period, I make no pretence to be systematic or comprehensive. That would be impossible in a volume of such length. Rather, in aiming to provide a general framework for understanding the nature of geographical endeavour, and describing how it changed through time, I particularly emphasize scholarship and episodes that appear to me to be especially significant. No doubt my choice will disappoint or displease some readers. But by seeking to place selected aspects of the Russian story into an international context I hope to show how far that story was distinctive and how far Russia's experience was just part and parcel of a common endeavour in the early modern period.[2]

Geographical endeavour in the early modern period

In what sense were the kinds of knowledge and activities to be examined in this book 'geographical'? The early modern period was for the most part a time before the formulation of the strictly defined scientific disciplines familiar today. Only in the early-nineteenth century were the specialized disciplines we now know organized with their own scientific societies, professional journals and university departments. Geography was a latecomer in the field. Chairs and departments of geography began to multiply in Europe only from the 1870s and 1880s, frequently accompanied by sharp disagreements about the scope and aims of the discipline. In Russia, the first department (*kafedra* or chair) of geography was founded at Moscow University in 1885.

However, this is not to suggest that no 'geography' was taught in European universities prior to the late-nineteenth century. The word 'geography', or 'writing about the earth', is Greek in origin and, following the rediscovery of a number of classical geographical texts, notably Ptolemy's *Geography*, during the Renaissance, the subject was taught in various forms in European universities and also inscribed in print in the form of gazetteers and geographical dictionaries (see, for example, Mayhew 2001; Withers and Mayhew 2002; Withers 2006; Stock 2019).[3] The actual content of 'geography' was far from well-defined, however. Scholars have emphasized the fact that early modern geography was characterized by two rather different traditions: a mathematical tradition derived from the Greco-Roman mathematician and geographer, Claudius

Ptolemy (c. 100–c. 170 CE), devoted to mapping and the identification of locations on the earth's surface, and a descriptive, textual tradition deriving from the Greek geographer Strabo (c. 64 BCE–c. 24 CE), dedicated to describing the differences between places. The problem was that, in the attempts to classify the sciences that were so popular in the eighteenth century, geography's place was uncertain since the two traditions were by no means closely linked.[4] This uncertainty has been perpetuated in the work of modern historians of science. Thus the fourth volume of the monumental *Cambridge History of Science*, which considers eighteenth-century science, finds no place for geography (Porter, 2003).[5] Other subjects, like mathematics, astronomy, experimental physics, chemistry and the life and earth sciences are included despite the fact that they too were only in the process of formation at the time. Geography's absence also characterizes other histories of science.[6] At most, such histories may devote a chapter to discovery and exploration, as in Porter's volume cited above. Geography's status in the early modern period may therefore have been especially uncertain.[7]

Be that as it may, this book is centrally concerned with a set of interrelated ideas and practices which, for reasons to be discussed, can be labelled 'geographical'. As noted earlier, the focus of this book is on those processes 'through which people came to know the world'. In classical and medieval Europe geography had been a mixture of myth and empirical experience (Kimble 1938; Hannam 2009; Chekin 2006; Kivelson 2008; Mel'nikova 1998). Thus European understanding of the world, and especially of its more distant parts, was strongly influenced by ancient and religious authority as well as by numerous myths and legends. The celebrated Hereford *mappa mundi*, or world map, for example, which depicts Jerusalem in the centre of the world, is a picture of the world as seen from a Christian point of view. However, at the same time Europeans were frequently obliged to undertake spatial exercises of a practical kind involving territories closer to home. One thinks here of Roman methods of centuriation, surveying lands designed for the planting of new colonies and the settlement of veterans, or of William the Conqueror's *Domesday Book* (1086), an inventory of the land and wealth of the Conqueror's recent acquisition of England. With the onset of the Renaissance in the fifteenth century, however, things began to change – the early modern era was a period when territory and space assumed an entirely new significance, requiring their systematic exploration, survey and control. This was the great age of discovery and exploration, when Europeans set out to explore the globe as a whole, to map the extent of its lands and seas and to describe their form and character. In other words, while the mythical never entirely lost its significance, a new emphasis was now placed on the empirical – the idea that scientific knowledge should be based on observation and experience rather than on received tradition and ancient authority.

A central argument of this book is that such practices as mapping, land survey and exploration, although usually considered by scholars under separate headings, are in fact all the interlinked product of this new empirically based perspective on the world – a product I have termed *geographical endeavour*. Although this novel perspective became particularly apparent across Western Europe from the late-fifteenth century, in Russia's case, because of the particular circumstances prevailing there, it only manifested itself from Peter the Great's time. However, as will become clearer later, echoes of the tendency first appeared in Russia before Peter.

What were the reasons for the new significance attaching to territory and space? Scholars have pointed to a range of factors that worked together towards this end, many of which are interlinked. They include commercialism, or the rise of the capitalist economy, growing competition between states leading to a greater emphasis on defence, the need to demarcate and defend boundaries more strictly, the pressure to raise additional revenues, the centralization of the state coupled with administrative reform, the construction or improvement of communications for trade, troop movement and other purposes, the search for and conservation of resources, internal security, imperial rivalries, national prestige, scientific curiosity and much else. Most historians have regarded these processes as an inherent part of modernization.[8] They led to a more rigorous application of geographical methods, such as mapping and exploration, to problems posed by space.[9]

Geography's historians have explored many aspects of the growing significance of space in the early modern period and their geographical implications (see, for example, Livingstone 1992; Bowen 1981; Glacken 1967; Ogborn 1998; Stock 2015). But relatively few have highlighted in detail the linkages between such phenomena and the rise of the early modern European state, or what some have chosen to call 'the fiscal-military state' (Glete 2002). Glete's examination of the early modern state is particularly relevant to the development of European continental states between the early-sixteenth and mid-seventeenth centuries, and provides a background for understanding some of the ways in which geographical endeavour changed during the period. Many of the processes he describes are applicable to Russia, though for a somewhat later period.

Numerous historians have regarded militarization, and competition between states, as the decisive factors leading to the state's centralization and bureaucratization during this period, but Glete suggests that, since war was not exactly a new phenomenon, the reverse may have applied. What is decisive in his view is the state's transformation into a new kind of organization, ensuring that it gained new power over its own territories, reducing or eliminating local autonomy (including the relative autonomy traditionally enjoyed by members of the elite and by peripheral regions), establishing a new bureaucracy consisting of professional administrators, constructing a standing army and (in many cases) a navy, reforming local administration and policing powers to enforce its rule locally, facilitating taxation and access to finance, asserting control over frontiers, enforcing standardization, and similar measures. All of these had geographical implications. What was decisive was the knowledge of its own territories that the state required to exert these controls. Geographical knowledge, in other words, equalled political power.

Maps, for example, were seen to be important instruments for attaining such power (Buisseret 1992; Barber 1997). Early modern states were keen to map their territories since maps were a means of surveillance and ultimately of control. One only has to think of William Roy's military survey of Scotland, begun in the wake of serious Jacobite rebellions in the first half of the eighteenth century and designed to facilitate the military subjection of the Scottish Highlands, to realise how significant they were in ensuring military security and internal policing (Skelton 1967). In a similar way they expedited the redrawing of internal administrative boundaries, essential if governments were to challenge the traditional authority of local elites and to make their power effective at the local level. Maps also helped to ensure the state's external security by demarcating and facilitating control over its frontiers and, where imperial expansion was occurring, by identifying and claiming new territories, often in competition with other states. Commercially, maps were important aids in the construction and maintenance of roads and waterways, the improvement of ports and navigation, the inventory of natural resources and the recording of economic activities. Maritime maps were essential tools in navigation.

At the local level, maps played a significant role in the planning and replanning of towns and cities, especially capital cities, thus adding to national prestige among other things (Keenan 2015). Maps also had a symbolic value in themselves and were often shown in evidence of a state's prestige, for example in providing a visible demonstration of a state's territories or the discovery of new lands (Edney 1997).

Closely related to (but by no means identical with) mapping was land or cadastral survey. In Western Europe this activity was often undertaken by private land or estate owners wishing to demarcate their lands from those of others or to improve the layout of their fields and other lands. But in colonial situations where new land was being allocated (see, for example, Thrower 1966; Andrews 1985) and in poorly mapped lands like Russia, it was often done by the state. In Russia there was a cadastral tradition before Peter the Great, since land was linked with state service (the legal principle being that those who held land should serve the tsar, for example in the military or bureaucracy) and also taxation. Under Peter, land lost the latter function but survey continued to be important since, until 1762, it was still linked to state service, and in any case it was necessary for conservation reasons (for example, in order to preserve forests for shipbuilding and fuel) and to demarcate properties. In addition to the maps that often accompanied land survey, its geographical significance lay in the wide variety of other information about the land which was often collected.

That the early modern era was the great era of geographical discovery and exploration has been emphasized above. Russia played a part in this process, beginning before Peter with the (partly) spontaneous exploration and settlement of the steppe lands to the south of European Russia and, more significantly, of the vast Siberian *taiga* to the east.[10] Much has been made in English-language literature of the importance of the eighteenth-century sea voyages, especially those across the Pacific, to the European understanding of the geography of the globe at the time (Withers 2007, 40; Pagden 1993; Sorrenson 1996; Knight 2014). Much less has been made of the land-based exploration of the vast territories of Eurasia. Under Peter there began the first scientific expeditions to the east and the north, and these were soon to be greatly augmented by those mounted by the Russian Academy of Sciences. Academy-sponsored expeditions studied the regions of north European Russia, Siberia, the Far East, the north coast and the Arctic, Alaska and the northern Pacific, Central Asia and even further afield. In the nineteenth century the Academy's activities were supplemented by those of the Russian Geographical Society and other bodies. All this added greatly to the geographical knowledge of the globe and was of the utmost importance to the Russian state in its quest for expansion and in its imperial rivalries with other powers.

Other early modern geographical activities, such as the publishing of geographical books, dictionaries, gazetteers, maps and similar aids, were important instruments in the hands of the state's rulers and its subjects in helping to bring some order to the 'ferment of knowledge' about the world that characterized the period.[11] As we shall see, however, publishing in Russia was attended by its own specific difficulties. These activities were nonetheless an essential part of geographical endeavour at the time.

Russia's empire in the early modern period

Before considering the social and political context in which Russian geographical endeavour operated in the period, something must be said about the variable territories which were the focus of its activities and, more particularly, about when and how those territories were acquired (see Figure 1.1).

At the beginning of the seventeenth century the Russian empire was already an enormous, multi-national realm spanning the Eurasian landmass, bordering the Polish-Lithuanian Commonwealth and Sweden's Baltic provinces in the west and stretching beyond the Urals and into Siberia in the east (see Figure 1.2). But its official title at this time was not the 'Russian empire' but the 'Muscovite state' (*Moskovskoe gosudarstvo*).[12] Not until 1721, when Peter the Great was proclaimed emperor (*imperator*), did Russia officially assume the designation 'empire'.

As was the case with many European states, the Muscovite state had had an intricate history, having arisen as a result of a complex process of war, conquest, amalgamation, dynastic manoeuvres and rivalries, and similar developments. The city of Moscow is first mentioned in the Russian chronicles for 1147 when it was in the principality of Vladimir-Suzdal', then forming part of the much bigger state of Kievan Russia (or Kyivan Rus'). The latter was a loose conglomeration of small and rival city states nominally answerable to Kiev and situated in the centre of what is today European Russia, Belarus, and the northern part of Ukraine (Martin 1995, 1–20, 41). Kievan Russia finally came to grief in 1237–40 as a result of the Mongol-Tatar conquest led by Batu Khan, grandson of Genghis. Having conquered the Russians and the other eastern Slavs, the Mongols established an empire centred on their capital of Sarai on the lower Volga, their empire becoming known as the Khanate of the Golden Horde (Hartley 2021, 31–8). For more than two centuries the Russian

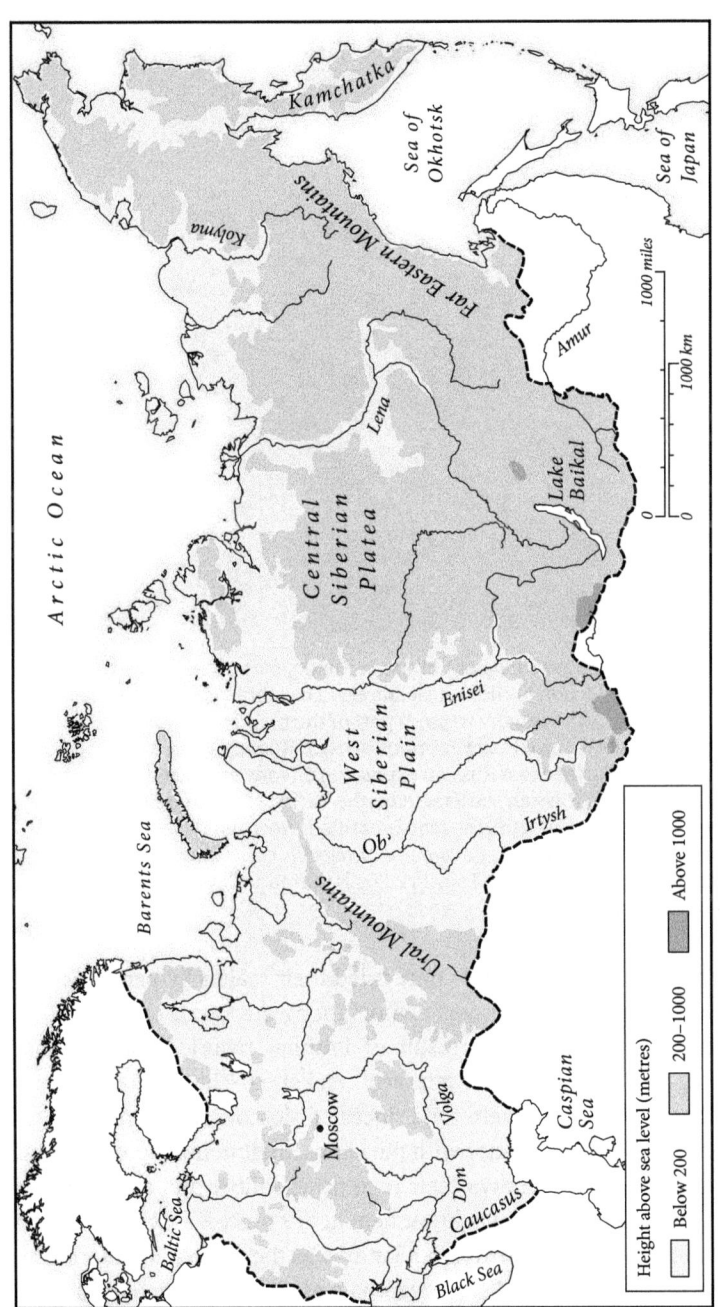

Figure 1.1 Russia in the late eighteenth century showing natural features: relief, rivers, seas and major physical regions. The boundary is that for 1796. Source: various. Map © D. J. B. Shaw, drawn by Martin Brown.

Figure 1.2 Isaac Massa's map of European Russia, part of the King's Topographical Collection at the British Library. The Library's catalogue dates this as after 1644. Although the western part of the map shows territories in northern and central Europe, the enormous size of Russia's European lands is clearly depicted. Further east Russian expansion already embraced much of Siberia, and the first Russian settlement on the Pacific was founded in 1649. According to the BL catalogue, the map is entitled: *Novissima Russiae tabula, Authore I. Massa. Sumptibus J. Janssonii, Amstelodami*. The map (shelfmarked at: Cartographic items Maps K. Top. 112.24) is reproduced by courtesy of the British Library board.

and other Eastern Slav princes only ruled their realms by permission of the khans of the Golden Horde, to whom they were forced to pay tribute. Gradually, however, as the result of internal rivalries and external pressure, the Golden Horde's grip was weakened. The eventual victors in the ongoing struggle were the princes of Moscow, who were able to use their position of influence with the khans, their military prowess and other advantages to overawe their rival principalities and states and to absorb them. Their greatest achievement in this process of what has been called 'the gathering of the Russian lands' was the annexation of the city republic of Novgorod in 1478. Novgorod was a great centre of trade and commerce with enormous dominions in the coniferous forest lands of north-west and northern European Russia, stretching north-east to the

Urals and beyond into west Siberia as far as the river Ob'. Its acquisition thus represented a huge territorial gain for Muscovy.

Having absorbed the rest of the Russian principalities by the early-sixteenth century, the rulers of Muscovy (or tsars) continued to expand their realm to the west and south, but more particularly to the east. Numerous factors underlay this territorial expansion, including the need for defence of what were often open frontiers, access to resources, commercial attractions and others (see Figure 1.3). Important episodes in the eastward movement were the conquest of the Tatar khanates of Kazan' (1552) and Astrakhan' (1556) on the Volga, which took place in the reign of Ivan the Terrible (r. 1533–84). This opened up the prospect of expansion across the Urals and into Siberia. Under the initial patronage of the merchant family Stroganov, bands of Cossacks[13] moved eastwards, crossing the Urals in the search for furs, minerals and other resources, and imposing tribute on the native peoples (Huttenbach 1988). A key moment in the occupation of west Siberia was the conquest of the Tatar khanate of Sibir', centred on the valley of the Irtysh, by the Cossack adventurer Ermak in the 1580s. The khanate had previously levied tribute on the indigenous Siberian peoples, who now became subject to the Russian tsar and his officials. Meanwhile, partly under the sponsorship of the state and partly spontaneously, Cossack bands moved ever further eastwards in the quest for furs and other resources, utilizing the river network as major routeways (Armstrong 1965; Martin 1986; Wood 2011; Hartley 2014). Behind the bands came the Russian state, founding the forts (*ostrogi*) and towns that were to become the state's control points over the new colonial territories. The eastward movement was extraordinarily rapid, with the first Russian settlement on the Pacific, Okhotsk, being founded as a fort as early as 1649. Thereafter territorial expansion became more difficult. South-eastwards from Siberia Russia came up against the opposition of the Chinese empire, and Russia's ambitions here were checked by the Treaty of Nerchinsk in 1689, which established a definite boundary in this region. North-eastwards towards the Bering Strait Russian penetration was hindered by fierce resistance from indigenous peoples. Only later in the eighteenth century was Russia able to secure this region. Further expansion followed as the Russians crossed the Bering Strait and secured Alaska. But here occupation eventually proved untenable and the territory was finally sold to the United States in 1867 (Gibson 1976; Jones 2014).

Although Russia's eastward expansion from the old Muscovite core proved most dramatic, expansion also occurred in other directions: to the west, the south and south-east of Muscovy. But in these cases territorial

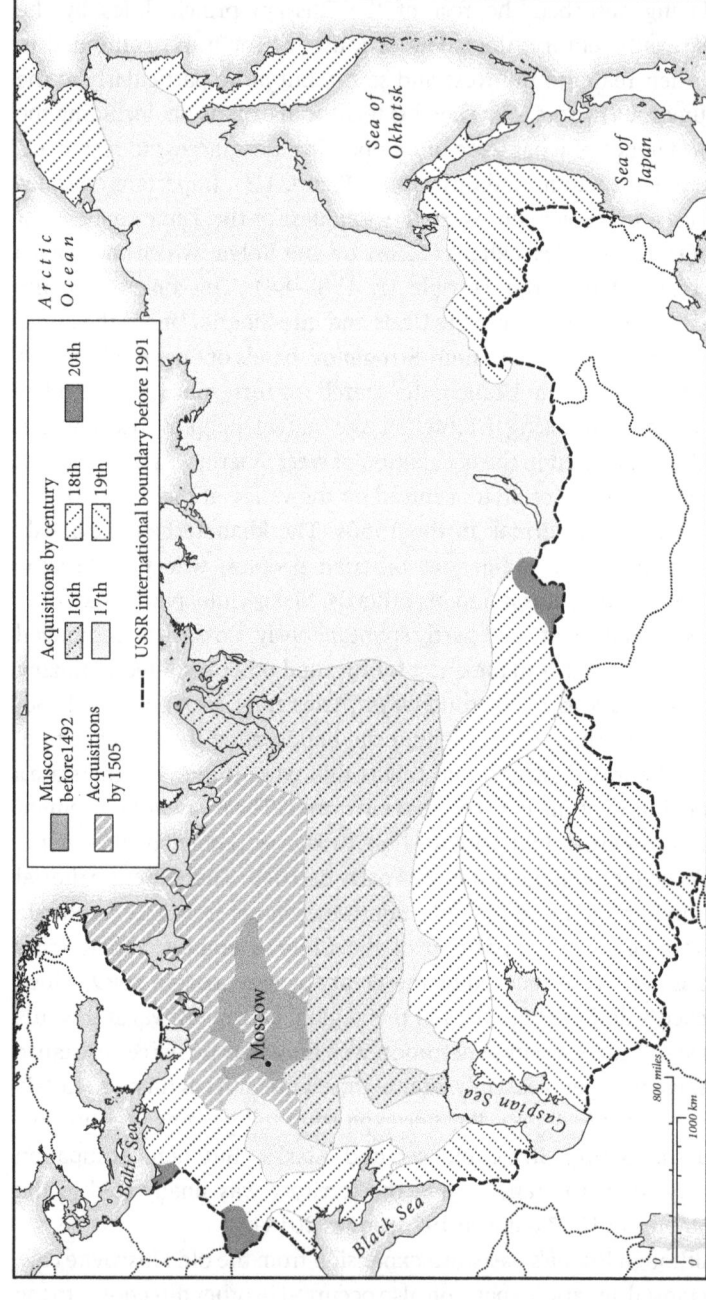

Figure 1.3 Russian and Soviet territorial expansion from the late fifteenth century to 1991. Source: various. Map © D. J. B. Shaw, drawn by Martin Brown.

acquisition was more problematic. To the west, for example, Russia came up against organized European states like Poland and Sweden, and thus entered into the competition between states that has been a central feature of European history. Southwards towards the open steppe the Russians were faced with the raiding activities of nomadic peoples like the Tatars and Kalmyks, and the occupation of new territory in this direction was only possible at all by means of the construction of fortified lines and towns and the recruitment of special mobile forces (Shaw 1983, 1989, 1991; Sunderland 2004; Morrison 2017).[14] Ultimately this assumed the character of a struggle between the Russians and the Turks. Further east, in the Caucasian region, there evolved a complex three-way tussle between Russia, Ottoman Turkey and Persia in the attempt to overawe and control the many indigenous peoples grouped into a variety of politically unstable states and kingdoms. Russia was the eventual victor in this struggle, but only in the 1860s was the region finally pacified (Atkin 1988; Baddeley 2010). Russian expansion southeastwards into what is today Bashkiria and Kazakhstan also came up against the military prowess of steppe nomadic peoples and required measures similar to those taken in the European steppe (Donnelly 1988; Kandirbai 2002; Vulpius 2016). Bashkiria and the northern part of Kazakhstan had been acquired by the end of our period, but the occupation of territories further south (southern Kazakhstan, Kokand, Khiva, Bukhara and neighbouring regions) took place only later in the nineteenth century (MacKenzie 1988; Becker 1988; Morrison 2020).

Over our period between the seventeenth century and the early part of the nineteenth, therefore, the Russian empire experienced an enormous expansion – according to one estimate, from about 7–8 million square kilometres in the 1680s to more than 20 million by the time of the Emancipation of the Serfs in 1861 (Taagepera 1988). This placed Russia as perhaps the second or third biggest empire in world history.[15] Some scholars have attempted to ascribe this imperial experience to one overriding factor, such as the Russian state's militaristic character and strategy. But in fact the experience bears comparison with that of many other imperial states and involved a variety of complex processes. It was far from being the entirely state-centred development that some have imagined. The overall point for this book, however, is to stress the enormous size of the territories at which Russian geographical endeavour was directed. Russia made a huge contribution to the history of modern European imperialism, a point not often recognized in the literature. Its contribution to the geographical understanding of a large section of the globe was commensurately great. Furthermore, because of its transcontinental character, Russia's empire is a case where the differences between state-building and empire-building are elided. Unlike the overseas empires established by many Western European states in the early modern period, Russia built its empire overland. Numerous scholars have therefore begun to question the generally accepted notions of 'empire' and 'imperialism' as oversimplified.[16]

At the same time it is important to stress that, despite their enormous extent, the territories thus acquired by the Russian empire were not particularly productive. Extending over the vast Eurasian landmass and situated relatively far to the north, the territory generally experiences a harsh, continental climate with long, hard winters and short but warm summers. Even in the reasonably benign environment of the mixed forest belt of European Russia, northern Ukraine and Belarus, the original homeland of the Eastern Slavs, agricultural potentials are frequently affected by late frosts in the spring or early frosts in autumn (see Figure 1.4). Rainfall is often unreliable. The mixed forest belt does not extend east of the Urals. Further south are the forest-steppe and northern steppe (grassland) belts which, with their rich black earth (*chernozem*) soils are the former empire's breadbasket, though subject to summer drought. Only a thin belt of forest-steppe and steppe extends eastwards beyond the Urals. Most of Central Asia is desert, and here agriculture is generally only possible in oasis lands along the major rivers. Finally, most of north European Russia and Siberia is covered by boreal or coniferous forest (the so-called *taiga*), and further north by tundra, with very poor soils and frequent swampy conditions. Historically, however, the poverty of the environment in the *taiga* was to some degree mitigated by its wealth of fur-bearing fauna and other resources. But in summary, considering Russia as a whole, the relative poverty of much of its natural environment can be said to be one of the factors that held back its development in the early modern period.

A final point is to consider the extent to which the lands gradually annexed by the Russian state were actually settled by ethnic Russians, since this has a bearing on the character of the empire. Elsewhere I have attempted to discuss this issue following the general model of European imperialism developed by Donald W. Meinig (Shaw 1999a, 4–10; Shaw 2023). In accordance with his scheme, I divide the old Russian empire (the former USSR) into four: a core territory historically settled by ethnic Russians (old Muscovy) together with their close associates, the Belarusians and Ukrainians, who live further to the west; a 'boreal empire', which corresponds with the vast coniferous or boreal forests of north European Russia and much of Siberia; the 'settlement empire',

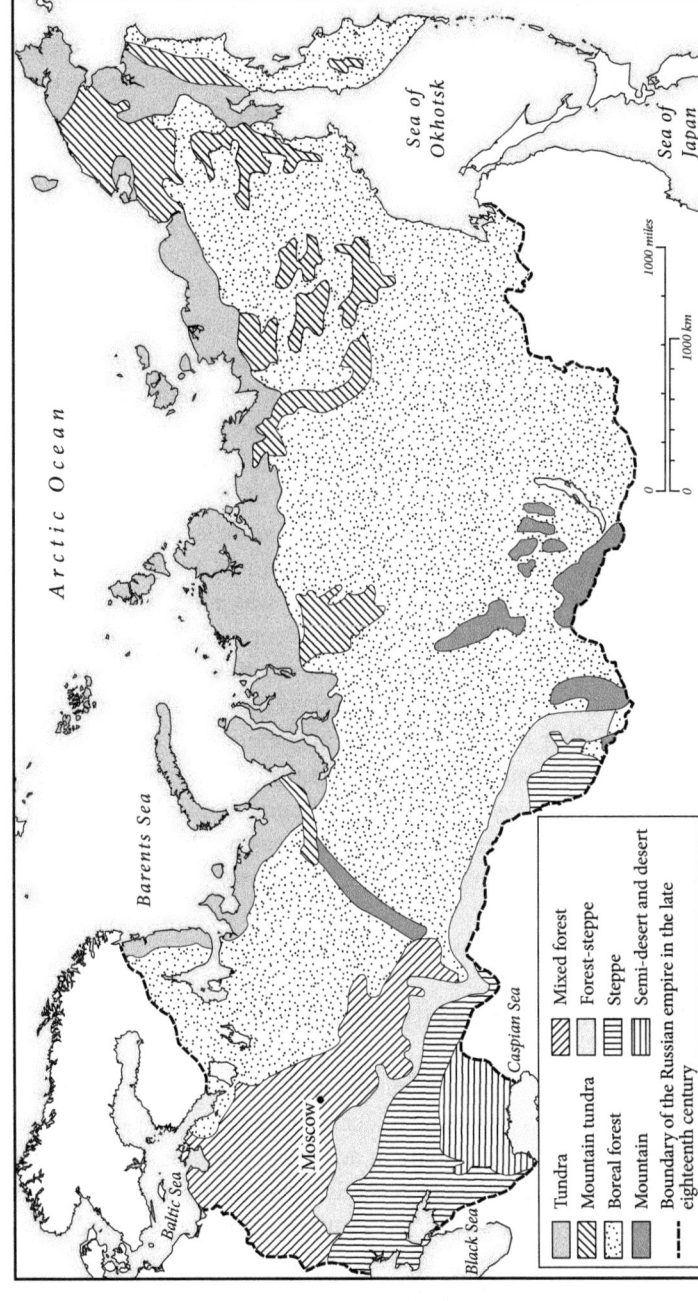

Figure 1.4 Russia in the late eighteenth century showing natural vegetation. Source: various. Map © D. J. B. Shaw, drawn by Martin Brown.

which largely corresponds with the forest-steppe and steppe of southern Ukraine, south European Russia, south-west Siberia and northern Kazakhstan; and finally what Meinig calls the 'nationalistic empire',[17] consisting of all those territories on the periphery of the old Russian empire and then the USSR that are now independent states: the three Baltic states, the Caucasian region south of the Caucasus mountains (now three states) and the five Central Asian states (see Figure 1.5). With regard to settlement, the core regions were the historical homelands of the ethnic Russians and, to the west, of the Belarusians and Ukrainians. The 'boreal empire', whose occupation by the Russians began in the late medieval period, long received relatively little Russian settlement because of their agriculturally unproductive character, and those who did migrate there shared the territory with the indigenous population. By contrast, the 'settlement empire' was gradually colonized by large numbers of Russian, Ukrainian, Belarusian and other agricultural settlers, a consequence of their fertile soils and other environmental advantages. The indigenous peoples, many of whom (with certain important exceptions) were pastoral nomads, were largely assimilated, pushed out or perished as a result of disease and for other reasons. Finally, the 'nationalistic' or 'outer' empire was already well-settled by non-Russian peoples, and so Russian occupation here assumed a character rather like that of many colonies of other European powers, exploited for the natural products and markets they provided or for their strategic value rather than for agricultural settlement. Thus, like other European empires, Russia's empire varied in the ethnic composition of its population according to geographical, environmental and other factors, but unlike most of the former empires, there was no clear geographical, ethnic or other division between the core territory and its subsequent acquisitions.

Science and society in early modern Russia

Although at one time it was commonplace for historians of science (including historians of the geographical sciences) to regard science as somehow *sui generis* or developing in accordance with its own internal rules and logic, they have more recently come to see it as a product of human culture, much influenced by the social, political and other contextual circumstances in which it occurs (see Livingstone 1992, 1–23; Golinski 1998; Shapin 1998; Latour 1987). This has abetted what has been referred to as a 'geography of science' agenda, or the recognition

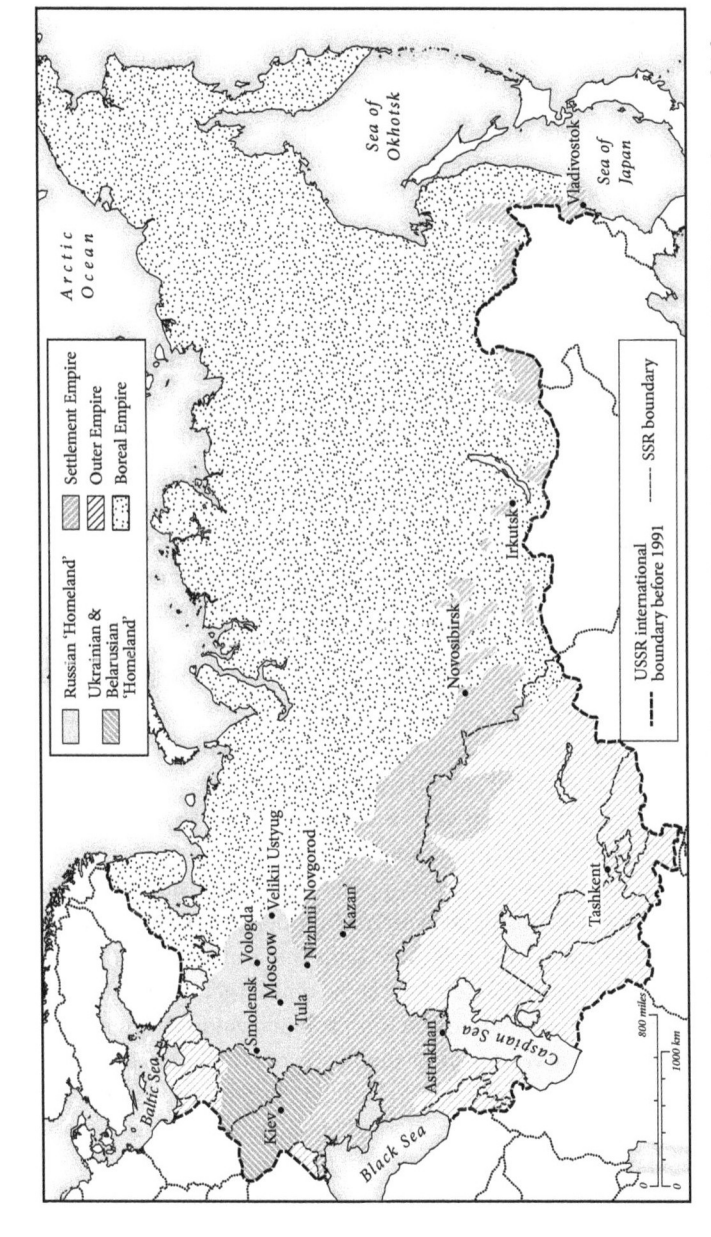

Figure 1.5 D. W. Meinig's scheme of European imperial expansion applied to Russia and the USSR. The scheme, which Meinig devised to describe different phases of European overseas expansion, is here modified by the present author to apply to the overland territorial expansion of Russia and the USSR. The map shows the boundaries of the USSR's constituent republics (Soviet Socialist republics or SSRs). Source: author. Map © D. J. B. Shaw, drawn by Martin Brown.

that scientific understanding and practice may vary from place to place in accordance with variations in the social and cultural context (Livingstone 2003; Finnegan 2008; Rupke 2011). This is the perspective adopted in this book. Science, or in this case geographical endeavour, is unlikely to take exactly the same form in early modern Russia that it took elsewhere in the world for the simple reason that Russian culture and society bore significant differences from those of other societies. It is therefore important to give some consideration to the character of the culture and society within which Russian geographical endeavour took place.

Past historians tended to stress early modern Russia's backwardness in scientific development by comparison with the countries of Western and Central Europe. Thus Alexander Vucinich, speaking of Russia before the sixteenth century, stressed the importance there of the 'Byzantine theological tradition', which was 'solidified by Russia's isolation from Western culture and its gradually developing body of secular and humanistic thought' (Vucinich 1963, 5). In general, it is true that the Byzantine tradition was suspicious of secular thought, including scientific thought, and that the Russian Orthodox Church battled against many of the new ideas emanating from the Renaissance and the Scientific Revolution in this period. Vucinich, for example, cites the long-standing importance in Russia of the writings of the eighth-century scholar John of Damascus and, of particular significance for geography, of the sixth-century *Christian Topography* of Cosmas Indicopleustes (Vucinich 1963, 4–10). Among other things Cosmas rejected Ptolemy's claim that the earth is a sphere and tried to ensure that scientific thought remained commensurate with theological belief. Empirical science thus failed to find ready acceptance by Russian thinkers, especially where such science seemed to challenge Christian tradition.

What were the reasons for this apparent obscurantism? After all, Christian belief was also strong in Western Europe, and yet that part of the continent experienced the effects of both the Renaissance and the Scientific Revolution, movements which at the time largely passed Russia by. Will Ryan, however, has pointed out the profound cultural differences that divided the Catholic West from Orthodox Russia (Ryan 1999, 9–11). Thus, although in Western Europe the Catholic Church, based in Rome, became a universal church with Latin as a common liturgical, ecclesiastical and legal language, Greek did not assume the same role in the East. Unlike the Catholic Church, the Orthodox churches of Eastern Europe, centred on Byzantium (Constantinople), were divided along national lines. Eventually Old Church Slavonic became the liturgical and literary language of the South Slavs of the Balkans and the East Slavs of Russia and their neighbours. Hence the Slavs were largely cut off from the classical Greek culture of Byzantium (including its philosophical and scientific texts) except by way of translations. And since the latter tended to be done by the clergy, who were naturally most interested in religious texts, few philosophical, scientific, historical or literary works were translated from Greek, and those that were translated were frequently garbled. In Russia intellectual isolation was worsened by the thirteenth-century Mongol-Tatar conquest, which cut the country off from the West and from the outside world in general. Summarizing the situation, Ryan states that 'Russian culture can still be characterized as medieval (with some oriental elements) up to the end of the seventeenth century' (Ryan 1999, 10). In contrast, from the time of the Renaissance the Catholic West had easy access to classical culture by way of Latin. This ultimately had profound consequences.

Although the difficulties faced by science in the context of early modern Russia should not be minimized, a Eurocentric overemphasis on these may lead to a failure to take account of the problems that also faced scientific progress in the rest of Europe, such as the long-standing influence of Aristotelian and Scholastic thought (Shapin 1996; Hannam 2009; Wilson 2017). In any case a static account of Russia hardly does justice to the fact that, by the seventeenth century if not before, many of the forces of modernization at work in Europe were also beginning to change Russia (Kotilaine and Poe 2004).

'Modernization' is, of course, a contentious concept that has been much debated by historians. Traditionally, Western historians of Russia have tended to measure Russian development or modernization against that of the West – thus, the Russian case was generally seen as simply a backward version of the Western one. According to this view, Russia was a case of retarded modernization. The disadvantage with this viewpoint is that the Russian story is always bound to disappoint, since although Russia borrowed many features from the West, it never became 'Western' – Russia remained forever Russia, while the West was taken to be the standard against which the degree of 'modernization' was to be measured. This book, however, takes a different approach. It accepts the idea that the early modern period was a period of economic and social change for many parts of Europe and that many such changes were initiated in the Western states before being followed by Russia. However, it rejects the idea that the West is the ultimate model of modernization (that 'modern' and 'Western' are synonymous). Rather we follow Dixon when he writes that he uses the modernization concept as 'a comparative analytical concept rather than as a measure of normative development'

(Dixon 1999, 7). In our view, for example, what Peter the Great wanted to do was not to 'Westernize' Russia, as so many scholars have argued, but to take advantage of the many technical and other advances invented or adopted in Western Europe in order to compete with those states and to fend off adversaries. In so doing, he sought to 'modernize' his realm. This approach is in keeping with the notion of 'multiple modernities', which suggests that, although many societies may be said to modernize, each does so in its own way, so that the resulting 'modernities' are never identical (Herf 1984).

Considering Russian modernization from a comparative perspective, it has already been indicated that the rise of the Russian state was characterized by the unification and centralization of a series of pre-existing principalities around the city of Moscow followed by the building of an empire. A similar process had taken place in several other European states. Russian contacts with the outside world were limited before the sixteenth century, but as the country entered into competition with other European states, it could not be hermetically sealed off, despite the suspicions of the Orthodox Church. Russia needed the technology and material goods which only the rest of the world could supply. In the military sphere, for example, the latest military technologies and ideas were required, and with them modern military skills that could only be furnished by the hiring of foreign military personnel. Similarly Russia needed trade contacts, and so the period witnessed the expansion of foreign trade both overland and by sea. Emblematic of the latter was the founding of the Muscovy Company in 1555 to develop Anglo-Russian trade (Stout 2015; Arel 2019).

Inevitably with such contacts came foreign ideas whose influence was strengthened by the presence of growing numbers of foreigners visiting or living in Russia. By the seventeenth century Western influences had multiplied despite the resistance put up by the Church and its allies. Elements of foreign scientific literature, for example, were now more common in translation, although their spread was hindered by the limitations of printing and publishing in Russia – notably by the fact that printing was a Church and government monopoly with limited opportunities for secular output (Marker 1985, 6–14). Sciences like mathematics, medicine and astronomy were perhaps those best known among the elite and, although Russia had no true scientists of its own, science had a small but growing band of enthusiastic followers. Such changing interests were reflected in various scientific practices. In geography, for example, the needs of the state fostered an expanding cartography, a growing interest in the character of Russia's territories, especially peripheral and little-known ones, as well as in those of neighbouring states, and an increasing number of geographical expeditions of various kinds. Such practices will be described in detail in Chapter 2.

However, despite these developments, there can be no ignoring the difference between Russia and much of the rest of Europe in terms of science and education, and the official acceptance of their significance in Russia prior to Peter the Great. Catholic and Protestant Europe had long recognized the importance of institutions like universities for the education of its elite and for the propagation of the faith (Rüegg 1992–2011). In medieval times such institutions were usually associated with the Church and were valued not least for the training of clergy. They made important contributions to the development of what was called 'natural philosophy', or science. In Orthodox Russia, by contrast, only two academies, offering a somewhat traditional curriculum, appeared in the seventeenth century (Hartley 1999, 125; Chrissidis 2004), and there were no universities prior to the reign of Peter the Great. Provision for primary and secondary education was extremely rudimentary before Peter. The overall result was that the Russian population was largely illiterate and remained so down to the end of our period (Hartley 1999, 140).

For a modernizing state, which is what Russia tried to be from Peter the Great's time, this was an intolerable situation. Henceforward concerted efforts were made to rectify it, though with limited results, especially by comparison with other states (Hartley 1999, 140). Why such disappointing results? Part of the explanation must lie in the particularities of Russian culture mentioned above. Unlike the Church in Western Europe, for example, the Russian Church played little or no role in education, even in the case of its own clergy. Far from the Russian clergy having a role in public education, it was the state that eventually took on this function, and also insisted that the Church educate its clergy. There was widespread indifference and even resistance to education on the part of the population as a whole. The great majority of the latter (about 90 per cent) were peasants living off the land, and most felt little need for or inclination towards education. Since in Peter's reign more than half of the peasants were serfs, they lacked the freedom to leave their estates and seek enlightenment elsewhere, even had they wished to do so. Russian serfdom had developed gradually over several centuries, reaching its culmination in the Code of Laws *(Ulozhenie)* of 1649 (Blum 1968; Smith 1968). It is one of history's ironies that a measure that might have aided Russia's modernization, in securing its defence and development by tying down a mobile population to produce the food and other resources that the state required, should have retarded its development in the longer term (Dukes 1982, 48).

If the overwhelming majority of the peasants were indifferent or even hostile to education, the situation among the nobility was not much better. The latter constituted a tiny proportion of the population, according to one account rising from a mere 0.5 per cent in 1744–5 to 1.4 per cent in 1833 (Dixon 1999, 93). It was far from a coherent social group, with relatively few wealthy individuals owning many serfs and a very large proportion owning only a handful. What held the nobility together was the service it owed to the state, a principle that was finally enshrined in the *Ulozhenie* of 1649. Peter the Great's Table of Ranks, promulgated in 1722, made state service compulsory for all members of the nobility, and only in 1762 were nobles emancipated from this obligation. Many, however, were too poor to avoid service, while the higher nobility saw in service an important way of consolidating their social status. State service, whether in the military or the expanding bureaucracy, could only benefit the country if servitors were educated and, as the school system developed, more and more nobles became educated, though there was continued resistance. Many continued to be educated at home in traditional fashion, often enough in a superficial way prior to entering service. Dixon notes that as late as 1834 an attempt, first instituted in 1809, to demand rigorous qualifications from those wishing to enter the bureaucracy had to be abandoned because of lack of cooperation from the nobility (Dixon 1999, 94).

In the event it was the service nobility who were to prove the most promising social estate or grouping from the point of view of education. Of the remaining social strata, the merchants hardly yet constituted a bourgeoisie, being undeveloped as a result of the weakness of Russian capitalism and very much under the thumb of the state. Russia was thus deprived of a class that played such an energetic role in the rise of science and education across much of Europe. The clergy, as we have seen, was traditionally uneducated and increasingly, through time, became a closed social grouping, though the state did recruit seminary graduates for its own administration. Of the rest of society, the *raznochintsy* or 'people of various ranks' – those who did not fit into any of the accepted social categories, including off-shoots of the military, of the clergy, the minor nobility and the rising professions (teachers, doctors and others) – proved more promising. In some readings, together with part of the lesser nobility, the nineteenth-century *raznochintsy* formed the core of the nascent intelligentsia. There remained, however, a huge gulf between the educated and cultured Russian minority, on the one hand, and most of the population on the other. It was in this above all that Russia stood out from other European states in this period.

Thus Russian society in the early modern period provided a difficult context for the rise of science. But it is important not to exaggerate the differences. For example, serfdom was common in various parts of Central and Eastern Europe in the seventeenth and eighteenth centuries (Pennington 1989, 97–102; Anderson 1987, 39–45), though there it was possibly more closely connected with capitalist development than with state-building as in Russia. Moreover, as already noted, Russia could not be hermetically sealed off from the outside world. Not only did people, ideas and goods penetrate Russia by such means as trade, recruitment and migration, but as Russia itself expanded, new territories with different peoples and cultures were incorporated within its realm. The annexation of Ukraine in the seventeenth century, for example, opened Russia up to Catholic influences, and both Catholic and Protestant ideas and beliefs followed Peter the Great's occupation of the Baltic provinces in the early eighteenth. The occupation of the European steppe eventually gave rise to the settlement there of many German and other colonists, and the partitions of Poland in the the late-eighteenth century ensured the growing significance in Russia of Catholics, Jews and others (Bartlett 1979). Similarly, Russia's expansion to the south and south-east only enhanced the significance of Muslim influences. All this meant that scientific development in early modern Russia took place in what was, in many respects, an increasingly multi-cultural context. In this sense, as shall be seen, early modern Russia was a society in flux.

Structure of the book

One of the key arguments of this book is that such superficially diverse practices as mapping, surveying, exploring and regional description are interrelated by virtue of the fact that all were part of the process whereby 'people came to know the world', signifying the new importance accorded to territory and space in the early modern period. To describe each of these activities in separate chapters would be to run the risk of splitting interrelated practices and of divorcing each practice from the broader social, political and other contextual circumstances in which it occurred. For these reasons this book adopts a chronological approach, acknowledging that Russian geographical endeavour changed and developed in numerous ways in the two centuries or so between the commencement of the Romanov dynasty in 1613 and the death of Alexander I in 1825.

I acknowledge that scientific development cannot be split into discrete chronological periods (and certainly not neatly according to monarchical reigns), but I hope that a chronological approach will provide a clear and perhaps familiar framework for the presentation and analysis of what is, after all, a rather broad range of material. This approach, which views scientific change in the context of political developments, among others, also serves to emphasize the significance of the state for science as for so many other aspects of Russian history.

The present chapter serves as an introduction to the book as a whole and outlines both the key issues to be addressed, and the background to the nature of geographical endeavour – and that of the Russian state and society – in the early modern period.

Chapter 2 focuses on the period from 1613 (or earlier where necessary) to the beginning of Peter the Great's reign. The emphasis is on those geographical practices that were typical of Russia before Peter's reforms. Firstly, consideration is given to what Russians knew of the rest of the world before Peter's reign – in other words at a time when Western Europeans were engaged in global exploration and publishing their findings in travel accounts, maps and atlases. The accent is on those elements of foreign geographical literature that were being translated into Russian. The mapping of Russia's own territory is then considered, with a discussion of the 'Book of the Great Map', an artefact of the 1620s. Since cadastral survey was a significant instrument for gauging landholding in the pre-Petrine period (landholding being the major basis for determining taxation and service assessments), attention then switches to this practice, using the 1615 and 1629 cadastres of Voronezh district by way of example. Finally, some important geographical literature of the period is discussed, namely itineraries, expeditionary accounts (notably that of Spafarii 1675–8), and cosmographies – specifically the 'Cosmography of 1670'.

The reign of Peter the Great (1682–1725) is the focus of Chapter 3. This period witnessed a sea change in Russian geographical endeavour. Peter, traditionally referred to as the 'Great Reformer', introduced a series of sweeping social, economic and political reforms that affected virtually the whole of Russian society, including the practices I have referred to as geographical endeavour. The chapter first considers the context and character of his reforms before describing their impact on those practices. In mapping and surveying, for example, the tsar placed these practices on a new, mathematical basis, and eventually decided that the whole empire should be mapped. His many educational and publishing initiatives are considered, with particular attention to the translation and publication of foreign geographical literature. Bernhard Varenius's celebrated *Geographia Generalis*, published in Russian in 1718, is subjected to an extended analysis. Attention then switches to Peter's statistical and land surveys, including his forest cadastres. Finally the expeditionary work of the reign is discussed, including expeditions to Central Asia and to Siberia and the Far East. In the latter case the expeditions of Evert Ysbrants Ides (1692–5) and of Daniel Messerschmidt (1720–7) are singled out for more extensive consideration.

Chapter 4 is devoted to the post-Petrine period during which Russia was successively ruled by no less than six monarchs (1725–62). Even though this period is often considered a dull interlude between the reigns of two 'great' sovereigns, Peter and Catherine, I argue that this was the period when many of Peter's reforms came to fruition. Two accomplishments particularly mark the time: the full introduction of mathematically based mapping, and Russia's first major geographical expeditions (the First and Second Kamchatka Expeditions of 1725–30 and 1733–43 respectively), both under the leadership of Vitus Bering. The chapter first considers the advances in cartography made during the period, particularly the activities of Ivan Kirilovich Kirilov, Joseph-Nicolas Delisle and Vasilii Nikitich Tatishchev, and the 1745 *Atlas Russicus*, also known as the *Academy Atlas*, which served as the period's major achievement in mapping. Discussion then centres on the two major expeditions mentioned above and particularly the second, frequently described as the 'Great Northern Expedition'. The exploratory work of Stepan Krasheninnikov and Georg Wilhelm Steller on the Kamchatka peninsula in the Russian Far East then comes under scrutiny via their respective publications. Consideration is finally given to other geographical publications of the time, notably to Petr Rychkov's 'Topography of Orenburg Province', which was to provide a model for later topographical descriptions.

The reign of Catherine the Great (1762–96) is the focus of Chapter 5. During this relatively long reign many of the geographical practices which had been introduced or reformed by Peter the Great matured and broadened, not least because of the territorial expansion that characterized the period. The chapter first discusses the advances in cadastral survey embodied in Catherine's General Survey, which comprised detailed survey maps and atlases together with lengthy economic notes. It extended survey work to much of European Russia and provided new insight into the microgeography of these regions. The Academy of Sciences expeditions of 1768–74 embraced not only the peripheral regions of Russia but also its inner reaches.

The work of these expeditions is described, together with a more detailed consideration of that led by Ivan Ivanovich Lepekhin, the only Russian expedition leader. The developing use of questionnaires to gather local information, and the resulting topographical descriptions that marked the period, are then discussed. Finally, Sergei Pleshcheev's *Survey of the Russian Empire* and the geographical dictionaries of Fedor Polunin and Lev Maksimovich are considered, as significant geographical publications of the time.

Chapter 6 rounds off our discussion of geographical endeavour in the early modern era by highlighting the period between the accession of Catherine's son Paul in 1796 and the death of his son Alexander I in 1825. An introduction considers some of the developments that influenced science in this period, such as the opening of new universities and scientific societies. New advances in cartography, including changes in organization and new methods like triangulation, are described. Consideration is then given to the further development of local and topographical studies, notably to Evgenii Bolkhovitinov's 'Historical, Geographical and Economic Description of Voronezh Province' (1800). From the late-eighteenth century Russian geographers and other scientists were influenced by the new fashion for statistics, which is considered in this chapter, emphasizing the work of Evdokim Zyablovskii and Konstantin Arsen'ev. There is an analysis of Afanasii Mikhailovich Shchekatov's 'Geographical Dictionary of the Russian State' (1801–9). Finally, Russia's widening global horizons are illustrated by a survey of Adam von Krusenstern's round-the-world voyage (1801–6), Russia's first circumnavigation.

Chapter 7, which serves as the book's conclusion, summarizes its contents and discusses its main findings.

Notes

1 The book's main title, *Reconnoitring Russia*, might ordinarily be taken to include the written accounts of the many foreign visitors who went to Russia for various reasons during the period – for example, the English-language accounts so ably listed and discussed by Anthony Cross (Cross 2014). Such, however, is not my concern. Rather my focus is on the scientific geographical activities undertaken either by subjects of the Russian empire or by foreigners in Russian service.
2 The term 'early modern' is commonly used by European historians to refer to the period between the sixteenth and eighteenth centuries. Here it will be taken as referring to the entire period covered by the book.
3 For Russian universities, see: Anuchin (1949), Berg (1956), Esakov (1983), and Solov'ev (1955). Various forms of 'geography' (usually mathematical geography related to navigation and mapping) were taught in Peter the Great's naval and other institutions – see Chapter 3.

4 See, for example, Yeo's discussion of maps and charts of knowledge in Yeo (2003).
5 However, the volume's editor, Roy Porter, comments on the desirability of having included geography and other subjects but for a lack of space and opportunity. See Porter (2003, 19, footnote 68).
6 See, for example, Hankins (1985), Goldstein (1980), Goodman and Russell (1991), Clark, Golinski and Schaffer (1999).
7 By contrast, Mayhew (2001) has stressed that early modern geography was 'precisely defined' and that 'there was an overwhelming consensus about its nature and relationship with other enquiries'. Mayhew argues that 'geography' at the time was a textual practice derived from Renaissance humanism. In his view the 'history of geography' should be solely concerned with this textual practice and be distinguished from other practices whose study constitutes the 'history of geographical knowledge'.
8 For the concept of 'modernization', see below in this chapter.
9 For suggestive comments on changing Russian attitudes towards territory in the early modern period, see Sunderland (2007).
10 For the word *taiga*, see Glossary.
11 For explanation of the term 'ferment of knowledge', see Rousseau and Porter (1980), 1–7.
12 Other titles were also in use.
13 See Glossary.
14 Also see Figure 2.2.
15 After the British and Mongol empires. See Taagepera (1988, 1, 4–5).
16 For more on this, see Turoma and Waldstein (2013); Shaw (2023).
17 For Russia I prefer the term 'outer empire'. See Shaw (2023).

2
Russian geographical endeavour before Peter the Great (sixteenth and seventeenth centuries)

> *Certainly the seventeenth century in Russia produced no true scientists, nor any profound contributors to science, but for the first time in Russia the secularization of wisdom had become an active process.*
>
> Alexander Vucinich, 1963

In October 1654 one Alexander Rowley was paid the sum of £50 for 'setting up a Sphere in Whitehall for the use of His Highness' the Lord Protector, Oliver Cromwell. As Cromwell's biographer Antonia Fraser remarks: 'the presence of a real-life map could only enhance the practical efficacy' of the Protector's imperial dreams, which had been growing in ambition since the conclusion of the Dutch war. 'Indeed', she continues, 'as England's foreign policy flowered, watered by Cromwell's enthusiasm, the Council of State also found it necessary to order new maps, new spheres, even a book called *The New Atlas*[1] in order to keep up with the Protector's expanding dreams, at times clearly beyond their own geographical knowledge' (Fraser 1973, 520).

Exactly 61 years later, in 1715, the celebrated Gottorp globe, a gift of the Duke of Holstein, was transported to St Petersburg and set up for the delectation and edification of Tsar Peter and his guests (Karpeev 2003). A combination of terrestrial globe and planetarium, it had been made in Holstein under the supervision of Adam Olearius (1599–1671), the famed traveller to Russia and Persia and later librarian to the Duke of Holstein, possibly about the same time that Cromwell was acquiring his globe. Perhaps like Cromwell, Peter's not inconsiderable imperial ambitions were further excited by the globe. Just as Cromwell had set his eyes on Hispaniola and Jamaica, Peter's were to fall on Madagascar just a few years later.

The story of the two globes seems to symbolize the intellectual distance that separated Russia and Western Europe before Peter's day. Peter acquired a globe that was already several decades old, yet which was presumably still a great novelty in Russia. The Gottorp globe was re-erected in a country only just beginning to open itself up to the outside world. At the time when Alexander Rowley and Adam Olearius had originally set up their globes, a public display of this kind would have been unthinkable in Russia.[2]

As noted in the previous chapter, traditional Western histories of Russia have placed much stress on the intellectual and scientific gap between Russia and Western Europe before Peter's reign. Hence many scholars have taken their cue from the words of Olearius, who visited Russia in the 1630s and 1640s:

> Although they know nothing of them, most Russians express crude and senseless opinions about the elevated natural sciences and arts when they meet foreigners who do possess such knowledge. Thus, for example, they regard astronomy and astrology as witchcraft. (Baron 1967, 131)

As the previous chapter noted, however, the differences between Russia and Western Europe in this period can be overstressed. Indeed, current scholarship, while noting the important changes (and difficulties) that Russia underwent in the sixteenth and first part of the seventeenth centuries, tends to see the middle of the seventeenth century as the point at which serious modernization began to occur.[3] In other words, Peter the Great did not build on a *tabula rasa*. Equally, however, in terms of 'those [geographical practices] through which people came to know the world', seventeenth-century Russian knowledge of the world, and indeed of Russia itself, remained patchy at best. For the Romanov dynasty, which came to power in 1613, this was a highly unsatisfactory situation. Russia had only recently emerged from the period of civil strife and foreign invasion known as the 'Time of Troubles' (1604–13). The new Romanov dynasty needed to secure control over its territory, strengthen its frontiers, counteract fissiparous tendencies and protect its resources. All this meant encouraging geographical endeavour.

This chapter will discuss some types of geographical endeavour that characterized the pre-Petrine period. First, consideration will be given to Russian geographical understanding of the rest of the world before Peter's reign, as exemplified in the influence of foreign geographical literature. Attention will then turn to the mapping of Russia's own territory, together with a brief discussion of the 'Book of the Great Map', an artefact of the 1620s. The process of cadastral survey will be considered, as illustrated by surveys of southern frontier regions. Finally there will be a review of some of the geographical literature of the time.

Russian knowledge of the world before Peter

The sixteenth and seventeenth centuries are frequently referred to as an age of discovery (for example in Parry 1981). It was in this era that European adventurers, in the wake of Columbus's celebrated 'discovery' of the New World in 1492, set out to explore the world's oceans and coasts and to conquer new lands in the name of their sovereigns. These endeavours gave rise to the publishing of new maps and atlases, superseding the often stylized and fictional productions of the Middle Ages (Harley and Woodward 1987; Harvey 1991; Chekin 2006). Thus the sixteenth century witnessed the publication of world maps, atlases and cosmographies by geographers like Martin Waldseemüller (in 1507), Gerardus Mercator (c. 1537 and 1569) and Abraham Ortelius (1570), and the first half of the seventeenth saw the publication of the work of the Blaeu family of cartographers, including their *Atlas Novus* or *New Atlas* (1635 and later) referred to above. This was also the period in which, in his revolutionary book *De revolutionibus orbium coelestium* (*On the Revolutions of the Heavenly Spheres*) (1543), the Polish clergyman Nicholas Copernicus presented the world with a new model of a heliocentric universe, though this took many years to become accepted. With these and other publications, by the end of the seventeenth century not only had a new model of the universe been widely accepted but many of the world's coastlines (with significant exceptions like the north-western parts of North America, eastern Siberia, lands in the southern ocean, and the polar regions), together with some parts of the continental interiors, had been explored and mapped (Sarazin 2015).

Furthermore, the sixteenth and seventeenth centuries witnessed the beginnings of national mapping. The year 1579, for example, saw the publication of Christopher Saxton's *Atlas of the Counties of England and Wales*, the first atlas to depict the two countries county by county. This restricted view of what was to become the United Kingdom was succeeded in 1611–12 by John Speed's *Theatre of the Empire of Great Britain*, which included both Scotland and Ireland as well, reflecting King James I and VI's strong desire to see his two kingdoms of England and Scotland fully united. Somewhat later across the Channel, following the foundation of the Académie des sciences by King Louis XIV in 1666, there began the great Cassini survey of France – 'the first modern map of a nation, using innovative scientific surveying methods to comprehensively represent a single European country' (Brotton 2012, 295). Thus there began what Jean-Yves Sarazin calls 'the golden age of French cartography' (Sarazin 2015, 10). Other national surveys were begun in the Netherlands and the Holy Roman Empire.

Relatively little of this geographical endeavour was reflected in sixteenth- or early-seventeenth-century Russia. Here, as noted in chapter one, modern scientific ideas were excluded not only by the influence of the Church but also by such factors as the lack of printing facilities open to secular use, and Russian reliance on Greek and Byzantine literature rather than Latin. Latin, the international diplomatic and scientific language of the time, was hardly known except among a handful of officials and a few scholars – only in the 1660s did Simeon Polotskii arrive in Moscow to establish a monastic school to instruct minor government officials in Latin (Okenfuss 1995). Muscovite ideas of the universe were still based on traditional Byzantine models. Only in the seventeenth century did Aristotelean and Scholastic ideas begin to penetrate, and Copernicanism remained practically unknown before the eighteenth.

Russian understanding of the geography of the earth was rudimentary in the sixteenth century. However, as Russian contacts with the outside world expanded and the country became more conscious of its need for foreign goods and skills, so the situation began slowly to change. More foreigners visited Russia and, especially from the time of Ivan the Terrible (r. 1533–84), Russian students were sent abroad to learn foreign languages. The capacity for translating foreign languages thus expanded (Sobolevskii 1903). In the geographical literature, sixteenth-century translations into Russian included the geography of Pomponius Mela and the chronology and cosmography of the Polish scholar Marcin Bielski, translated in 1584 and containing a discussion of the New World (Bielski 1597). More significant was the literature translated in the course of the seventeenth century, including the work of Ortelius (possibly early-seventeenth century, from a Polish edition), that of Mercator (probably translated directly from Latin in about 1637), and the first four volumes of the text to the Blaeu *Atlas Novus* (possibly in the 1650s). As ever, the spread of such important geographical sources among Russians was hampered by the problems of publishing and the difficulties of reproducing maps using only woodblock prints. It thus remained a geography very much confined to the elite.[4]

If Russian understanding of the world's geography was quite restricted in the seventeenth century, understanding of Russia itself was not much better. Whereas France, Britain, and certain other countries were beginning to undertake national mapping surveys, moving gradually towards mapping on a strictly mathematical basis, such efforts were as yet only just beginning in Russia. There, although some attempts were made to map the empire as a whole on a non-trigonometrical basis, mapping was for the most part episodic and impressionistic. Only towards the end of the seventeenth century did regional maps of a slightly more modern kind begin to appear. It is to mapping that we must now turn.

Russian mapping in the sixteenth and seventeenth centuries

The extent and significance of Russian mapping in the pre-Petrine era has been the subject of much scholarly debate. Maps are notoriously fragile objects and many were lost in the fires that so frequently beset timber-built towns, in wars and civil disturbances and in other ways. The point at which Russians began to make maps, and their overall significance to government and other aspects of life, are thus by no means clear. Unfortunately the lack of clear evidence has meant that this whole area of enquiry has been bedevilled by rival claims based largely on nationalist rhetoric. On the one hand there have been those scholars, usually Russian, who have sought to bolster the idea that Russia by no means lagged behind Western Europe in cultural development and have advanced hypotheses of a highly speculative nature in consequence. On the other hand their opponents have sometimes been keen to emphasize the notion of Russia's relative backwardness. Ideological as well as purely scholarly motives are clearly involved.[5]

Fortunately much light has been thrown on this question by the American scholar Valerie Kivelson in her brilliant study of pre-Petrine maps, *Cartographies of Tsardom* (Kivelson 2006). Kivelson's work is focused on what she calls the 'expressive functions' of maps, in other words how they reflect the assumptions and attitudes of their creators, as well as on their 'transformative power', or how they influence the ways in which those who read them experience space, place and power. The present book, by contrast, focuses on mapmaking as a practice through which people 'come to know the world'. Yet Kivelson's study has much to tell us about the latter. Thus, based on the catalogue of

Vladimir Svyatoslavovich Kusov, she notes the present-day existence of around a thousand maps or *chertezhi* (literally 'sketches') dating from the seventeenth century to be found mainly in Russian archives and repositories (see Kusov 1993). These include both foreign maps of Russia and those drawn by native cartographers. In addition, there are various inventories (*rospisi*) of maps that were catalogued in the archives of the main departments of state such as the Military Chancellery (*Razryadnyi prikaz*), the Service Lands Chancellery (*Pomestnyi prikaz*), the Siberian Chancellery (*Sibirskii prikaz*) and the Foreign Affairs Chancellery (*Posol'skii prikaz*).[6] Six such *rospisi* exist for the period 1570–1670 (Kusov 1993, 6). Many of these maps no longer exist but the *rospisi* testify to their considerable significance in the pre-Petrine period.[7]

Scholars have often commented on the apparent lateness of the adoption of the mapmaking habit by the Russians, and some have seen this as further evidence of the country's cultural backwardness. Thus only three existing maps are known to have been made before the mid-sixteenth century: a twelfth-century map carved into a stone slab in Tver' province, north of Moscow, a late-fourteenth- or early-fifteenth-century map, possibly of the Kirillo-Belozerskii monastery in northern Russia, and a property map also from Tver' province and dated 1533 (Kivelson 2006, 14). There is also evidence of a now-lost property map drawn up as part of a legal dispute in 1483 (Lebedev 1956, 200). Few maps, it seems, were drawn by Russians prior to the late-sixteenth century. However, Russian tardiness in mapmaking may be more apparent than real, for mapmaking was in fact a relatively unusual practice in Western Europe as well before the sixteenth century. As P. D. A. Harvey has written: 'It simply did not occur to people in the Middle Ages to use maps or to see landscape or the world in a cartographic way' and: 'Maps were practically unknown in the Middle Ages' (Harvey 1991, 7–9). Instead, he points out, medieval people 'often produced written descriptions where we would be more likely to draw a map' and suggests that this 'points to a way of thought quite different from our own' (Harvey 1987, 8–9). The change to a cartographic way of thinking, or to one of seeing and representing the world spatially, required what has been termed an 'epistemic shift' (Kivelson 2006, 15). That shift may have occurred somewhat later in Russia than it did elsewhere in Europe, but not that much later.

According to Kivelson, more than half of the presently existing maps from the pre-Petrine period are large-scale maps of local areas, generally drawn up in connection with property disputes. Most are in the archive of the Service Lands Chancellery (*Pomestnyi prikaz*), the department of government responsible for the allocation and supervision of lands apportioned to those engaged in state service. The great majority of such maps that can be dated were drawn in the second half of the seventeenth century, especially in its last quarter. Such maps typically depict local topographic features such as villages, rivers and streams, churches, trees, roads, fields and, where relevant, property boundaries. As Kivelson notes, many are painted in attractive colours. While some of the maps give an indication of orientation (often by showing the position of the summer sunrise), others are multidirectional. None are drawn to a consistent scale or give any other evidence of geometrical sophistication.

The geographical distribution of early property maps, which has also been analysed by Kivelson (2006, 2–4), shows a distinct bias towards the central parts of the Muscovite state – the regions around Moscow – with a few outliers such as Vologda towards the north, Novgorod and Pskov to the north-west, Voronezh to the south, and Kazan' to the east (see Figure 2.1). Since the maps depict only small territories or districts, and were often drawn by local, unskilled people on the orders of higher authority, their view of the world is a limited one. But, as stressed by Kivelson, they represent a local perspective based on local knowledge. At this stage, in other words, Russian mapping was by no means simply top-down.

The second type of map analysed by Kivelson is the regional map depicting sizeable territories. In the Russian case there are numerous such maps for the sixteenth century but most are of Western origin, based no doubt on Russian sources of information. Examples include maps by Paolo Giovio (1525) and Sigismund von Herberstein (1549). For the seventeenth century the most prominent names were those of Hessel Gerritsz and Isaac Massa (maps of all Russia, 1613–14 and 1612–13 respectively), Tomasz Makowski (Grand Duchy of Lithuania, 1630s), Guillaume de Beauplan (several maps of Ukraine beginning in 1639) and Nicolaes Witsen (Asiatic Russia, 1690) (Bagrow 1975, 51). Not until late in the sixteenth century do the Russians seem to have begun to draw regional maps themselves. In the reign of Ivan the Terrible government officials began to collect Western maps and atlases, whilst Tsar Boris Godunov (r. 1598–1605) evinced a personal interest in maps and seems to have commissioned a 'Great Map' (*Bol'shoi Chertezh*) of his realm as a whole. Although this was subsequently lost, as was a 1627 replacement, the latter's accompanying text, known as the *Kniga Bol'shomu Chertezhu* ('Book of the Great Map'), survived. The 'Book', and its various early editions, were exhaustively analysed during the Soviet period by Kseniya Nikolaevna Serbina (Serbina 1950).[8]

Figure 2.1 Larger towns in mid-seventeenth century European Russia. Source: various. Map © D. J. B. Shaw, drawn by Martin Brown.

The 'Book of the Great Map' is a significant artefact of early Russian mapmaking. Its origins are clear from the book's introduction. In the year 1627, in the wake of a great fire in Moscow in May 1626, the tsar ordered the recovery of 'the old map of the entire state of Muscovy and of all surrounding states' from the archives of the Military Chancellery. The map, which had been drawn 'long ago under previous sovereigns' was found to be decayed and difficult to use. Officials thus ordered a new map to be drawn based on the old one, and in addition a second map showing the territories lying south of Moscow and down to Crimea – from where, especially by way of four routes or tracks (the Muravskii, Izyumskii, Kal'miusskii and Nogai), Tatar nomads regularly launched raids against the Russian state (Figure 2.2). This second map was to show the fords or river crossings that Tatar raiders regularly used, the system of fortified points and military patrols whereby the Russians attempted to defend their frontier, and similar information. Finally, to accompany both maps, a descriptive inventory or book was to be written indicating distances and other details from the two maps. As noted above, the composition of written descriptions to accompany maps was a common practice of the period.

Although the exact date of the original 'old' map of Muscovy has been disputed, the evidence seems to point to the late 1590s, or slightly later under Tsar Boris Godunov (Postnikov 1989, 20). As noted above, this map, and the copy made in 1627, were both subsequently lost, as were all original copies of the 'Book of the Great Map'. However, partly because the latter was in regular official use throughout the seventeenth century, many copies exist in the archives, and it was finally published by the celebrated writer and journalist Nikolai Ivanovich Novikov in St Petersburg in 1773 (Serbina 1950, 36).

In the absence of the maps that it describes, the 'Book of the Great Map' is the definitive source for what must have been a monumental accomplishment of Russian cartography, describing a huge swathe of territory that constituted the Russian state in the 1620s and the regions beyond. The 'Book' provides important testimony to the extent of Russian knowledge of its territories in the period, and also to the limitations of that knowledge.[9]

In the seventeenth century Russian regional mapping became ever more significant. Unlike the property maps discussed above, regional maps were usually commissioned directly by agencies of the state to serve the state's military and strategic purposes. They were not drawn to a fixed scale or projection but generally around a network of routes – usually rivers. The accent was on general direction, the relative location

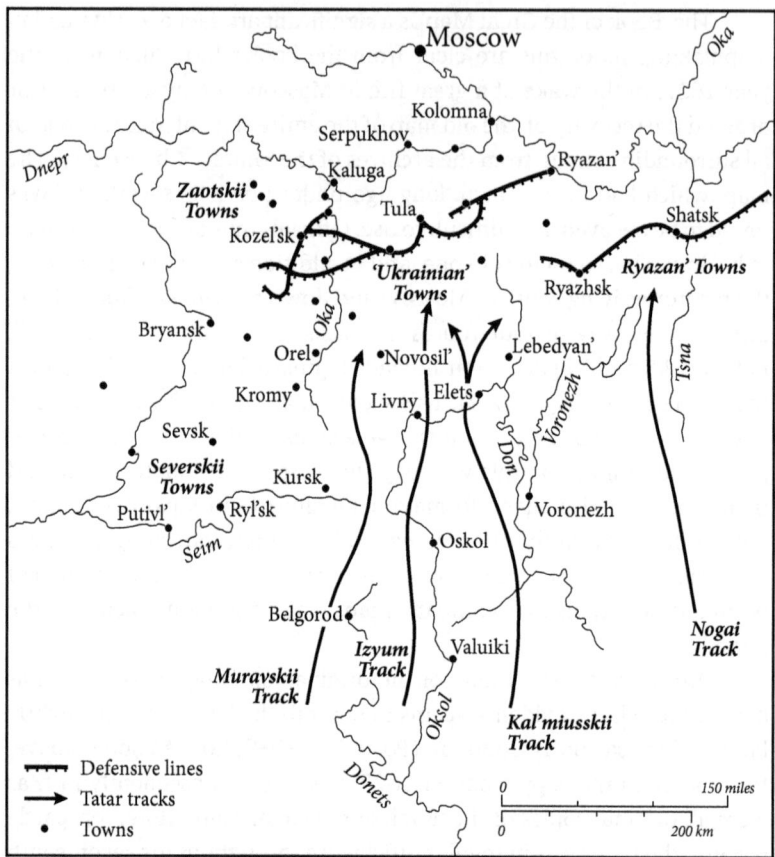

Figure 2.2 Russia's southern frontier in the late sixteenth century showing principal towns, defensive lines and Tatar tracks. Source: author. Map © D. J. B. Shaw, drawn by Martin Brown.

of important features, and distance. The foci of their interest include borders, river and overland routes, towns and fortified points, smaller settlements including those of indigenous peoples, forests, steppelands, and other features. Particular attention was paid to border regions and especially to Russia's expanding empire east of the Urals. Many seventeenth-century maps of Siberia exist, especially of the routes to China (which was of great commercial importance). The first map of Siberia to have survived is the Godunov map of 1666–7, commissioned by the governor of Tobol'sk, the region's administrative centre. More and more regional maps were drawn toward the end of the century, culminating in the major cartographic work of Semen Ul'yanovich Remezov (c. 1642–c. 1720).

Remezov, who was born and educated in the west Siberian city of Tobol'sk, produced what Kivelson has described as 'a dazzling corpus of cartographic material' between the 1690s and the early-eighteenth century (Kivelson 2006, 21, 133–45).[10] Outstanding among this body of work are his three atlases of Siberia: the *Khorograficheskaya kniga* ('Chorographic Sketchbook', 1697–1711), the *Chertezhnaya kniga* ('Sketchbook', 1699–1701), and the *Sluzhebnaya chertezhnaya kniga* ('Working Sketchbook', 1702–30). Together with Remezov's other work, these constitute the ultimate achievement of Russian cartography prior to the mapping reforms introduced by Peter the Great. Kivelson has discussed how, despite working in a remote location, Remezov evinced a remarkable interest in the achievements of Western science, including advances in cartographic methods, which are reflected in his atlases and other work. And yet, for reasons that are not entirely clear, his work also retained many Muscovite mapping traditions. As Kivelson asserts, his work ultimately 'seems a fairly uncontaminated expression of a pre-Petrine cartographic style and aesthetic' (Kivelson 2006, 137). Particularly reflective of a pre-Petrine ethos, according to her, is Remezov's depiction of his Siberian homeland as a place steeped in religious significance, a providential landscape or 'peaceful angel'. Indeed, in her view Remezov frames his entire Siberian opus in a biblical and historical chronology that reflects its place in the divine purpose. Thus his work is marked by the religious and mythical ideology that moulded so much European cartography in the medieval period (Harley and Woodward 1987; Brotton 2012, 82–113).

Cadastral survey

As well as maps, cadastres – or surveys of property and land – were compiled by many centralizing states in the early modern period, including Russia. Such surveys usually formed the basis of taxation and military service obligations. As Kivelson writes: 'Without detailed surveys of land and ownership, states had no way to attach responsibility to particular people and properties. Cadastres served a crucial agenda of centralizing monarchies by making territories, populations and resources "visible" or "legible" to the governing regimes' (Kivelson 2006, 18). Cadastres generally served the three-fold purpose of registering, valuing and delimiting landed properties (Karimov 2007, 16). As I shall argue below, they were a significant aspect of geographical endeavour in the early modern period.

Russian cadastral surveys described spatial units midway in scale between the large-scale property maps and the small-scale regional maps discussed by Kivelson. At this stage, however, the typical Russian cadastre was a written document, and few were accompanied by maps. From at least the late-fifteenth century the Muscovite state, notably the *Pomestnyi prikaz* or Service Lands Chancellery, began to send its officials and surveyors into the provinces to measure and record landed properties and enter the results into cadastral registers (*pistsovye knigi*). The focus of such endeavours was usually the town and its surrounding district (*uezd*), the basic territorial-administrative unit of the Muscovite state. The data recorded generally included not only details of the landholdings and their owners but also other materials: descriptions of towns, villages and other populated places, land use, the composition of the population, economic activity, assessments of wealth and tax owing, and much else. Several thousand cadastral registers have been discovered in Russian archives covering much of the territory of the Muscovite state as it existed between the late-fifteenth and seventeenth centuries (Kochin 1936, 145; Merzon 1956, 7).

Although censuses of population with fiscal and military aims had been conducted in the Mongol period, if not earlier (Merzon 1956, 4–5; Eaton 1967, 55), land and property surveys were being undertaken in Novgorod, Muscovy and perhaps other principalities by the fifteenth century (Eaton 1967, 56–8; Karimov 2007, 50). Whatever the variations among these different surveys, the emergence of the unified Muscovite state towards the end of that century led to an expansion and greater standardization of the work. Thus, after the incorporation of Novgorod into the Muscovite state in 1478, its territories were thoroughly surveyed and much land was confiscated to the benefit of Muscovite servitors. As to standardization, taxation came to be based on a unit of assessment known as the *sokha*. The Russian word *sokha* denotes the light or scratch plough used on the mixed forest soils of central Russia, but for taxation and service purposes it came to denote a specific area of tilled land or a specific amount of labour, property and other sources of wealth. The standardization of the *sokha* unit in the mid-sixteenth century meant that, on land held by servitors, a *sokha* was equivalent to 800 chetverts[11] of 'good' land, with reduced amounts for Church, crown and 'black'[12] land. On land of 'medium' and of 'poor' quality, the number of chetverts in a *sokha* was increased commensurately. In this way the there was an attempt to vary the basic tax unit according to ability to pay.

According to Eaton (Eaton 1967, 60), several hundred cadastral registers were compiled in the sixteenth century, though few have survived and many are incomplete. The following century witnessed numerous difficulties for the conduct of cadastral surveys, not least being the period of chaos, civil strife and foreign intervention known as the Time of Troubles (1604–13). As a result of the losses of population and wealth sustained, the government was forced to undertake a series of emergency surveys, the results of which were recorded in so-called *dozornye knigi*, or registers, which usually had a provisional character (Merzon 1956, 9). Then in 1619 a new general survey was ordered, and begun the following year. Many of the resulting cadastres were subsequently lost in the great Moscow fire of 1626 and a further survey followed in 1627–31. Later in the century the taxation base moved from land to non-noble households, a process culminating in Peter the Great's inauguration of the poll tax in 1718.

We can gain some impression of the character of early-seventeenth-century cadastres from an examination of the 1615 cadastre of Voronezh district, which has been analysed in some detail by the present author (Shaw 1991). It was composed by a group of scribes under the supervision of Grigorii Kireevskii in the summer of that year and is the first extant survey and description of the area. It is not a full cadastral survey (*pistsovaya kniga*) but a register, a *dozornaya kniga*, implying a hurried surveillance as stated above. Even so, the work undertaken at Voronezh in 1615 seems to have been more thorough than many similar surveys, perhaps reflecting the fact that this was the authorities' first chance to take stock of the area since the town's foundation in 1585–6.[13]

The special character of Voronezh and its district in the early-seventeenth century derives from the fact that they lay on Russia's southern military frontier, a system of fortified towns and ultimately of fortified lines designed to defend the state against the raiding tactics of the nomadic Tatars.[14] The town was founded as part of a broader movement in the 1580s and 1590s to secure the valleys of the Don, Oskol and Severskii Donets rivers, and thus to push the defensive frontier decisively to the south (Shaw 1983, 124–5). This endowed Voronezh and its district with a distinctive social geography. Unlike central Russia, much of the population consisted of 'state servitors', in other words people who held their land in return for the military service they provided along the frontier. Servitors belonged to one of two classes: a middle class with hereditary status (forerunners of petty nobility), and a lower class of 'contract' servitors (servitors *po priboru*), subdivided into different categories. The latter had been recruited from various elements such as Cossacks, runaway serfs and others who, in the eighteenth century, came to occupy an intermediate social status between the peasants and the lower nobility.[15]

The 1615 cadastre begins with a description of the town. Situated on the high right bank of the river Voronezh, and stretching down to the river bank, the town had a fine view over the 'Nogai side' to the east. It consisted of two parts: the smaller *gorod* or inner town, containing the central administrative and military offices and a cathedral church, and the much larger outer town or *ostrog*. Both parts were fortified with wooden ramparts, all carefully described in the document. In the *ostrog* were situated the residential quarters (*slobody*) of most of the inhabitants, the majority of whom were state servitors and their dependants. Separate quarters existed for each category of servitor, such as the musketeers (*strel'tsy*), the regimental Cossacks, and others.[16] The head of every household (*dvor*) is named (as are the cottars or serfs who lived with them)[17] and each house is located geographically, thus providing an official list of those owing service to the state. Also in the *ostrog* was a quarter for 'quitrent-paying' (*obrochnye*) people, mainly traders and craftsmen who performed no state service but paid a tax in lieu. The amounts of money payable by such traders, as well as by those dwelling in two further 'quitrent-paying' settlements down by the river bank, are carefully recorded. Also recorded are the dues owed by those who kept shops (*lavki*) in the town, many of whom were in fact servitors rather than designated traders. Close by the town was the Assumption Monastery with its various outbuildings and monastic cells. The monastery had its own quarter for quitrent-payers, who paid their dues directly to the monastery.

In addition to the town's population, the status of its various inhabitants, and how much tax was due from its traders and those who had shops, the cadastre also notes other significant properties and sources of wealth: the churches and their valuable furnishings, barns, and sources of income such as bathhouses, malt-houses, a tavern and a ferry.

As we have seen, the servitors held their land conditionally in return for military service. The town's servitors typically held their land in several scattered parcels, presumably because there was insufficient land close by the town. The 52 *belomestsy* atamans,[18] for example, had 9 chetverts apiece in the town fields and in two adjacent glades, and the remaining 41 chetverts in various scattered glades and 'wastes'[19] (*Materialy* 1891, 21). Out of a total of 15,000 chetverts in the hands of the town-dwelling servitors, about 6,000 were located in outlying parcels. The total amount of land held by each category of servitor and its location are indicated. In addition the cadastre describes rights to hayland and meadow, together with their location. Rights to the forest are also specified. The availability of timber was clearly not an issue in 1615 as the cadastre states that 'by the town of Voronezh is a large forest of firewood and construction timber by the rivers Voronezh and Don into which all the inhabitants of Voronezh may go for fuel, timber and for all their necessities' (*Materialy* 1891, 24).

The musketeers, atamans, Cossacks and others who constituted the majority of the town's population in 1615 ranked as members of the lower service class.[20] Government policy favoured the settlement of such servitors in towns, leaving lands in the rural districts (*uezdy*) for the higher-ranking middle-class servitors. In Voronezh district in 1615, however, this policy had been only partly successful. Thus four settlements in the rural district were populated by atamans.

The 51 settlements listed in the 1615 cadastre in the district consisted of villages, hamlets[21] and new settlements (*pochinki*) plus the four ataman settlements indicated above (Figure 2.3). Settlements varied greatly in population, in numbers of landholders and in the amount of land attached to each. Most were located in the river valleys, ensuring the settlers access to land of different types – arable, meadowland and hayland – and also forest. Apart from the occasional drought, the forest-steppe environment in which Voronezh is located was generally suited to the traditional farming practices of the Russians, a marked contrast with the pure steppe located farther south, which was settled later (Shaw 1983; Moon 2013).

With the exception of the atamans, most of the land in the rural district was thus held by members of the middle service class, the majority of whom had the rank of 'junior boyar' (*syn boyarskii*). Although the middle-class servitors were designated servitors 'by patrimony' (*po otechestvu*), or hereditary servitors, on the southern frontier that designation was often in fact a fictional one.[22]

An important feature of the middle-class servitors living in Voronezh district in 1615 was the fact that the majority held only small amounts of land. Thus of 295 middle-class servitor landholders recorded in the 1615 cadastre, 223 held less than 70 chetverts. This relative poverty was reflected in the number of serfs each landholder possessed. In 1615 only about half of the junior boyars of Voronezh district seem to have had serfs at all. It thus appears likely that many were forced to cultivate their land themselves, with their families or using casual labour. A similar picture was characteristic of other

Figure 2.3 Voronezh district in the early seventeenth century. Based on Shaw (1991) and reproduced by permission of the *Slavonic and East European Review*. Map © D. J. B. Shaw, drawn by Martin Brown.

districts on the southern frontier in the seventeenth century. In other words, the social geography of the southern military frontier was quite different from those parts of Muscovy where at least some landholders had relatively large and long-established estates and significant numbers of serfs.

In conclusion the 1615 cadastre of Voronezh and its district suggests the multiple purposes fulfilled by cadastral surveys in this period. Primarily the cadastre was a fiscal document, a record of property and of other sources of wealth and of taxes and rents payable on those sources. Second, it was a record of who held the land, in what capacity and (by implication) what services they were to perform and/or what taxes they were to pay. Third, and in consequence, the cadastre was a register of social status. Fourth, cadastres were military documents, describing towns, their fortifications and similar features. Finally, as geographical descriptions, cadastres provided information on individual towns and the character of surrounding settlements, together with the location of landholdings. They also gave general indications of land use, including the location of tilled land, hayland and forest. In the case of the tilled land, the quality of the land on individual holdings and the intensity with which such land was used were often indicated.

From a geographical point of view, the major shortcoming of the cadastre was the fact that, at this stage, there were few if any accompanying maps. There is no known map, for example, to illustrate the 1615 Voronezh cadastre, nor that of 1629. The same is true of other cadastres of this period. As noted already, few Russian maps appear to have existed prior to the late-sixteenth century. Even so, Russian scholars are frequently in two minds over the extent to which cadastral surveys were linked with mapping in the sixteenth and seventeenth centuries. Yet there seems little reason to postulate the widespread practice of cadastral mapping for this period. The West European evidence suggests that such practices were not the norm until much later (Kain and Baigent 1992). But whatever one's opinion of the significance of cadastral mapping in pre-Petrine Russia, Karimov does make one point that seems indisputable – through the cadastral registers and other sources available to the state's officials, the government's access to detailed geographical information at the local level was by this time often extensive, if hardly comprehensive (Karimov 2007).

Geographical literature in the seventeenth century: itineraries, exploration, travel and cosmography

The final part of this chapter will consider several genres of geographical literature that characterized the pre-Petrine period. These genres include itineraries, literatures associated with travel and exploration, and cosmography. Once again, in an era in which printing had yet to be widely adopted, we are considering literatures that were largely available only to officials and associated members of the elite.

Itineraries

Two pre-Petrine itineraries (road-books or *dorozhniki*) were investigated by the Soviet scholar V. A. Petrov (1950). These were the *Poverstnaya kniga* ('Verst-Book') and the *Opisanie rasstoyaniyu stolits narochitykh gradov slavnykh gosudarstv zemel'* – *grada Moskvy* ('Description of the Distance from Moscow to the Most Important Cities of Foreign States'). Petrov locates the origins of such works in the growing need of the recently centralized Muscovite state for geographical knowledge, particularly in respect of its territory, communications and the geographical relationships between Muscovy and foreign neighbours (see also Franklin and Bowers 2017). Both works exist in many copies, a fact Petrov explains in terms of the need for constant reworking and updating as well as their wide use by officials and possibly others. In some manuscript copies both works appear together under a common title, leading some commentators to speculate that they had a common origin. However, based on his study of the sources, Petrov believes them to be separate creations composed at different times. He dates the origins of the 'Verst-Book' to the early part of the seventeenth century (though later versions were still in use well into the eighteenth), and the 'Description' to 1667, the work of Andrei A. Vinius, then a translator working in the Ambassadors' Chancellery.[23] In Petrov's opinion the development of the 'Verst-Book' is linked to seventeenth-century reforms to the official postal service (*yamskaya gon'ba*) and the network of postal roads, which ensured the speedy dispatch and delivery of government communications across all parts of the Muscovite state.

Although the 'Book of the Great Map', discussed earlier, was not a description of routes in the strict sense, it did have elements of a *dorozhnik*, or itinerary, such as listings of distances between places. Even so, as Petrov asserts, 'the information concerning the locations of towns and the distances between them [contained in the 'Book'] could not meet the need for a full gazetteer containing a systematic listing of Russian towns, a precise indication of the distances between them, and a description of the most important overland and water routes' (Petrov 1950, 75). Hence the appearance of the 'Verst-Book' which, according to Petrov, was designed to fulfil this need. The version of the 'Verst-Book' published by Petrov in his study dates from the 1680s (Petrov 1950, 102–48). It gives firstly the distances from the capital to a number of crown villages in the vicinity and to nearby districts, measured in the traditional Russian measurement of the verst, equivalent to about 1.1 km. Then comes a list of the first postal stations along major roads together with their distances from Moscow. Finally, along nine major highways radiating from the capital, the principal cities and settlements are indicated together with the distances of each from the capital, and also their distances from other towns and important points, not all of which lie on the highway concerned. It is not always clear why the particular towns and points listed have been selected, since not all are of major significance. Cross-country routes between the highway towns and the other points listed are not generally described. Presumably this reflects the difficulty of describing in written form a complex lattice of routes. The 'Verst-Book' is thus not an itinerary in any straightforward sense.[24] Some indication of its contents is apparent from Text Box 2.1 below:

Trinity Sergeevskii monastery
From Trinity monastery: to Dmitrov 30 [versts], to Aleksandrov sloboda 30, to Vladimir through Kirzhach 120, to Suzdal' 110, to Yur'ev Pol'skii 70, to Kashira 90, to Uglich 100, to Troitsa on the Nerl' 60, to Pereslavl' Zalesskii 60
Pereslavl' Zalesskii
From Moscow to Pereslavl' Zalesskii 120
From Pereslavl' Zalesskii: to Kolyazin monastery 90, to Rostov 60, to Suzdal' 80, to Uglich 90, to Romanov 120 ...

Text box 2.1 Extract from the 'Verst-Book' indicating towns, routes and distances in the neighbourhood of Moscow, probably dating from the 1680s (Source: Petrov 1950, 102–48).

Turning to the 1667 *Description*, Petrov places this in the context of the Peace of Andrusovo with Poland, which marked the end of the 1654–67 war with that country and Muscovy's annexation of part of Ukraine, Belarus and adjacent territories. According to Petrov, this event signalled

Russia's final arrival on the European stage and the growing importance of diplomatic relations (including in some cases official postal services) between Russia and its neighbours. It thus became important to list the distances and routes between Moscow and the capital cities and other important centres of neighbouring states for the guidance of travelling ambassadors, postal officials and others. The *Description* lists 54 foreign cities in alphabetical order together with their distances from Moscow and an indication of the route. Some sense of its contents is given in Text Box 2.2 below (Petrov 1950, 149–50):

Adrianople, a city under the rule of the Turkish Sultan, a distance from Moscow overland of 1,800 [versts].
Alexandria, a great city in Egypt under the rule of the same Sultan, a distance from Moscow via Azov and from there by sea 4,000, or by the Volga via Astrakhan' and from there via Persia overland 3,800.
Antioch, a city in Syria, a distance from Moscow via Azov and from there by sea 4,500, or through Persia overland 3,500.
Amsterdam, the leading city in Holland, stands at a distance from Moscow via Riga and from there by sea 2,900, or via Arkhangel'sk and from there by sea 3,800, or overland via Poland and the [Holy Roman] Empire (*Tsezarskaya zemlya*) 2,100.

Text box 2.2 Extract from the *Description* (c. 1667) indicating the capitals of principal states, their distances from Moscow and the routes to access them (Source: Petrov 1950, 149–50).

Of particular interest, as testifying to Russian geographical knowledge of the world at this particular time, is the most distant city listed, in Text Box 2.3:

Maxico [*sic*.], the leading city in America, of the Spanish king, stands at a distance from Moscow via Riga and from there by sea 14,000.

Text box 2.3 Extract from the *Description* (c. 1667) indicating the capitals of principal states, their distances from Moscow and the routes to access them (Source: Petrov 1950, 156).

In the absence of detailed road maps, itineraries provided important geographical guidance for the Muscovite state and its officials. To what extent they were used by ambassadors and other travellers in the field, however, is uncertain.

Exploration and travel

Surveying Russian travel literature in the sixteenth and seventeenth centuries, N. I. Prokof'ev points to the first official reports and accounts of ambassadors, which began in the sixteenth century, and then the official reports of travellers and explorers, as having particular significance as indicators of geographical endeavour in the period (Prokof'ev 1988, 5–20). Since, in the sixteenth and seventeenth centuries, Russian exploration and conquest were directed primarily toward the new lands being occupied and exploited in Siberia and the Far East, those areas are the main focus of travellers' accounts. And since Russian expansion to the east was motivated not only by the quest for furs but also by a desire to develop trade relations with China, those areas also provide the background for numerous ambassadors' reports. Both ambassadors' reports and the accounts of explorers and travellers are therefore the subjects of this section, with a particular emphasis on Siberia and the Far East.

As regards ambassadorial journeys and accounts, most of Russia's near neighbours, as well as some not so near, were the objects of such visits from the sixteenth century, if not before, and these have been surveyed by Lebedev (1949, 106–64, 175–95). In the seventeenth century numerous embassies were sent eastwards to Mongolia and China, with commercial motives playing a central role. Lebedev regards three of these as having particular significance: those of Ivan Petlin (1618–19), Fedor Baikov (1654–58) and Nikolai Spafarii (1675–78), in part because of the amount of information on landscapes and peoples contained in their reports.

The Spafarii expedition, which has been examined by the present author, is particularly notable for the amount of geographical information it provided on Russia's eastern regions and China (Shaw 2021, 229–32; Kizel' and Solov'ev 1960a). Nikolai Milesku Spafarii (Nicolai Spathari) (1636–1708), a soldier, diplomat and scholar of Moldavian noble origin, was sent by the Patriarch of Jerusalem to Moscow in 1671 to help strengthen ties between the eastern churches. In Moscow he worked for a time as translator in the Ambassadors' Chancellery before being ordered by the Russian government in 1675 to lead an embassy to China. The purpose of the embassy seems to have been to settle frontier disputes along the then ill-defined Russo-Chinese border, and to secure trade relations (Kizel' and Solov'ev 1960b, 134–5). Among the instructions issued by the Chancellery to Spafarii were: to compose a detailed description of the Chinese state; to discover the best route to China, whether by river or overland; and to provide a detailed description of his journey to the Chinese border. He was also to compose a detailed map of the region. This is testimony to the Russian government's limited knowledge of Siberia's geography and its concern to verify earlier accounts.

Spafarii left Moscow in early spring 1675, arriving in Tobol'sk on 30 March. He left the latter on 2 May, accompanied by an entourage of 150 people, including a military escort. He reached Nerchinsk, close to the disputed border with China, on 4 December, subsequently proceeding to Peking, the Chinese capital. He returned to Moscow on 5 January 1678. Among the texts he submitted to the government on his return were a detailed description of the Chinese state, and a journal of his journey from Tobol'sk to the Chinese border. The latter was published by the Russian Geographical Society in 1882 (Spafarii 1882). In addition he submitted an official ambassador's report (*stateinii spisok*) on the course of his diplomatic mission (Kizel' and Solov'ev 1960b, 289–506).

Spafarii's journal gives an account of the route he took and the dates he arrived at, and left, significant points. Other than the fact that he carried details of the routes taken by earlier travellers, and no doubt acted on the advice of others, including perhaps that of Yurii Krizhanich (see below), we cannot know why he took the particular route he did. On the road between Lake Baikal and Nerchinsk, moreover, he tells us that he passed through places 'where formerly no-one had been' (Kizel' and Solov'ev 1960a, 11) – his exact route is uncertain. In fulfilment of his instructions Spafarii gives many topographical and ethnographical details of the phenomena he encountered, including the physical features, populated places and peoples he saw or met with, and details of the precise distances (either in versts or in days of travel) between points along his route. A striking point is that Spafarii's account ranges far beyond the regions which he himself had visited, drawing on earlier accounts and material taken from European geographies. This can only reflect the extent of Spafarii's own knowledge as a European scholar and the ways in which Russia was already being influenced by European thought prior to Peter the Great. According to its Russian editor, Spafarii's account was used by the authorities to correct the Godunov map of Siberia, drawn in 1667, and formed a basis for the later cartographic work of Semen Remezov (Spafarii 1882, 3–4). It thus constituted an important addition to the Russian state's knowledge of its eastern territories in the late-seventeenth century.

With regard to explorers' and travellers' accounts, many are to be found in the archives, dating especially from the mid-seventeenth century. Lacking the formal and official status of ambassadors' reports, these vary in character but the records we possess usually have at least a semi-official status (spontaneous expeditions, which certainly occurred, often left little or no evidence). Local governors were under pressure from Moscow to expand the practice of tribute-taking, and frequently sent out armed detachments to explore new regions and to enforce tribute (*yasak*) from the native peoples, usually in the form of furs. The formula typically used for such excursions was an interesting one: native peoples were generally classified into the 'pacified' (or *yasak*-paying) and the unpacified (non-*yasak*-paying). The latter were 'invited' to place themselves 'under the sovereign's great tsarist hand' and 'under his tender rule' and pay the *yasak* (Kivelson 2006, 188–9). If they refused, retribution would follow. In other words, imposing the *yasak* equated to extorting protection money – a rather unsophisticated form of blackmail. Needless to say, such practices often gave rise to disorder, violence and murder. In more recent times scholars have become more aware of such downsides to exploration, in contrast to the purely heroic accounts typical of earlier times.[25]

By the middle and later years of the seventeenth century it was the eastern and far-north-eastern regions of Siberia that were being explored and their peoples 'pacified'. Among the more famous ventures were those of Ivan Moskvitin (1636–9/40), the first Russian to reach the Pacific; Kurbat Ivanov, the first Russian to discover Lake Baikal (1643); Vasilii Poyarkov, who explored the lands along the river Amur (1643–6); Mikhail Stadukhin, the first Russian to reach the Kolyma and other far-north-eastern regions (early 1640s); Semen Dezhnev, believed to have been the first Russian explorer to round Cape Dezhnev (East Cape, the most easterly point of Eurasia), by ship in 1648 (Fisher, 1981); Erofei Khabarov, who explored the Amur region in two expeditions (1649–50 and 1650–3) involving military clashes with both the local peoples and the Chinese; and Petr Beketov, who visited the region beyond Lake Baikal in 1653.

The much later venture of Vladimir Atlasov (1697–9), the Russian explorer of Kamchatka, has been discussed elsewhere by the present author (Shaw 2021, 232–5). Unlike Spafarii, Atlasov seems unlikely to have had any kind of higher education. He appears to have served for many years as a *yasak* collector in Siberia and was then appointed commander of the fort of Anadyr', near the Pacific coast, in 1695. Two years later Atlasov was sent with a large party of servitors and hunters on the tsar's service 'for the finding of new lands and for the bringing of new, non-*yasak*-paying peoples under the high hand of the great autocratic sovereign' ('Skaski' 1988; Berg 1924). Having some knowledge of the existence of the Kamchatka peninsula brought by earlier explorers, he proceeded down the full length of its west coast, but with diversions to the Pacific side and to the valley of the river Kamchatka which runs south–north through the peninsula's south-central part before entering the ocean. In the course of his adventures, Atlasov met local Koryaks, Kamchadals (Itelmens) and Kurils (Ainu), imposing the *yasak* and engaging in armed clashes, even extending to the occasional massacre. He returned to Anadyr' in 1699, proceeding with his booty to Yakutsk, where he gave his first oral report, written down in 1700. He was then ordered to Moscow, where in February 1701 he gave a second oral report, this time to the Siberian Chancellery (*Sibirskii prikaz*).[26] The latter formed the basis of the written report discussed elsewhere by the present author (see above). Although it is somewhat unsystematic – as might be expected from what is basically an oral account – the report is quite comprehensive and gives the impression that it is based on the answers given by Atlasov to specific questions. The report focuses on people rather than on the physical geography, though here and there it does discuss aspects of the latter, such as the peninsula's celebrated volcanoes, its highly unstable climate and the plants and animals upon which the indigenous peoples depended. The account's key significance, however, lies in its rich ethnographic descriptions covering many facets of the lives and cultures of the native peoples. Though probably uneducated and possibly even illiterate, Atlasov was clearly a keen observer and provided the Russian authorities with much valuable information on their distant colonial possession.

Regional description and cosmography

Dmitrii Lebedev writes that 'the lack of essays of a specialist geographical character written by actual scientific travellers does not mean that there were no manuscripts in pre-Petrine Russia which addressed geographical issues to greater or lesser extent' (Lebedev, 1949, 196). Quite what he means by manuscripts 'of a specialist geographical character' is unclear, unless he is referring to those produced by scientists whose only purpose was that of precise geographical observation and description. But, as he rightly says, there were many accounts of journeys undertaken and new lands explored, including chronicles and such productions as *The Life of the Archpriest Avvakum* (Avvakum 1924) and the *History of Siberia* by Yurii Krizhanich (Pushkarev 1984).[27] There is an obvious overlap between ambassadors' and travellers' accounts on the one hand and geographical descriptions of regions of the Russian empire on the other. Thus Spafarii's account, Yurii Krizhanich's *History* and Atlasov's discussion all contain rich descriptions of the physical landscapes and peoples of Siberia, despite the very different purposes their texts served. Clearly the Russian government, no less than those of other imperial powers, was keen to expand its territories and to discover as much as possible about them. Russia may not as yet have possessed the scientific infrastructure that was being developed in such states as Britain and France, but it was moving in exactly the same direction. By the late-seventeenth century, regional description was becoming a standard part of geographical endeavour in Russia, whether as an accompaniment to itineraries such as Spafarii's journey, to journeys of exploration like Atlasov's, to maps and atlases, or to some mixture of the three. The collections of documents published by Titov (1890) and in *Zapiski russkikh puteshestvennikov* ('Notes of Russian Travellers') (*Zapiski* 1988) constitute a fair reflection of some of the more important materials produced in this period.[28] One also thinks of Remezov's cartographic work and with its textual accompaniments, embracing Siberia.

Although most of the geographical accounts discussed so far concern Russia, or one or two neighbouring countries such as China, the seventeenth century also witnessed the appearance in Russia of a new type of geographical literature – the cosmography. Cosmographies embraced not just individual countries, or even the earth as a whole, but the entire universe as it was understood at the time. Thus the beginning of the Russian translation of the Blaeu atlas, which probably dates from the 1650s, explains that cosmography studies both the heavens and the earth and consists of two parts: astronomy, which studies the heavens and heavenly bodies, and geography, which studies the earth (Lebedev 1949, 211–12). As noted above, numerous Western cosmographies and atlases had been translated into Russian in the sixteenth and seventeenth centuries, informing Russians about the character of the globe and of their place in it. An important example is the so-called *Kosmografiya 1670g.* ('Cosmography of 1670'), a uniquely Russian production (*Kosmografiya 1670g.* 1878–81). This was analysed by Nikolai Charykov towards the end of the nineteenth century (Charykov 1878–81).

The full title of the 'Cosmography of 1670' (or the '76-chapter Cosmography' as it is sometimes called) is the *Kniga glagolemaya Kosmografiya sirech', opisanie vsego sveta zemel' i gosudarstv velikikh* ('Cosmography or Description of the Lands and Great States of the Whole World'). The manuscript itself declares that it was finished on 4 January

1670 in Kholmogory, a town situated near the White Sea. However, on the basis of detailed research, Charykov argues that it was composed between 1655 and 1677 in Moscow (Charykov 1878–81, 41–2; Lebedev 1949, 214). In its origins, the *Cosmography* seems emblematic of the eclectic culture of late pre-Petrine Russia. Thus in part it contains many citations of classical and medieval European authors and travellers, and Latin forms are given to names. Elsewhere the predominant references are biblical, with many mythical and legendary elements. Here the influence of such Byzantine writers as Cosmas Indicopleustes is evident. Charykov concludes that the 'Cosmography' is based on three sources. First, of the 76 chapters, 69 are clearly derived from the Russian translation of Mercator's *Cosmographia,* replete with classical and West European references. Mercator's work was translated into Russian in about 1637 by Bogdan Lykov of the Ambassadors' Chancellery. However Mercator's creation was not incorporated into the 'Cosmography of 1670' unmodified, especially since only a limited amount of information about Russia had been available to Mercator. Furthermore, unlike Mercator's *Cosmographia,* the Russian one of 1670 contains no maps. A second source for the 'Cosmography of 1670' is the West European literature that came to Russia by way of Poland and Ukraine, exemplified by the *Cosmography* of Marcin Bielski. The third source is the Byzantine and Russian material of a strictly Orthodox and national character, which Charykov calls the 'Short Cosmography'. He believes that this was composed before the beginning of the seventeenth century and was originally a stand-alone composition, later incorporated into the 76-chapter work. The 'Short Cosmography', he argues, may have been the most popular cosmography in seventeenth century Russia, and was widely reproduced into the eighteenth.

It is notable that the 'Cosmography of 1670' considers the world as divided into four parts: Europe, Asia, Africa and America. Information about the latter is clearly taken from West European sources. But Charykov and others have argued that the Russo-Byzantine material also contained much that was valuable, particularly regarding the geography of Russia itself and that of its near neighbours. Lebedev describes the 'Short Cosmography' as 'an original expression of Russian geographical thought of the late-sixteenth or early-seventeenth century' (Lebedev 1949, 215). In conclusion, Charykov describes the 'Cosmography of 1670' as:

> … an attempt by a Russian seventeenth-century writer to combine in one compact and full text all the best and most interesting

geographical information contained in those Byzantine, Russian, Latin and Western sources that were most widely distributed in Russia at the time and from which Russian readers of the pre-Petrine era could extract information on cosmographical and geographical issues. This attempt fully succeeded. (Charykov 1878–81, 80)

Conclusion

From the accession of the Romanov dynasty in 1613 there was a growing concern on the part of Russia's rulers to centralize and strengthen the state. This meant gathering more spatial and geographical information about the state's territories and taking action based on that information. It also meant developing a more sophisticated understanding of Russia's place in the world, so as to enhance defensive measures where necessary, to secure needed resources, and to take advantage of trading opportunities with China, Western Europe and elsewhere. In such ways the new dynasty sought to secure its position and to avoid the anarchy that had characterized the preceding period.

Thus it is apparent that, even before the radical reforms of Peter the Great, Russia was not a static society but one undergoing modernization. This became particularly apparent by the latter half of the seventeenth century. All the facets of geographical endeavour described in this chapter – the mapping, cadastral survey, exploratory ventures, geographical description, and translations of foreign geographical literature – are evidence of modernization. Yet in the minds of Peter and other elite Russians these accomplishments fell short of requirements and far short of what was being achieved in Western Europe. Russian maps, for example, lacked a mathematical basis and were far from comprehensive in their coverage. They also faced difficulties in their publication. Russian cadastres also suffered from an unsophisticated mathematics and were dropping out of use by the late-seventeenth century to the detriment of demarcation between landholdings. Exploration was conducted on an *ad hoc* basis without any overall plan or coordination. The translation and publication of geographical literature suffered from the same publishing problems as those confronting maps. Russian geographical endeavour therefore faced many problems. Many of these issues were to be addressed by the 'Tsar-Reformer'.

Notes

1. *Atlas Novus* – see below.
2. However, Peter's father, Tsar Alexis, who exhibited a personal interest in astronomy and astrology, had an astronomical ceiling painted in his palace at Kolomenskoe and had an armillary sphere erected on the roof (Ryan 1999, 23).
3. See, for example, several of the essays in Kotilaine and Poe (2004).
4. Woodcuts were introduced to Russia in the later-sixteenth century, and engraving and etching on metal began in the seventeenth, but only in the reign of Peter the Great were such modes of reproducing illustrations properly established. See Cracraft (1997, 24–6, 149ff.).
5. For one example of the contentious nature of this whole area, see Baron (1992).
6. The chancelleries were early equivalents of modern-day government ministries.
7. See also Shaw (2005, footnote 32); Rybakov (1974).
8. I have discussed Serbina's analysis of the 'Book' in Shaw (2005).
9. For a detailed analysis, see Shaw (2005).
10. See also Gol'denberg (1965).
11. One chetvert, as an area measure, was one half of a desyatina, or about 1.35 acres (0.546 hectares).
12. 'Black' (*chernaya*) land was land belonging to the tsar in his capacity as sovereign (that is, not personally). It was subject to normal tax obligations.
13. A second cadastre, this time a full *pistsovaya kniga*, was compiled in 1628–9. The 1615 cadastre and extracts from that of 1629 were published by the local provincial statistical committee in *Materialy* (1891).
14. The two main Tatar groups active in the area were the Crimean and Nogai Tatars.
15. Known as the *odnodvortsy*. See Shaw (1990a; 1990c).
16. The different categories of servitor reflected their varied origins and duties.
17. Dependants were probably named in order to ensure their legal enserfment.
18. Atamans were higher-ranking Cossacks. *Belomestsy* ('white place') atamans and Cossacks were free of certain state impositions.
19. The word 'waste' (*pustosh*') was used to describe unsettled land which might be cultivated or otherwise actively used.
20. Except for the Cossacks, they generally served in the infantry.
21. Villages (*sela*) usually had churches; hamlets (*derevni*) did not.
22. See Zagorovskii 1969, 26. Shortages of manpower to defend the frontier encouraged the government to recruit from many different social elements (runaway serfs, Cossacks and others) despite laws purporting to maintain the exclusiveness of the different servitor groups.
23. The Ambassadors' Chancellery was the department of state responsible for foreign affairs.
24. Different versions of the 'Verst-Book' give inconsistent geographical information. The version transcribed by Petrov is not always geographically accurate.
25. See, for example, Kennedy (2014).
26. The Siberian Chancellery was the department of state overseeing Siberian affairs.
27. Yurii Krizhanich (1618–1683) was a Croation priest and scholar who was exiled to Tobol'sk in west Siberia in 1661 for what were deemed his heretical views on Slavic Church unity.
28. See also Andreev 1960.

3
'The Great Designs of the Tsar': the era of Peter the Great (c. 1694–1725)

> *The occasion of his first falling upon the thoughts of shipping, and of his travelling to inspect the improvements of other countries, was owing chiefly to his early genius and curiosity to enquire into the reason and causes of things; which method in his common conversation, he still uses with indefatigable application in the minutest things. And next was also owing to an accident that happened, which led him to a liking and pleasure in conversation with foreigners.*
>
> John Perry, 1716 (1967)

By the late-seventeenth century Russia was gradually opening itself to the outside world, and this fact was reflected in many fields, not least that of geographical endeavour. Even so the gap between Russia and the rest of Europe in science, technology and culture remained a wide, and possibly widening one, which rendered Russia vulnerable to the ambitions of the increasingly powerful and expanding powers to its west. This was a gap that Tsar Peter I (born 1672), whose formal reign commenced in 1682 but who began to rule about 1694, was determined to close. After having discussed the overall background to the new tsar's reforms, this chapter will consider the impact of those reforms on a number of facets of geographical endeavour: mapping, Peter's educational and publishing initiatives (with particular emphasis on the translation and publication of Bernhard Varenius's *Geographia Generalis* in 1718), the geographical contribution to Peter's purported 'well-ordered police state', and expeditionary work, especially that of the German Daniel Messerschmidt (1720–7).

Peter the Great's reforms: their context and characteristics

Given the autocratic and highly personal character of Russian government in the late-seventeenth century, the personality and outlook of the tsar himself are vital to an understanding of his policies. Peter's personality and life have been subject to searching scrutiny by historians,[1] and only a brief summary of their findings is possible here. Peter's views seem to have been much affected by the events of his youth, when political instability meant that the future tsar and his mother were forced to spend much of their time in exile from the court. In the event Peter found himself free to consort with the inhabitants of the 'German suburb' (*nemetskaya sloboda*), situated close to one of his residences just outside Moscow and the place where foreign soldiers, merchants, adventurers and others were obliged to reside. By seeking the company of such men as the Swiss Franz Lefort and the Scot Patrick Gordon, Peter was exposed to the ideas and outlook of a European world quite alien to that of most seventeenth-century Russians. Peter's prior education had been of the narrowly religious kind that was then deemed appropriate to members of the ruling family. The tsar was no intellectual, and to the end of his days he remained a basically practical man with a limited grasp of abstract ideas. Even in this, however, Peter was unconventional – previous tsars led lives of seeming religious piety sequestered in the Moscow kremlin. By contrast, before he began to rule Peter indulged his passions for sailing, shipbuilding, military manoeuvres and war games. As ruler he was able to put such childish hobbies to practical use. Throughout his life Peter proved himself keen to learn at first hand from others and himself to practise many of the arts he observed. Perhaps the most startling indication of this comes from his journeys abroad, undertakings which had no precedent among earlier Russian rulers. Especially significant in this regard was the celebrated 'Grand Embassy' to the Netherlands, England, Germany and Austria in 1697–8 when the tsar worked for a time as a shipbuilder and craftsman. On such occasions he was keen to meet technicians, intellectuals and practical men, some of whom he recruited to work in Russia. There is much to suggest that over the course of time Peter was increasingly impressed by European accomplishments beyond the narrow concerns that had first arrested his attention. His policies to modernize Russia thus became ever more ambitious and, being a man of restless energy, he was personally involved in the drive to apply them.

It is almost certainly a mistake to imagine that Peter was motivated by a carefully defined ideology, such as a well-constructed policy to

'Westernize' his country. Although he was no doubt impressed by the wealth and apparent power of the foreign countries he visited, initially at least his reforms grew out of the pressures and demands of warfare. Indeed, during Peter's reign Russia was almost continuously at war, notably against the Ottoman Empire (1695–1700, 1710–11), in the Great Northern War against Sweden (1700–21) and the war against Persia (1722–3). Early reforms were evidently formulated in haste, but after the victory over the Swedes at the Battle of Poltava (1709) many appear to have been constructed in the light of foreign models, especially those provided by the northern and western countries that Peter had visited and which had so impressed him with their military, technical and cultural achievements (Butler 2021). Thus what began as a series of *ad hoc* measures with little real interconnection eventually became a determination to transform the realm. Step-by-step reform of the army, and the gradual building of a navy (essential for the military campaigns against the Turks and the Swedes), began to have implications for such matters as government administration and finance, systems of recruitment, and the provision of armaments, equipment and supplies. These matters in turn interconnected with economic, social and cultural issues. War, for example, placed enormous strains on the uncoordinated and even chaotic government administration inherited from Peter's predecessors. Greater coordination and centralization were secured by the establishment in 1711 of the Senate, a body that gradually assumed competence over different areas of administration. Its activities were supplemented from 1718 by the more specialized colleges, forerunners of ministries, arguably based on Swedish models. Administrative reform connected with reform of the Church, which lost some of its autonomy and with it some of its ability to act as a conservative force in the state. Also connected with the stresses and strains of war were Peter's reforms of regional and local government (1708–10, 1718–19), which had the aim of expediting military recruitment and taxation, and strengthening law and order. The first reform divided Russia into eight, later thirteen provinces (*gubernii*) and the second one further subdivided these into fifty *provintsii*. A new system of districts (*uezdy*) was also introduced at lower levels.

The implications of Peter's reforms for Russia's economy, society and culture were profound. Notable economic changes included the reform of government finances, involving the imposition of a poll tax (1718), industrial development (such as that of the Urals iron industry), attempts to improve agriculture, and the encouragement of foreign trade (here, the founding of St Petersburg, Russia's new port and capital on the Baltic, was especially significant). In the social arena, two important changes included the imposition of a Table of Ranks to tighten the system of compulsory state service for the nobility (1722) and further restrictions on the peasantry, notably those arising from the poll tax and from the new military recruit levy (1705). Finally, in the cultural sphere, the tsar's sweeping reforms touched on many areas designed to reduce the differences between Russia and Western Europe: dress reform (for the nobility), calendar reform, the development of St Petersburg as a distinctly European city in form and appearance, the encouragement of science and education, language and printing reform, and others. Altogether the Russia that emerged at the end of the reign in 1725 was a very different place from that which had existed previously. Even so not all Peter's reforms were successful, and some were reversed after his death. Indeed, in some ways his policies widened the gap between Western Europe and Russia, particularly in strengthening the bonds of serfdom and the imposition of the Table of Ranks on the nobility. What Peter wanted was not a Europeanized Russia, but a modern and thus a strong one. Perhaps inevitably, however, in this he was only partially successful.

Under Peter, Russia began to assume the contours of a modern European state, able to play a significant role in European affairs. Thus his conquest of Ingermanland from the Swedes and construction of his new capital there, and his occupation of the Baltic provinces and other acquisitions in the west, ensured Russia's access to the sea and moved it closer to Europe. At the same time Russian activities in Central Asia, Siberia and the northern Pacific, to be described below, consolidated its imperial hold over these territories. Russian geographical endeavour under Peter was a key component of state- and empire-building in this period.

Geographical endeavour under Peter: mapping

I have often heard the tsar say that he intends to send people on purpose to take a true map of his country, as soon as he has peace and leisure to apply his mind to it.

John Perry, 1716 (1967)

Although it has been suggested above that Peter's early education was a religious one and that as tsar his initial approach to learning was essentially pragmatic, there is no doubt that he displayed real intellectual curiosity and shared with many of his intelligent contemporaries a fascination with the intellectual and technical discoveries of his day. His geographical interests were no doubt stimulated by the broad horizons that were then opening up, and the availability in Western Europe, if not yet in Russia, of literature, maps and other materials testifying to the existence of a new world. Peter himself, unlike his forebears, was an incessant traveller both within Russia and abroad. His geographical interests were undoubtedly also fostered by his love of ships and sailing. This devotion is underlined both by Peter's childhood experiences and by his attitude towards his navy. As Anderson writes: 'Throughout his adult life the fleet was his greatest passion, the greatest single focus of his hopes' (Anderson 1978, 88). The tsar's interests in all naval affairs, and his participation in shipbuilding and other associated practical pursuits, was an outstanding feature of his character (Hughes 1998, 80–9).

Peter proved anxious to meet and correspond with such eminent foreign geographers as Nicolaes Witsen and Guillaume Delisle, and discuss cartographic and related problems with them. He subsequently invited the astronomer and geographer Joseph-Nicolas Delisle, half-brother of Guillaume, to accept a position in the new Academy of Sciences. On the personal level, the tsar collected many books, atlases and maps. According to Luppov (1973, 170), at his death Peter left a personal library of 1,351 maps and 1,621 books, some 8.8 per cent of which are described as geographies, cosmographies or atlases. Only on religion (many no doubt inherited), naval and military affairs, and history and heraldry did he have more books. Peter's geographical interests are also evidenced by the report that he himself read through a draft translation of Varenius's *Geographia Generalis*, expressed his dissatisfaction on several points, and ordered corrections (Lebedev 1950, 354).

No doubt it was Peter's practical interest in military matters and his eagerness to learn from foreigners that led him at an early stage to appreciate the significance of surveying and mapping for navigation and warfare. As we have seen, Russia had experience of mapmaking, but Russian maps were crude and inaccurate by the standards of the day. Moreover their improvement was hampered by a lack of trained surveyors and cartographers. Peter was determined to overcome this problem by employing what little talent there was in Russia, by recruiting foreign expertise and by training new specialists. In 1695 during the first Turkish war, for example, Peter's siege of Azov, the Turkish fortress near the mouth of the Don, failed because the Russians lacked a navy to prevent the enemy from supplying it by sea.[2] Peter therefore set to work to build a fleet of galleys and barges at Voronezh, further up the Don, employing foreign experts in boatbuilding and siege warfare, and also surveyors to map the siege works and fortifications around Azov and sections of the Don river. One of the first fruits of this work was a map of southern Russia and its adjacent territories prepared by the mathematician James Bruce (Yakov Bryus), a Russian of Scottish descent, and the surveyor Yu. A. Mengden (Filimon 2003, 23–6) (Figure 3.1). The map was published by Jan Tessing in Amsterdam around 1696–9, probably the first Russian map to be published (Bagrow 1975, 98–100).[3] Work along the Don, the coasts of the Sea of Azov and parts of the Black Sea continued into the early years of the new century. One of the cartographic monuments to this period is the *Nauwkeurige afbeelding vande Rivier Don* ('Atlas of the Don'), published in Amsterdam about 1703 (Cruys c. 1703). This work bears the name of the Dutchman Cornelius Cruys, soldier and surveyor, who had been recruited in Amsterdam during Peter's Grand Embassy.

With the outbreak of the Great Northern War against Sweden in 1700 the work of surveying and mapmaking took on new directions. The war stimulated the survey of the Baltic coasts and the mapping of the seas and adjacent territories. Notable achievements included a nautical atlas of the Baltic (1714), a general atlas of the Baltic Sea (1719–23) and the mapping of the Baltic provinces taken from Sweden, including the area around St Petersburg. In addition to the severely practical tasks of aiding the movement of Russian armies and ships and easing the problems of administration, such cartographic endeavours also served to further Russian claims to these peripheral regions. Much the same could be said of Peter's efforts to map the Caspian Sea. Under Peter, these began in 1699 and continued beyond the end of his reign.

As the years went by and the pressures for change became more apparent, the need for proper surveys and maps moved well beyond narrow military and naval concerns. Maps were now seen as vital documents for government at all levels. As the *General'nyi Reglament* ('General Regulation') of 1720 stated in establishing colleges:

> In order that each college should have an authentic list and information concerning the condition of the state and of the provinces belonging to it, it is necessary that there should be general and particular maps or charts in every college – depicting all borders, rivers, towns, settlements, churches, hamlets, forests and so forth. (Gnucheva 1946, 20)

Figure 3.1 A simplified version of the Mengden-Bruce map of south European Russia (1699). The map has been modified and simplified to emphasize territories significant to the defence of southern Russia. Based on Kordt ed. (1899–) map 74. Map © D. J. B. Shaw, drawn by Martin Brown.

Considerable survey and mapping work was also involved in Peter's many construction projects, such as the building of roads and canals, of new factories like the ironworks in the Urals, and especially of the city of St Petersburg. Peter was responsible for the introduction to Russia of new principles in town planning and architecture, first applied to the new capital and then to other places. Border changes and more stringent standards of demarcation also meant the paying of more careful attention to the frontiers, as with the Turkish frontier in 1704–5, the Swedish in 1722, and the Chinese just after the end of his reign. Peter gradually came to the view that nothing less than a full geographical survey of the whole of Russia would meet the growing needs of the state. This ambition was no doubt encouraged by the tsar's meeting with the celebrated cartographer Guillaume Delisle in Paris in 1717, with whom he discussed the problems of such an undertaking, and by his correspondence with the philosopher and polymath Gottfried Wilhelm Leibniz (Kuentzel-Witt 2018). The growing number of trained geodesists (surveyors) in Russia by this stage also seemed propitious. In 1715 Peter ordered that geodesists be trained in mapmaking so that they could be sent in pairs to each province of the empire to compile a general map. A comprehensive Senate decree on this matter was issued in December 1720, followed up by detailed instructions to the geodesists allegedly written by the tsar himself (Lebedev 1950, 204). However, the work proceeded slowly and by the end of the reign the Senate had received maps for only about 12 per cent of the empire's districts. The full fruit of these endeavours came only some years later in the compilation of the first Russian atlas in 1734 by Ivan Kirilovich Kirilov.

Peter's educational and publishing initiatives

Peter's policy of reform was heavily dependent on the availability of specialists trained in a variety of fields ranging from navigation, shipbuilding and metallurgy to cartography and mining. Inevitably, therefore, the tsar was obliged to establish institutions where such training might be acquired.[4] One such institution was the Moscow School of Mathematics and Navigation, founded in 1701 (Hans 1950–1, 532–6; Ryan 1991). The principal instructor was Henry Farquharson of Marischal College in Aberdeen, who was assisted by two young graduates of the Royal Mathematical School at Christ's Hospital in London, Stephen Gwyn and Richard Grice. The curriculum of the Moscow School was based on that taught at Christ's Hospital and included such subjects as mathematics, navigation, fortification, astronomy, geography and geodesy. Several of the school's graduate geodesists worked under Farquharson and Gwyn on a survey of the Moscow–St Petersburg road in 1707–8 (Aleksandrovskaya 1989, 142).

Although the school began to take on a higher educational role after 1710, it soon lost this to the St Petersburg Naval Academy established in 1715. Farquharson and Gwyn were transferred to the new institution, whose curriculum was designed to produce more advanced graduates. Subjects taught included reading and writing, arithmetic and geometry, artillery and fortification, navigation and geography, drill with muskets, fencing and drawing. According to Aleksandrovskaya (1989, 142), courses in geography (including elements of mathematical geography, map reading and simple introductory studies of the map of the globe) were taught in all Peter's specialized schools. It is also important to note the considerable number of young Russians sent abroad during the reign to complete their education (Okenfuss 1973). This policy did much to disseminate geographical and other scientific ideas in Russia as well as practical knowledge of many kinds.

For Peter, education and science were seen to be important not only as a means of producing the specialists required by his reforms but also as a way of enhancing Russian prestige. Towards the end of his reign Peter's desire to be seen as a patron of the sciences, as well as the need to advance science in Russia, took concrete form in the initiation of the Academy of Sciences. Among the many influences bearing upon the tsar in this endeavour was that of the German philosopher Leibniz, with whom Peter began to correspond in 1697. Leibniz was a proponent of science, believing in the unity of scientific knowledge based upon mathematics and logic, and holding that the growth of human knowledge would glorify God. A leading figure in the establishment of the Berlin Academy in 1700, Leibniz saw Russia as providing a vital site for the spread of Christianity and rationality as well as an important link to the east. Russia was also regarded as a significant potential source for scientific data. Leibniz urged Peter to open Russia up to scientific discovery and, in a memorandum sent to the statesman Petr Pavlovich Shafirov in 1716, argued among other things for the advancement of geographical knowledge, a systematic survey of plants, animals and mineral ores in Russia and its southern neighbours, and the translation of scientific and technical literature (Vucinich 1963, 47). Detailed planning and recruitment for the Academy involved the participation of Leibniz's disciple, Christian Wolff. When the Academy was finally opened just after Peter's death in 1725, geography with navigation was grouped with theoretical mathematics, astronomy and mechanics in one of the three classes of specialism. The chair of astronomy and geography was occupied by Joseph-Nicolas Delisle who, together with his colleagues, was to make a major contribution to the mapping of Russia.

As well as establishing institutions where modern science and practical skills might be taught and encouraged, Peter's policy of reform required the printing and dissemination of relevant literature. Before Peter's reign printing was a Church and government monopoly, and largely given over to devotional literature and some government output. A new beginning was made in 1697–8 when the tsar, during his visit to Amsterdam, contracted with the Dutch printer Jan Tessing to establish a Russian press for the publication of maps, charts and secular books. The Mengden-Bruce map of southern Russia, mentioned above, was one of its few accomplishments. Within a few years several secular presses had been set up in Russia itself, most notably the Moscow press of V. O. Kiprianov, who was a graduate of the School of Mathematics and Navigation and who operated under the sponsorship of James Bruce. Kiprianov's press quickly became a leading centre for the publication of maps and geographical materials, though other presses were also active in geographical publishing. Peter's introduction of a new and simplified civil orthography in 1707 was a positive development for secular publishing (Marker 1985, 21). Likewise, the hiring of foreign engravers like the Dutchman Adriaan Schoonebeek, who was recruited during the Grand Embassy, considerably facilitated the publication of maps.

The move towards modern, mathematically based mapping was enabled by the publication of textbooks like the *Arifmetika* (1703) by Leontii Magnitskii, who may have been an early student of Farquharson (Ryan 1991, 82). According to one scholar, the period between 1700 and Peter's death in 1725 witnessed the publication of 33 history and geography books and 14 of science and technology (Marker 1985, 25). Science here included arithmetic, geometry, astronomy, navigation and also geography, which was understood in its mathematical sense.

The dissemination of modern geographical thought was also facilitated by the translation and publication of foreign literature. The first textbook of geography to be published in St Petersburg was entitled *Geografiya, ili kratkoe zemnogo kruga opisanie* ('Geography, or a Brief Description of the Earth's Circle', see *Geografiya* 1710). This was seemingly based on a Dutch original. Other notable publications included translations of Christiaan Huygens's *Cosmotheoros* (1717), which helped to propagate the Copernican heliocentric system, Bernhard Varenius's *Geographia Generalis* (1718), of which more below, and Johann Hübner's *Kurtze Fragen* (1719). With regard to the latter, in November 1716 James Bruce wrote to Peter, who was in Amsterdam at the time, to inform him that two scientific books had been translated, one of which was:

> ... a geography, whose author is called Hübner, which, on account of its usefulness, will be very much wanted by everyone for the knowledge of all states, and also of laws, customs and of their neighbours, in addition to which the names of their rulers are made known. (Pekarskii 1862, 299–300; Shaw 2007a)

Quite apart from the practical importance of Hübner's work, the sources also give us a clue about what Peter saw as its broader significance. Thus, in a letter from Bruce to Peter dated 6 May 1717, the former asks whether the tsar would agree to the book, 'except for the description of the Russian state, which is inaccurate', being printed in Moscow rather than St Petersburg. The request arose because of the dilatory nature of printing in the capital (Pekarskii 1862, 302). Reference to the inaccuracy of the description of Russia evidently reflects Petrine sensitivities over Russia's reputation. In other words, Hübner was valued for what it could teach Russians but not for what it had to say about Russia itself. In the Russian edition Hübner's references to 'Muscovy' are thus expunged in favour of 'Russia'. Peter was evidently concerned to dispel European as well as Russian ignorance, and to instruct Europeans in the new European geography – one that embraced Russia as an integral part of Europe. Hübner's clear indication that Europe's boundaries embrace at least the central and northern parts of what would be recognized today as European Russia could only find favour with the tsar (Shaw 2007a, 67; Cracraft 2004, 210–11).

Bernhard Varenius's *Geographia Generalis* and Peter's geographical programme

> 'Our Most Sagacious Monarch' ordered that 'this most learned and wise Geography book' be translated from the original Latin into a Russian text for the benefit of students and readers.
> Translator's Preface from Varenius (1718),[5] quoted in Cracraft (2004, 206)

Peter's decision to order the translation and publication of Bernhard Varenius's *Geographia Generalis* can be regarded as a significant step in the introduction of modern geographical thought to Russia, and indeed of modern science more generally (Shaw 2007b). Varenius was born in 1622 at Hitzacker on the Elbe and was educated at several German universities and at Leiden in the Netherlands, where he graduated doctor of medicine in 1649. From 1646 he lived in Amsterdam. In 1649 he published two books on Japan, and in 1650 his *Geographia*. He appears to have died in the same year in unknown circumstances (Schuchard 2007a).

The *Geographia Generalis* soon became widely known. Three Latin editions were published in Amsterdam by Louis Elsevier in 1660, 1664 and 1671. These formed the basis for editions edited by Isaac Newton, published in Cambridge in 1672 and 1681.

The first translation into a contemporary language was Richard Blome's English-language edition, entitled *Cosmography and Geography*, published in London in 1682, 1683 and 1693. These appear to be based on the Amsterdam version. The Newton Latin editions were re-edited and republished by James Jurin in Cambridge in 1712 and then translated into English and published as *A Compleat System of General Geography* by 'Mr. Dugdale' and Peter Shaw MD in London in 1733 (Varenius 1733). Further editions of this translation appeared in 1734, 1736 and 1765.

The 1718 Russian edition of *Geographia Generalis*, entitled *Geografiya general'naya*, was chronologically only the second edition to be published in a contemporary European language. This early translation is no doubt explained by the general ignorance of Latin in Petrine Russia as well as the tsar's wish that the book be read as widely as possible. The translator was Fedor Polikarpov of the Moscow Printing Office and the book was published, according to the title page, 'by command of his Most Sacred Tsarist Majesty' in Moscow in June 1718. It appears to be based on Elsevier's Amsterdam edition of 1664 (Cracraft 2004, 206).

Varenius's book was also translated into other European languages (Schuchard 2007b, 234). Thus it appears that it was in wide circulation in Western Europe in the first half of the eighteenth century. Despite one scholar's caveat about assuming that Varenius's English editions constituted 'a standard textbook' or were in 'huge demand' among students or the learned (Mayhew 2007, 243; see also Aleksandrovskaya 1989, 26), and the fact that the book was nearly sixty years old when it was chosen for translation into Russian, it was clearly considered a valuable resource by scholars across Europe at the time.

Unfortunately, there is no direct evidence about exactly why Varenius's book was chosen for translation. But it might be possible to address this issue in part by considering what role it probably played in

Peter's policy to modernize Russia. In his introduction, and following an already established tradition, Varenius states:

> We divide *Geography* into *General* and *Special*, or *Universal* and *Particular*. We call that Universal Geography which considers the whole Earth in general and explains its properties without regard to particular Countries; but Special or Particular Geography describes the Constitution and Situation of each Single Country by itself. In this Book we shall exhibit Universal Geography.[6]

Thus Varenius's book is quite different from Hübner's work – which was, by Varenius's definition, essentially a 'special geography'. Whereas Hübner's work is basically descriptive, Varenius, like many of his contemporaries (and like Newton) regarded geography, and particularly general or universal geography, as a branch of mathematics:

> Geography is that part of mixed Mathematics [*uchenie matematicheskoe, smeshenoe*] which explains the State of the Earth, and of its Parts, depending on Quantity viz. its Figure, Place, Magnitude and Motion, with the Celestial Appearances etc. (Varenius 1733, 2)[7]

Peter was acutely aware of his country's mathematical backwardness – which put Russia at a disadvantage in all kinds of ways – and strove to overcome it. Varenius's book gave a fresh, mathematical vision of the world, unprecedented in Russia. In the Russian context it must have seemed like a vision of modernity.

The book's mathematical approach comes out strongly in Book One of the work, or what Varenius called 'the Absolute or Independent Part' (*chast' sovershennaya*), that is, 'what respects the Body of the Earth itself; its Parts and peculiar Properties e.g. its Figure, Magnitude and Motion, its lands, seas, rivers etc.' Here, after a chapter devoted to 'Preparatory Propositions from Geography and Trigonometry' (with a brief lesson in the latter), there follow chapters on such topics as the sphericity of the earth, its dimensions and how they are measured, its internal composition, and the major divisions of its surface into continents and oceans. Perhaps of particular significance to Peter were chapters five and six where, in the opinion of one scholar at least, the reality of the Copernican system is firmly established (Staffhorst 2007). There then follow chapters on such topics as mountains (including how heights are measured), the ocean (including tides), rivers, mineral springs, the air and atmosphere, and winds. In these chapters, of course, the discussion is more descriptive than mathematical.

The mathematical character of Varenius's geography reaches its apogee in Book Two, or the 'Relative Part' (*chast' razsmotritel'naya'*), namely 'Appearances and Accidents that happen from Celestial Causes'. Here much of the mathematical structure essential to the realization of what might be called Peter's geographical project is given: the background to mapmaking, navigation, practical astronomy, location finding, the calculation of time, and what were known as 'climates' (in Russian *strany* or *kraya*) – the differing length of day and night in different seasons and at different latitudes. Thus the first chapter in this section is devoted to a definition of terms (globes, maps, the poles, the axis of the earth, the meridian, horizon and so on) and to a description of the apparent motions of the sun and stars. The following chapters discuss the concept of latitude and how to find it on maps or at a given place, the zones into which the earth's surface can be divided relating to the differing length of the day in different places, and the measurement of time.

If Peter would no doubt have valued the second part of Varenius's book for providing the mathematical basis for a whole range of geographically related activities, the importance of Book Three or 'The Comparative Part' (*chast' uravnitel'naya*) must have seemed self-evident, for the emphasis is on the actual practice of mapmaking and on the practicalities of navigation by sea. Beginning with a discussion of the making and uses of maps and globes, including how to make maps 'in the mathematical style', how to take bearings and calculate distances, the section proceeds to consider the arts of navigation and of steering a ship (including how to build and correctly load ships) and many related practical matters.

Varenius's *Geographia* therefore provides a comprehensive and systematic analysis of the universal or mathematical geography of the globe according to the scientific understanding of the day. But it is far more than this. It is also an account of how to put that mathematical geography to use in the solution of a host of basic geographical problems. Its potential significance for Peter's modernizing project, including the educational part of that project as reflected in the translator's preface quoted above, was readily apparent. Cracraft has pointed out how the tsar himself took a personal interest in the translation, being unimpressed with the first draft when it was submitted in the autumn of 1716. As noted above, Peter did not like Polikarpov's use of Slavonicisms to translate what the latter termed Varenius's 'elevated and beautiful Latin'. Polikarpov was therefore ordered to improve the translation 'not with high Slavonic locutions, but with the simple Russian language – of the

Ambassadorial Office', or as it was known, Chancery Russian (Cracraft 2004, 208). The tsar was evidently most concerned that the book should be understood by its readers. Eloquence of expression was not a priority.

Cracraft has spoken of Varenius's significance to the development of geography in Russia and more broadly of his importance for science. Cracraft's essentially linguistic analysis points to the way in which numerous scientific terms and their related concepts, well understood by educated Europeans of the day, were introduced to the Russian language, and to Russian scientific culture at large, by Varenius via Polikarpov 'in a mixture of extant Russian (or Slavonic) terms and assorted neologisms'. Thus, in his view, the book made a fundamental contribution to the development of geography in Russia, 'to the subsequent acquisition, expansion and diffusion in Russian of geographical knowledge about both Russia itself and the rest of the world' (Cracraft 2004, 210). As such it also made a fundamental contribution to the Petrine project.

Towards the 'well-ordered police state': statistical and cadastral survey under Peter

Chapter 1 argued that it is important to place Russian geographical endeavour in the early modern period into the context of state-building. European states in this period were all engaged in the process of reinforcing their territorial control in the light of their quest for resources, defensive capacity, administrative efficiency and similar needs. One scholar who has taken a particular interest in the interconnections between spatial control and the exercise of political power in the development of the modern state is Anthony Giddens (1985). Giddens has emphasized the types of rule that are pivotal to states. In his view, rulers have access to two forms of control in exercising their power: control over resources and control over behaviour. Central to both are the ruler's access to, and control over, information flows. Giddens argues that the ruler's control over information flows very much depends on the exercise of *surveillance* (the collection and storage of information about society and its members, and supervision of the activities going on in society). Effective rule requires surveillance accompanied by the application of sanctions (including violent ones if necessary) to those who disobey or whose behaviour transgresses designated boundaries (Shaw 1999b).

One scholar who has attempted to apply this type of analysis to early modern Russia is Marc Raeff (1983). Raeff argues that in the West the ultimate effect of the Renaissance and Reformation was to give rise to a belief in 'man's unlimited capacity for self-improvement through rational activity'. In consequence, Europeans began to look upon the state as a human creation that could be fashioned to serve rational ends, representing a transition in the role of government from one that is essentially negative (primarily concerned with security and social stability) to one that is positive and active, abetting social transformation and 'the aggressive promotion of the country's potential, social and material' (Raeff 1983, 204). Raeff argues that Peter the Great increasingly borrowed from European absolutist states like Sweden and the Germanies the concept of the 'well-ordered police state'.[8] Typically absolutist rulers used the law in a most detailed and comprehensive way to educate and guide their subjects into thinking, and behaving, in the desired fashion, and in general to promote the power and well-being of the state. Peter, for example, often prefaced his decrees with explanatory passages designed to cajole his subjects and persuade them of the wisdom of the measures being taken (Behrisch 1999). In Russia's case, however, the gap between the mental outlook of the ruler and that of most of his subjects was particularly wide, and the tsar's admonitions, read out in church and other public places, frequently found an unreceptive and uncomprehending audience.

The need for accurate, systematic and up-to-date information on all parts of Russia was thus essential to the surveillance that was central to the success of Peter's reforms. Along with other European states of the period, therefore, Peter's Russia strove to develop mechanisms for the collection of many kinds of statistical data and of related types of information, including map data (Ptukha 1945). This whole process was inherently spatial, and provided the basis for the future geographical description and survey of the Russian state. Thus, in addition to the cartographic endeavours described above, Peter's government ordered the systematic survey of forest resources (1703), collected information from provincial governors on merchants and trading activities (1718), assembled detailed data on manufacturing (1719), collected materials on towns, stimulated and co-ordinated the search for minerals, commenced the first population census in connection with the poll tax (1718),[9] and ordered the Church to keep records of births, marriages and deaths (1721). The aims were common to European states of the period: internal pacification, compiling records of resources and wealth, taxation, population surveys for military recruitment purposes, and so on. In Russia, however, such efforts were all too frequently frustrated by the indolence and poor education of the officials tasked with collecting the data as well as by financial constraints.

One important facet of the 'well-ordered police state' was the tradition of land survey, which continued under Peter, albeit with some major modifications (Karimov 2007). Since landholding was no longer the basis for determining taxation and service obligations (once it was replaced by a poll tax on most of the population apart from the nobility and clergy, and a revamp of the compulsory service obligation on the nobility), the purpose of land cadastres changed. Peter's reforms entailed increased demands on local resources, and especially on Russia's forests. Despite the apparent vastness of the latter, timber was not necessarily abundant in the places where it was most needed. Timber was required for Peter's ambitious naval programme as well as for the new metallurgical works in the Urals and other projects. Surveying forest resources to assess the extent and quality of the timber available, and the imposition of conservation measures, therefore soon became part of Petrine practice.

The eighteenth-century forest cadastres were carefully studied by Aleksei Karimov (Karimov 1999 and 2007). Most of these are in the Naval Archive in St Petersburg, since the Admiralty was soon designated the central organization for overseeing Russia's forests, irrespective of their ownership. A decree of 1703 had introduced restrictions on the use of forests, even those in the ownership of monasteries and other landholders. The decree subjected all high-quality forests to the control of the Admiralty, amounting in effect to the nationalization of the forests. These restrictions were removed only in 1782.

Although forests were surveyed in a very general sense in the seventeenth-century cadastres, they were not subject to the accurate and precise surveys applied to arable and hay lands. The first case of a more precise forest survey was that conducted in the Voronezh district in 1698–1701. This was undertaken in connection with the shipbuilding on the Voronezh wharves that took place during Peter's first Turkish war. Karimov's research shows that the resulting survey was strongly influenced by the traditional Russian methodologies employed in the seventeenth century (Karimov 2007, 62–3). The Voronezh surveys were fragmentary and unsystematic, but a noticeable departure from the traditional cadastres (*pistsovye knigi*) was the fact that the material was presented according to the forests' locations in relation to navigable rivers.

More systematic, as well as showing greater Western influence, were the forest surveys of the 1720s. By this time the Russian focus had shifted to the Baltic in connection with the Swedish war. Forests in the neighbourhood of St Petersburg and in Novgorod province were subject to survey and the resulting material was recorded in great detail in survey books (the so-called 'Val'dmeister' books, indicating a strong German influence) and maps. Eventually, as Karimov indicates, forest surveys were extended in a systematic way to cover much of European Russia.

Expeditionary activity under Peter the Great

Expeditionary activity under Peter the Great proceeded along much the same lines as in previous reigns, and with similar motivations: the desire to explore and assert Russian sovereignty over new lands (including imposing *yasak* upon the native peoples), geopolitical and strategic motives such as securing Russia's borders and access to important land and sea routes, diplomacy and its associated trading links, and the acquisition of significant natural resources. But a new element now began to enter the frame – what we might call the 'scientific' – the careful description of lands and peoples, their classification, and the collection of material objects and other kinds of data. Interest in the 'scientific', of course, was very much the result of the modernizing influences encouraged by Peter. The problematizing of what is meant by 'scientific', however, is an issue inherent in much of what follows.

In addition to this new scientific element, the direction in which expeditionary activity advanced also changed somewhat. Much seventeenth-century activity was focused, as we have seen, on the eastern parts of the empire and on relations with China. By Peter's time the outermost wave of Russian influence was reaching the eastern fringes of Asia, its adjacent islands and the north-eastern Pacific. But under Peter, Russian interests also began to turn southwards towards Central Asia and the possibilities of developing diplomatic links and trading relations with such lands as Persia and India (Donnelly 1975). The Petrine geographical perspective was thus significantly broadened.

An exhaustive discussion of expeditions under Peter was provided by Lebedev (1950, 29–167) and the details need not be repeated here. The following discussion will therefore encompass only some of the principal characteristics of that activity before focusing on two expeditions – those of Evert Ysbrants Ides and of Daniel Messerschmidt – as key achievements of the reign.

Russian interest in Central Asia had already been much enhanced by the capture of Astrakhan', at the mouth of the Volga, in 1556. The Volga route gave the Russians direct access into the Central Asian region. By the reign of Peter's father Alexis (r. 1645–76) the significance of trade with Central Asia was reflected in Moscow's trading quarter (the *Kitai gorod*), where many eastern goods were traded wholesale and to which many embassies from that region together with accompanying merchants were directed. According to Donnelly, no fewer than 41 Central Asian embassies visited Muscovy in the seventeenth century, with eight Russian embassies proceeding in the reverse direction (Donnelly 1975, 205). Other trading centres for Central Asian goods included Astrakhan' itself and intermediate markets along the Volga such as Nizhnii Novgorod and Samara, as well as several towns in west Siberia. Not only Russians but also other Europeans were interested in the Eastern trade, and Russia began to act as something of a bridging point between Western Europe and Asia, bypassing Portuguese (and later Dutch) control over the sea route around Africa and the difficulties of dealing with the Ottoman Turks if travelling through the Levant. However, those wishing to develop relations with the Central Asian khanates experienced numerous problems, such as the lengthy journeys involved, the difficult environment, and the chronic lawlessness and warfare that beset the region.

Peter's ambitions in Central Asia were much greater than those of his father. As well as seeking to strengthen Russia's geopolitical position with respect to the trade with Persia and India, Peter found many attractions in Central Asia itself. Gold was rumoured to exist in the river sands of the region, raw silk was available along the western and southern coasts of the Caspian Sea, and cotton textiles, wool, finished silk, dyes, fruits and spices were also produced locally. The tsar hoped that, by taking advantage of the region's internal strife and asserting Russian sovereignty, not only would Russia benefit from Central Asia's own resources and products but also from the access it provided to Persia, India and other important lands. In all these ways Russian imperial ambitions had much in common with those of other European imperial powers active in various parts of the world in this period (Lehning 2013).

Despite the relative proximity of Central Asia to Russian territory, Russian knowledge of the geography of the region was limited. Peter evidently regarded the Caspian Sea as a key to control of the area, and for a tsar obsessed with his navy one can understand why. Russian domination of the sea, and the possibility of finding a river route from there to India, were among his principal aims. Russian mapping of the sea was begun by a Dane by the name of Skjelkrup in 1699, but unluckily he seems to have been taken prisoner by the Persians and died soon afterwards (Berg 1946, 167). Peter then appears to have commissioned Captain Meier, a German, to continue the work (1699–1703). Whether or not his map was ever completed seems uncertain. But the real breakthrough in Russian geographical understanding of the Caspian came through the map commissioned by Peter in 1715. For the first time, and unlike contemporary Western maps, this showed that the Amu Darya (Oxus) flows not into the Caspian but into the Aral Sea. When an engraved map of the entire Caspian Sea was presented by Peter's librarian, Johann Daniel von Schumacher, to a meeting of the Académie des sciences in Paris in 1721, it allegedly caused a sensation (Shaw 1996, 169).

The story behind the map is an interesting one. In 1713 Peter received information from a Turkmen that gold had been discovered in the sands of the Amu Darya, and that the river, which had formerly flowed into the Caspian Sea, could easily be diverted to do so again (Berg 1946, 171ff; Donnelly 1975, 210–12). The tsar was evidently not only tempted by the gold but also impressed by the possibility of sending a Russian fleet across the Caspian and up the Amu Darya into the heart of Central Asia and possibly as far as India. In May 1714, therefore, he signed a decree organizing an expedition to Khiva, to be led by the Russified Kabardian prince Aleksandr Bekovich-Cherkasskii. After an abortive start from Astrakhan' in the autumn of 1714 the prince set out again the following spring with a large number of ships and men. Having arrived at Karagan Bay on the east coast of the Caspian, he questioned local Turkmen concerning the former course of the Amu Darya and whether it could be diverted to flow that way once again. The Turkmen responded positively, and Cherkasskii sent a party of men to reconnoitre the former river mouth.[10] In the meantime the expedition surveyed the east coast of the Caspian as far south as Astrabad Bay. Having received a favourable report from his reconnoitring party, Cherkasskii returned to Russia to report to Peter.

The tsar decided to pursue the policy further and allocated a large sum of money and a considerable body of men to the venture. Cherkasskii returned to the Caspian in 1716 and began to build forts at various points along the east coast. In the following year he set out for Khiva but the Khivan khan, assuming that the Russians meant war, attacked and eventually massacred most of the Russian party. Clearly Peter's Central Asian ambitions had been thwarted.

Although Peter did make some further attempts to develop Russian relations with Central Asia (Donnelly 1975, 212–14), and he did finally control the Caspian Sea, the dream of establishing Russian supremacy over the region and of finding a river route to India failed. Nevertheless, Russian understanding of Central Asia's geography had been considerably advanced, as reflected in the map of the Caspian commissioned in 1715. It is also interesting to reflect that, in his plans for diverting the Amu Darya, Peter now displayed a new attitude towards nature. Together with his building of a new capital city on the swampy delta of the river Neva and his attempts to build new canals in various places, Peter demonstrated his belief that Russia's future should mean not only adapting to nature but, where necessary and possible, changing nature itself to meet the state's needs. No previous tsar had thought in these terms.

With regard to Siberia and the Far East, expeditionary activity centred, as noted already, on the easternmost parts of Asia, though with the gradual development of a scientific perspective attention also began to be paid to achieving a more systematic and profound understanding of already known regions.

Exploration of new territories only served to whet the appetite for further discovery. St Petersburg constantly pressed its governors and servitors to question the local inhabitants about new lands and the prospects for developing trade with distant places, to impose the *yasak* on 'unpacified' peoples, to follow up on rumours about unknown regions and native groups, and to send reports and maps. Local officials were instructed to build fortified posts (*ostrogi*) to guard strategic locations and ensure the security of Russian occupation. None of this meant that local initiative played no role but, as in many other areas of Petrine government, the centralization of activity was now much more important than formerly.

As a result of the Atlasov expedition (1697–9), which was briefly discussed in Chapter 2, Russians became familiar with the geography of Kamchatka, but many unanswered questions concerning the distant peninsula remained to be addressed. The overland journey to Kamchatka from Yakutsk, a major administrative centre of eastern Siberia, was long and difficult, taking up to six months to accomplish. Not until 1716–17 was a satisfactory sea crossing between Kamchatka and the mainland established. Meanwhile travellers had become aware of the existence of other lands and islands nearby: for example the Komandorskie (Commander), Shantar, and Kuril island groups. In 1720 the geodesists Ivan Evreinov and Fedor Luzhin were sent out to Kamchatka, and in May of the following year they sailed along the northern Kurils, surveying, mapping and secretly collecting as much information as possible on Japan (which at that time was closed to all foreigners except the Dutch). In 1722 Evreinov returned to European Russia and met Tsar Peter in Kazan', presenting him with a report of their journey and a map of Siberia, Kamchatka and the Kurils.

Beyond Kamchatka lay the Chukotka Peninsula jutting out into the Bering Strait and, beyond that, Alaska. Russian knowledge of all these regions in Peter's day was quite sparse. The Russian occupation of Chukotka was still contested, and whether or not there was a strait between Asia and North America was still considered uncertain despite Dezhnev's voyage of 1648. Rumours of a 'Big Land' lying further east circulated even in pre-Petrine times. However, according to one account, reliable information about its existence began to be acquired under Peter. In 1711 an expedition led by the Cossack Petr Popov and others was sent to Chukotka to collect the *yasak* from the natives and to enquire about other, non-*yasak*-paying peoples. Popov returned with valuable information about the 'Big Land', its inhabitants and their way of life, and its landscapes and resources. Although no Russian sighted Alaska during Peter's reign, and no maps were drawn, Russian knowledge of the territory was thus considerably enhanced (Lebedev 1950, 89–93; Berg 1924, 52–4).

Another offshore land that sparked the Russian imagination under Peter was Japan. Russian interest in Japan dates from the seventeenth century, when rough representations of that empire began to appear on Russian maps as well as textual allusions in various Russian reports – for example those of Spafarii and Atlasov. Lebedev relates the story of a Japanese captive by the name of Denbei who in 1701 was ordered by Peter to be sent to Moscow to be interrogated in the Siberian Chancellery (Lebedev 1950, 137–41). Denbei was questioned not only about the products available in Japan and possibilities for trade but also about many other aspects of Japanese life – its overall geography, its armed forces, the appearance of its towns, its religion, its monetary system, calendar and other matters – testifying to the wide variety of issues that interested Russian officialdom. Information about that country was also elicited from other Japanese subjects who happened to fall into Russian hands during the reign. Clearly Russians had been impressed by stories and legends about Japanese wealth and power, and this no doubt help to explain the mounting of the Evreinov-Luzhin expedition mentioned above.

As in the seventeenth century, Russian interest in China, as well as Mongolia, continued under Peter. Numerous embassies and trading missions were directed to China with the aim of strengthening diplomatic and commercial ties. As before, ambassadors and the leaders of trading missions were furnished with instructions ordering them to obtain a wide range of information about China as well as about their journeys there across Siberia, including details of the routes taken.

The latter were meant to verify earlier accounts and to discover new or improved itineraries. Peter's reign therefore witnessed a considerable improvement in Russian knowledge of the geography of both China itself and of intervening Siberia. The rest of this chapter is concerned with two Petrine expeditions that added considerably to the geographical understanding of Siberia in particular: that of Evert Ysbrants Ides (1692–5), belonging to the first part of the reign, and what is alleged to have been Russia's first 'scientific' expedition, that of Daniel Gottlieb Messerschmidt (1720–7), which took place at the end.

Evert Ysbrants Ides (Eberhard Isbrand Ides) was a Danish or possibly German trader (c. 1657–c. 1708), who from 1677 was engaged in commercial activity in Russia. In 1692 the Russian government decided to send him on a diplomatic and trading mission to China, partly in order to confirm the 1689 treaty of Nerchinsk (Lebedev 1950, 148–60; Alekseev 2006, 418 ff.). It may be that Ides also had his own commercial links with China. He was accompanied on his journey by several officials from the Ambassadors' Chancellery and by a physician whose job it was to collect roots, seeds, grasses and medicinal plants. As was normal for the period, Ides was furnished with detailed instructions concerning his diplomatic and commercial aims, including secret instructions to reconnoitre and map the Chinese frontier and to find out about the trading activities taking place in Peking. Ides's route took him by way of Tobol'sk, Narym, Eniseisk, Ilimsk and Lake Baikal to cross the Chinese border near Nerchinsk, and then to Peking. He returned to Russia in early 1695.

Although Ides's mission seems to have accomplished little on the diplomatic front, his detailed day-book gives much information about his journey across Siberia and his experiences in China. Since Europeans were greatly interested in the little-known geography of Siberia and in trading routes to China, the book soon attracted international attention. It was first published in Amsterdam in 1704 in Dutch (Ides 1704). Later translated editions appeared in London (1706) and Frankfurt (1707) with French editions being published in 1718 and 1727.[11] The only early Russian edition was issued by Nikolai Ivanovich Novikov in 1789.

Ides's day-book gives a detailed account of his journey across European Russia to the Urals, providing a vivid impression of the problems of overland travel in the late seventeenth century (Ides 1748). Leaving Moscow by sled in March 1692, his journey via Vologda, Tot'ma, Sol'vychegodsk, Kaigorod and Solikamsk was greatly delayed by the spring thaw. He had intended to cross the Urals via the town of

Verkhotur'e but found the way there impassable, and thus proceeded by the river Chusovaya. However, he found the river

> ... far less agreeable than the beautiful Kama, which is a fine river abounding with all sorts of fish, and from Solikamsk to this place, adorned with very fine large villages and towns, several very extensive saltworks, fertile corn grounds, fruitful lands, spacious fields beautified with all sorts of flowers, woods etc., all beautifully pleasant. But though the banks of the Zawaja which falls westward into the Kama, are not less beautiful and fruitful, yet we found our passing this river very tedious, for by the high water we made but very small progress in several days, being obliged to be towed along with a line; however, at last, after twelve days, and tiresome tugging against the stream, we came to, and touched at a pleasant shore on the 25th of May, amongst the first Siberian Tartars, called Wogulski.[12] (Ides 1748, 920)

As he crossed Siberia, Ides was impressed by the wildlife he encountered. In western Siberia, for example, he observed:

> This and the neighbouring places do not afford any quantity of other skins than those of red foxes, wolves and bears; but a few miles distant is a wood called Heetkoy-Wollok which abounds with the very finest grey squirrels that keep their colour both summer and winter; they are as large as the common squirrels, besides which the leather prepared from them is very strong, and they are not to be found anywhere in the whole Muscovite Empire besides. It is forbidden under a great fine to sell them to merchants, for they are ordered to be preserved for the use of the tsar. (Ides 1748, 921)

At Tobol'sk, 'the chief city of Siberia', where he arrived on 1 July, he noted there are fish and '... plenty of all sorts of wild beasts, as elks, stags, deer, hares etc. and of wild fowl, viz. pheasants, partridges, swans, wild geese, ducks, and storks, all of which are cheaper than beef'. Near Surgut on the Ob' a month later were sables and 'black fox-skins, which are the very finest and richest anywhere', and which are 'caught by dogs'. Hereabouts grey and red foxes, hyenas, beavers and lynx were also to be found (Ides 1748, 921–3).

Lebedev was particularly impressed by Ides's treatment of the human geography of Siberia as containing much 'new and valuable' material. It is difficult to disagree with this assessment, since rich and detailed accounts are given of such things as the appearance, costume, religion, marriage and burial customs, dwellings, modes of hunting, diet and other aspects of the ways of life of the various peoples he encountered. The whole is enhanced by a series of attractive and informative illustrations. At the same time, and despite Ides's contention that he aimed at objectivity (Ides 1748, 952), he could not resist giving vent to some startling prejudices, probably not untypical of the period. Thus, although their lands deserved to be reckoned 'amongst the most charming in the world', the already mentioned 'Wogulskian Tatars' are described as 'stupid heathens' whilst the 'Samoyeds'[13] are 'gross idolaters' (Ides 1748, 920, 953). Ides is particularly scathing about the latter peoples. After making derogatory remarks about their diet, he tells us: 'And notwithstanding all this, they inhabit a country that richly abounds with wild game, fish and flesh; but most of them are too idle to provide themselves with it' (953). This point is followed by other derogatory comments on the Samoyeds' appearance, religion and customs.

That said, the importance of Ides's work to Russian geographical understanding is undoubted. Ides, though himself a foreigner, was in Russian service and his expedition was mounted under the aegis of the Russian government. Its combination of foreign skills and Russian experience made it a particularly valuable contribution to Russian geographical understanding under Peter.

Without doubt the most significant expedition of Peter the Great's reign was that of the German scholar Daniel Gottlieb Messerschmidt, which took place between 1720 and 1727. Lebedev describes this as a 'genuinely scientific expedition' whilst Novlyanskaya states that Messerschmidt 'was the first scholar to undertake a scientific study of Siberia' (Lebedev 1950, 77; Novlyanskaya 1970, 5). This suggests that Messerschmidt undertook his journey not primarily for practical reasons like Ides, but in order to study nature for its own sake. His broad approach to science is emblematic of what Pickstone calls 'natural history', or the holistic understanding of science that was characteristic of the eighteenth century (Pickstone 2000).

Messerschmidt was born in September 1685 in the Polish city of Danzig, where his father was in Polish service. He began studying medicine at university in Jena in 1706.[14] Two years later he moved to Halle, where he continued his studies of medicine together with zoology, botany and eastern languages. At this time Halle was well known for its specialisms in natural history and linguistics and was a centre for Russian and other eastern studies (Winter 1953). Graduating as doctor of medicine in 1713, Messerschmidt returned to his home city of Danzig, where he practised as a physician.

Messerschmidt seems likely to have been recruited into Russian service by Tsar Peter during the latter's visit to Danzig in 1716. He arrived in St Petersburg two years later and signed a contract with the Apothecaries' Chancellery to undertake a scientific expedition to Siberia. The tsar's decree of November 1718 specified that the expedition, now overseen by the Apothecaries' Chancellery (the government's medical department), was to be principally concerned with the collection of medicinal herbs, seeds and similar resources (Novlyanskaya 1970, 10). But it soon became clear that Messerschmidt's own ambitions encompassed a much wider spectrum of interests, including not only the physical environment but also ethnography, the languages of indigenous peoples and even archaeology. Contrary to the assertions of some scholars, it seems unlikely that Messerschmidt was provided with exact instructions. Even his route across Siberia and his timetable seem to have been left to the doctor's discretion (Novlyanskaya 1970, 10–17).

Messerschmidt's journey across Russia was delayed by various bureaucratic difficulties, and he arrived in Tobol'sk in west Siberia only in December 1719. Here he suffered a further holdup until March 1721. A bonus for Messerschmidt, however, was the presence in Tobol'sk of a group of Swedish prisoners of war, most notably Philipp Johann von Strahlenberg (also known as Tabbert), an educated soldier who had spent his captivity studying the environment of the local area. He was able to advise Messerschmidt about Siberian nature, accompanied him for the first part of his expedition, and eventually played a key role in publicizing his scientific work (Borisenko 2022).

Leaving Tobol'sk at the beginning of March 1721, Messerschmidt's expedition proceeded to follow a roundabout route across Siberia, taking advantage of the region's great rivers where possible. The group eventually arrived at Nerchinsk near the Chinese border in July 1724. Messerschmidt's return journey began almost immediately at the urging of Johann Doedat Blumentrost, head of the Apothecaries' Chancellery, and took a somewhat more direct route across Siberia. Messerschmidt finally arrived back in St Petersburg towards the end of March 1727.

During his seven-year expedition Messerschmidt fulfilled an enormous programme of study (Heesen 2000). This encompassed not only the collection of 'rarities and medicinal herbs' envisaged in Peter's original 1718 decree, but also many other things: collections and descriptions of many types of plant, classified according to the then current systems (notably that of the French botanist Joseph Pitton de Tournefort), descriptions and classifications of fauna, collections and an attempted classification of minerals, reports on weather, the locations of places and routes, many drawings of flora, fauna, antiquities, indigenous peoples and their habitations, many maps, histories and archives relating to local peoples, accounts and discussions of their languages and ways of life, incidences of disease, and much else. During his journey, Messerschmidt sent regular reports to St Petersburg, and collections of materials were boxed up and sent back to the authorities. St Petersburg thus acquired an enormous amount of both written and material evidence on the geography of its eastern territories, more than could easily be processed at the time. Unfortunately much of it was lost during a fire in the Academy of Sciences in 1747. Part of the written archive survived, however, and is housed in the Russian Academy of Sciences Archive in St Petersburg. A great deal of material found its way into Peter's *Kunstkammer*, or 'His Majesty's Cabinet of Curiosities', where it formed the basis for future scientific studies (Shaw 2021, 241–2). Messerschmidt had thus fulfilled the previously mentioned request, which Leibniz had sent to Shafirov in his 1716 memorandum, that Peter open Russia up to scientific investigation.

One of the most important artefacts of the Messerschmidt expedition is his travel journal, a daily diary which he kept religiously throughout his journey, recording his activities and his observations of nature and of the people he encountered. This has been published only relatively recently (Messerschmidt 1962, 1964). A detailed examination of this journal has been published by Anke te Heesen, depicting what it tells us both about Messerschmidt personally, including his attitude to the locals, and his meticulous way of working (Heesen 2000).

Despite the absence of detailed instructions to guide him, Messerschmidt can be said to have introduced European research methods to Russia. As a result of his endeavours, the Russian authorities, and especially the growing band of naturalists or scientists, gained an enormous amount of information about Russia's eastern territories, including their human inhabitants. He thus made a major contribution to how Russians 'came to know the world'.

Messerschmidt's life's work ended in tragedy. Peter the Great had died early in 1725 to be succeeded by his widow, who took the throne as Catherine I. Catherine died in turn in 1727, and there ensued a political struggle among the nobility. Messerschmidt had made enemies, perhaps because of his stern character and refusal to return from Siberia when he was first instructed to do so. An argument developed over access to his written accounts and collections, which were retained by the

Apothecaries' Chancellery and the new Academy of Sciences. In 1729 Messerschmidt returned to Danzig but lost further notes and materials in a shipwreck on the way. Only in 1731, after the accession of Empress Anna and through the good graces of several scholars and officials (such as Vasilii Nikitich Tatishchev, Gerhard Friedrich Müller and Archbishop Feofan Prokopovich) was he allowed to return to Russia, but even then was denied full access to his collections. He died in 1735, and it was almost certainly because of the dispute that the greater part of his work remained unpublished. That said, his written and material collections continued to be used throughout much of the rest of the eighteenth century, laying the foundation for the First Kamchatka Expedition (1727–30) led by Vitus Bering and for subsequent expeditions, including those by Johann Georg Gmelin, Peter Simon Pallas, Johann Gottlieb Georgi and others. In 1730, furthermore, Strahlenberg published his celebrated account of the geography of the northern and eastern part of Europe and Asia, citing the work of Messerschmidt by name and calling it to public and even international attention (Strahlenberg 1730). As Aleksandrovskaya writes: 'the results of [Messerschmidt's] journey were well known in the eighteenth century and had no small influence on the development of reliable conceptions of the geography of Siberia' (Aleksandrovskaya 1989, 41).

Conclusion

The reign of Peter the Great experienced a sea change in Russian geographical endeavour, a change that was to have profound consequences for that endeavour over the rest of the eighteenth century and beyond. As we have seen, at the end of the previous century Russians' understanding of the geography of their own empire (to say nothing of the rest of the world), though slowly improving, remained patchy at best. Maps were unscientific, generally inaccurate and their spatial coverage restricted. With the exception of officialdom, access to maps and to other sources of geographical information was practically non-existent. Few indeed were the Russians who exhibited any geographical curiosity, and those who did usually had strictly practical ends in view. Compared to Western Europe, Russia's contribution to the expansive 'Age of Discovery' was a limited one.

By the end of Peter's reign in 1725 much had changed. Through the recruitment of foreign specialists, mapping had been placed on a scientific and mathematical basis, and a start had been made to the systematic mapping of the empire's territories. Russia was now training its own band of specialists, proficient in mapping, surveying and other geographical skills, and the foundations of general education had been laid. The printing and publishing of maps and foreign geographical materials now became possible, and the first geographical survey of Russia was completed (though not yet published) in 1727 (Kirilov 1977). Expeditions began to take on a scientific character, and interest in the outside world – especially in neighbouring lands like Central Asia, Persia, India, China and Japan – grew. Russian exploration of north-east Asia and its nearby seas and islands eventually made a major contribution to the 'Age of Discovery', and thus to global geographical understanding. Russian geographical endeavour, in other words, was transformed.

This transformation entailed a number of features that were to affect Russian geographical endeavour over the long term. First, by the end of Peter's reign it had become clear that Russia had entered the European cultural realm, at least as far as science is concerned. The recruitment of foreign specialists to work in Russia, the training and education of Russian specialists, the translation of foreign literature, the sending of Russian youth to be educated and trained abroad, all ensured that henceforth Russian geographical endeavour would have a European rather than a traditional, home-grown character. This was in spite of the evident difficulties of transferring European experience directly into Russia. Second, rather than the largely practical aims that characterized geographical endeavour in the pre-Petrine era, geographical practice now embraced science in its broadest sense – meaning a curiosity about the world, its varied character and contents, and attempts to make sense of the world through accurate mapping, illustration, the collecting and classifying of objects, measurement and the like. This does not mean that the practical – territorial control, military defence, navigation, trade, the acquisition and exploitation of resources and so on – now passed out of the picture. As before, Russian geographical endeavour continued to reflect mixed motives, but now science became one of those motives. And third, both the tsar and the educated elite now began to look on science as a source not only of power but also of prestige. Peter's concern to ensure that publications, including translations of foreign works, conveyed the right image of Russia (for example, using the name 'Russia' rather than 'Muscovy' or, even worse, 'Tartary'), his desire to display examples of Russian scientific achievement (for example, his presentation of the new map of the Caspian Sea to the French Académie des sciences in 1721), and finally, at the end of the reign, his founding of the Academy of Sciences in order to foster Russian contributions to world science, all testify to the growing importance the tsar and the educated elite now placed upon scientific prestige. It was an attitude that was to persist.

Notes

1. In English see especially Hughes (1998).
2. For Peter's abortive attempt to build a new capital, Petropolis, at Azov, see Boeck (2008).
3. The map appears to have had several editions. For a detailed discussion, see Bagrow (1955).
4. Igor Fedyukin (2019) and others have emphasized the important role played by private individuals or 'projectors' in the founding of such institutions.
5. The original Russian edition is listed in the references below as Varenius (1718).
6. Here and elsewhere I have used the text of the Dugdale-Shaw English-language edition, which is available in the British Library (see Varenius 1733). Comparison with the 1718 Russian-language edition (Varenius 1718) shows relatively little variation in their substantive content.
7. 'Mixed mathematics' would today be termed applied mathematics (see Brown 1991). Here and elsewhere, Russian quotations are taken from the 1718 Russian-language edition.
8. However, the concept of 'the well-ordered police state' has been challenged by some scholars as too simplistic. See Wakefield (2009).
9. The first population census, which counted males only, was taken in 1719. From this time onward censuses were known as 'Revisions'.
10. This is the Uzboi system, a series of dry stream channels through which the Amu Darya once flowed to the Caspian. Interestingly, the idea of diverting the Amu Darya also found favour with Stalin, but was abandoned after his death.
11. See also Ides (1748).
12. Voguls, or Mansi. The identity of the Zawaja river is uncertain.
13. The Nenets people and other peoples dwelling in north-west Siberia.
14. For details of Messerschmidt's life and activities, see Winter and Figurovskii (1962), Novlyanskaya (1970) and Winter (1971, 3–14).

4
The post-Petrine period: the Academy of Sciences, the 1745 atlas and the Great Northern Expedition (1725–62)

> *Johann Georg Gmelin is important to us not because he was a man of extraordinary intellect and scientific achievements, but because he was the originator of one of the strong scientific traditions in the history of the Academy. This was the tradition of the scientific study of the country's natural resources – a mighty intellectual current upon which much of the Academy's glory rested until well into the nineteenth century.*
>
> Alexander Vucinich, 1963

Although Peter the Great may be said to have provided the basis for numerous forms of modern geographical endeavour, it took many years for his efforts to bear fruit. In terms of mapping, expeditionary work, geographical publishing and the other processes whereby Russians 'came to know the world', at the end of Peter's reign much remained to be done. Unfortunately his sudden death in early 1725 plunged Russia into more than three decades of political uncertainty and even turmoil. Having decreed in 1722 that Russia's rulers had the right to nominate their successors, Peter failed to nominate his own. In the event he was succeeded by his widow, who ruled as Catherine I for two years (1725–7), her ascension to the throne having been engineered by Prince Aleksandr Menshikov, a close associate of Tsar Peter. Thereafter Russia experienced the reigns of five other rulers before that of Catherine II ('the Great') (r. 1762–96), a German princess who had no rightful claim to the Russian throne. And yet, despite this era of 'palace revolutions', 'the tragicomedy at the top should not be allowed to obscure important developments which affected the country at large' (Riasanovsky 1969, 268).

Among those important developments, as this chapter will show, were those directly affecting geographical endeavour.

Perhaps the most significant was the founding of the Academy of Sciences, the decree for which was signed by Peter in 1724 and which opened just after his death in 1725. Peter's project for the Academy, which was sent to the Senate for discussion in January 1724, specified that the new institution was to be 'an edifice that will not only serve to spread the sciences of the present day to the glory of the state, but also through the teaching and propagation of the same be of use to the nation in the future' (*Materialy* 1885, 15). The Academy was soon to acquire other aims, such as the duty to comment on the veracity and usefulness of new discoveries and inventions, and to undertake specific investigations on government orders (Kopelevich 1977, 159). However, such concerns quickly assumed secondary importance by comparison with what was to become the Academy's prime activity for much of the eighteenth century: to survey and map Russia's vast territory with a view to ascertaining its resource endowment and to promoting the empire's security and development. Indeed the emphasis given to science and geographical endeavour during this period arose directly from Russia's changing geopolitical situation. Peter's victory over Sweden in the Great Northern War and later Russia's participation in the Seven Years' War (1756–63) ensured its status as a great European power. The task now was to bolster this status by securing the empire's borders and taking full advantage of its wealth of resources.

This chapter will lay special emphasis on developments in two major fields of geographical endeavour that experienced particular advances at this time: mapping and exploration. Building on Peter the Great's record in the modernization and mathematical transformation of Russian mapping, the period witnessed cartography's further expansion and development, although not without controversy. Important roles were played by the government's Senate and by the Academy of Sciences, which opened a geographical department in 1739. Russian cartography's major achievement at this time was the publication of the country's first national Atlas in 1745, widely known as the 'Academy Atlas'. As regards geographical expeditions, the period was marked by the mounting of two major expeditions, the First and Second Kamchatka Expeditions (1725–30 and 1733–43), the latter often known as the Great Northern or Great Siberian Expedition. These two ventures placed Russian expeditionary work on a new scale, heralding the introduction of what has been termed 'Enlightenment exploration' (Withers 2007, 88). This chapter will also give some consideration to geographical publications of the period, a continuation of Peter's policies to encourage geographical understanding among the educated classes.

Post-Petrine mapping

Mapping in the post-Petrine period built upon the foundations laid by Peter the Great (Gol'denberg and Postnikov 1985). Its key feature was its centralized character, whereby cartographic activities were planned and directed by the state. To begin with, the major institution overseeing mapping activities was the Senate, where Ivan Kirilovich Kirilov (1695–1737) was secretary from 1721 and chief secretary from 1727. As noted in Chapter 3, Peter the Great's order of 1720 commanded that geodesists be sent to every province to compose maps of the area (Fel' 1950, 7; Lebedev 1950, 204). Kirilov subsequently became responsible for overseeing the work of the geodesists and for collecting the completed maps with a view to composing an atlas and to publishing a description of the Russian state. He issued a series of instructions to the geodesists to ensure the standardization of the work. Kirilov subsequently received permission from the Senate to publish the maps, which appeared as the *Atlas Rossiiskoi Imperii* ('Atlas of the Russian Empire') in 1734. This consisted of 37 maps, including a general map of Russia, the first to portray the country on more or less accurate lines.

Also central to Russian mapping in this period was the French astronomer and cartographer, Joseph-Nicolas Delisle (1688–1768), half-brother of Guillaume with whom Tsar Peter had discussed cartographic problems on his visit to Paris in 1717. It seems likely that Guillaume recommended his sibling to the tsar, who was recruiting specialists for his intended Academy of Sciences. After protracted negotiations Joseph-Nicolas arrived in St Petersburg in 1726, some twelve months after the tsar's death (Appleby 2001). Peter had had the intention of giving Russian cartography a more modern and mathematical basis and there was no doubt that Delisle could provide this. Under the aegis of the Académie des sciences, founded in 1666, and using new or refined technologies such as the telescope, logarithms and more sophisticated astrolabes, French cartographers led the world in mapmaking, particularly in the further development and application of triangulation. Under the leadership of Jean-Dominique Cassini, they set out to compose an entirely new and more accurate map of France. Eventually the whole country was surveyed, an accomplishment known as the Cassini survey, and a new map, consisting of 182 sheets at a scale of 1:86,400, was published. The Delisles – the two brothers along with their father Claude – were important participants in this venture (Konvitz, 1987).

It is hardly surprising, therefore, that Joseph-Nicolas, once appointed to the chair of astronomy at the St Petersburg Academy of Sciences, was eager to map Russia on an accurate, mathematical basis. He was soon to assume control of the Russian mapping project, being sent 33 maps by Kirilov at the Senate. To achieve greater cartographic accuracy, Delisle's first task was to determine the latitudes and longitudes of major Russian cities, beginning with St Petersburg itself. Determinations of longitude were in part derived from observations of the movement of Jupiter's satellites, a method perfected by Cassini, supplemented and made more accurate by using the solar parallax method. Delisle also attempted to introduce triangulation to Russia, measuring a baseline between Peterhof, on the coast of the Gulf of Finland south-west of St Petersburg, and Dubki on the opposite shore. He developed plans to extend this initiative along the Baltic coast and also north of the capital to Arkhangel'sk (Archangel) and Kola. In the event, however, this initiative was defeated by lack of funds, instruments and manpower. Delisle's attention was soon diverted on to other matters.

Vasilii Nikitich Tatishchev (1686–1750), who hailed from an impoverished gentry family in the Pskov region of north-western Russia, was also to make an important contribution to the modernization of Russian mapping (Iofa 1949; Evteev 1958; Daniels 1973; Aleksandrovskaya 1996, 157–9). Initially serving as a soldier, he became assistant to James Bruce, suggesting that he was a man of some talent and education. In 1719 Tatishchev was instructed by Peter and Bruce to commence a full survey and geographical description of Russia, a huge undertaking that proved impossible to fulfil since he was quickly diverted to other projects. In 1720 he was sent to the Urals, where he organized mining activities, established factories and engaged in mapping work, and then spent two years in Sweden, where he undertook various political duties and acquainted himself with Swedish mining and cartographic techniques. Returning to the Urals in 1734, Tatishchev continued with his duties there, which now included the exploration, defence and settlement of the region. In 1737, following the death of Kirilov, Tatishchev was appointed head of the Orenburg Expedition in the Urals – despite its name, an administrative and defence organization rather than an exploratory one – and in the same year he succeeded Kirilov as responsible for all cartographic activity in Russia. In this connection in 1738 he issued an instruction (*nakaz*) to geodesists in the provinces of Kazan', Siberia and Irkutsk designed to tighten up mapping activities in those regions and place them on a more centralized and scientific basis. This had also been the substance of a report (*donoshenie*) he sent to the Senate in the previous year proposing an acceleration of cartographic activities. As head of the Orenburg Expedition and governor of Astrakhan' (1741–2) he was able to send the Academy of Sciences a series of maps (sometimes referred to as the 'Tatishchev Atlas') composed under his supervision. Tatishchev is also noted for a questionnaire of 198 questions designed to be sent to provincial governors and their subordinates that would collect a wide variety of information to supplement that contained in the maps, and to aid future mapmaking. Unfortunately he was unable to escape the many political turmoils of this period and spent the last few years of his life in exile on his estate north-west of Moscow.

Delisle's plans for the strict, mathematical mapping of Russia would have taken years to accomplish and have occasioned huge expense. In practice, Russian mapping was a compromise between traditional methods like eyeline surveys, traverses following routeways and the measurement of directions using the compass, and stricter mathematical methods like the determination of astronomical points and of distances using the surveyor's chain. Maps were accompanied by written descriptions, based in part on the questioning of locals. The descriptions were designed to compensate for the limited amount of information conveyed by the maps. Although Delisle believed that modern maps needed an accurate, scientific basis, his ideas were opposed by scholars and administrators like Kirilov and Tatishchev who, being more conscious of Russian realities – the country's vast expanse and the lack of equipment and trained personnel – sought a compromise between traditional and modern approaches. In other words, they believed it was better to have rather inaccurate maps than no maps at all.

The 1745 'Academy Atlas'

The 1745 *Atlas Russicus* or 'Russian Atlas' (*Atlas Rossiiskii*), 'consisting of nineteen special maps presenting the Russian Empire with neighbouring lands ... with appended thereto a general map of this great empire' was a signal achievement of post-Petrine cartography. In view of its sponsorship by the Academy of Sciences, it is also referred to as the 'Academy Atlas' (see *Atlas Russicus*, 1745).

The background to the atlas has been discussed by Postnikov (1989, 49–51). Although work on provincial maps continued after Peter's death in 1725, it was not until 1735, with a Senate decree ordering maps and geodesists to be transferred from the Senate to the Academy of Sciences 'to compile a general map', that work on the composition of an atlas can be said to have begun. Four years later in 1739 the Academy of Sciences created its geography department to continue this work. Leonhard Euler (1707–1783), the celebrated Swiss mathematician, physicist and cartographer who had arrived in St Petersburg in May 1727, was appointed head of the department in 1740. In addition to his many mathematical studies, Euler accomplished much in the fields of cartography and astronomy and argued that the 'general map' of Russia should be based on larger-scale regional and district maps that should be published alongside the general map, thus in effect becoming an atlas. To facilitate the composition of the atlas, maps had been collected not only from the Senate but also from other government departments engaged in survey and mapmaking of various kinds. Many of the maps acquired, however, were found to be defective in lacking sufficient astronomically determined points, and many geodesists needed training to remedy this defect. In 1738, therefore, a new set of instructions was issued by Delisle and Euler indicating how this might be done.

The atlas was published in Latin and Russian editions and furnished with an explanatory text and index in German and French (Fel' 1960; Bagrow 1975; Kokkonen 1992). The general map of Russia is drawn at a scale of 1:8,400,000. Thirteen sheets cover European Russia at a scale of 1:1,527,000, and Siberia and the eastern territories are covered by six maps at a scale of 1:3,360,000. The standard symbols are derived from European cartography of the period. The projection is devised by Delisle himself, derived from Mercator. The physical landscape is depicted in very general form (elevation, drainage patterns, vegetation) and the human settlements are fitted into a rigid hierarchy.

Although the atlas was positively received internationally, no doubt in part because information on the geography of Russia that had previously been available was so limited, it also attracted some criticism. Tatishchev, for example, noted that not all available sources had been consulted (such as the materials gathered by the Petrine geodesists), some places and physical features had been omitted, and no account had been taken of Russia's different peoples. Other problems noted included mistakes in the drawing of some state borders and lack of attention paid to information gathered by the Second Kamchatka Expedition. Not surprisingly, perhaps, the historian Gerhard Friedrich Müller, a specialist on Siberia, pointed to some of the Siberian maps as especially problematic.

Kokkonen has argued that the efficient adoption of modern cartographic methods in Russia was relatively rapid due to the state's centralized nature, whereby local barriers could easily be overcome. Equally, however – as the dispute between Delisle on the one hand and Kirilov and Tatishchev on the other illustrates – modern mapmaking methods could not be applied in Russia without considering Russian conditions. Translating French mapping methods directly into Russia was unrealistic; in fact not until the twentieth century was anything as comprehensive as the Cassini survey of France accomplished. Once again this illustrates how cultural translation from the West to Russia was a far from straightforward process.

Post-Petrine exploration

Just as the post-Petrine period witnessed attempts to conduct Russian mapping on a more scientific basis, with greater attention paid to mathematical precision and standardization, so the same can be said of geographical exploration and survey. The previous chapter drew attention to the fact that the Messerschmidt expedition to Siberia was the first Russian expedition that can be said to have had a scientific basis. But although this set a pattern for the future, it was a relatively small-scale affair. The post-Petrine period, by contrast, was characterized by two major expeditions, known as the First and Second Kamchatka Expeditions, which were both bigger in scale (especially the second) and more far-reaching in their goals. As the eighteenth century proceeded, European geographical expeditions tended to become larger in scale, more cosmopolitan in composition and more focused on exact observation and reporting – or what has been termed 'Enlightenment exploration' (Withers 2007, 88). The two Kamchatka expeditions, and especially the second, can be said to be examples of this trend.

Peter the Great signed the decree for the First Kamchatka Expedition (1725–30) in 1724 shortly before his death. As expedition commander he appointed the Dane, Vitus Bering (1681–1741), with another Dane, Martin Spangberg, and a Russian, Aleksei Chirikov, as deputies. Bering had considerable naval experience and had served in the Russian navy since 1704. The expedition's central purpose, however, has been disputed by scholars, since Peter's instructions were quite vague (Urness 2003, 20). In contrast to traditional ideas, which suggested that the expedition was designed either to explore the eastern end of a projected north-east passage from Europe to the Pacific, or to find a sea route between Kamchatka and North America, Urness has argued that its principal purpose was to map Siberian territories east of Tobol'sk to the Pacific coast. Indeed, the drawing of an accurate map of those regions was perhaps the expedition's major achievement (see Frost 2003, 58–61). Urness does not discount the possibility that the expedition was also designed to discover whether or not there was a land bridge between east Asia and North America, the subject of earlier correspondence between Peter and Leibniz. In the event, although the flotilla of three ships (two newly built and one repaired) sailed north and then north-west into the Chukchi Sea before returning to Kamchatka, the North American coast was not sighted. This suggests that the issue of a land bridge was not the expedition's main focus.

The Second Kamchatka Expedition (1733–43), or Great Northern Expedition, was by contrast an enormous enterprise allegedly involving, in one way or another, more than three thousand people and costing the Russian state a huge slice of its income (Hintzsche and Nickol 1996, 200; *Vtoraya* 2001; *Vtoraya* 2009). Bering appears to have proposed this second expedition on his return to St Petersburg in February 1730, presumably because his first expedition had failed to achieve all its goals, such as resolving the question of the existence of a land bridge, or a strait, between eastern Asia and North America. Bering's proposal, however, coincided with political turbulence surrounding the accession of Empress Anna (r. 1730–40) and it was not until April 1732 that approval was given. The expedition was split into three components. The first or northern component was tasked with mapping Russia's north coast as far as Anadyr', situated close to the Bering Strait, and then finding a sea route to North America. The second component under the command of Martin Spangberg was to sail south from Okhotsk and find a sea route to Japan and China. Both the first and the second component were supervised by the Admiralty. The third component, which was approved in June 1732, was overseen by the Academy of Sciences and reverted to the methods employed earlier by Messerschmidt – in other words rather than being primarily concerned with navigation and mapping, its focus was on the collection and identification of plant and animal specimens, ethnography, historical artefacts and evidence, and also with the determination of astronomical points. The Academy appointed three scholars to lead this component: the German naturalist Johann Georg Gmelin (1709–1755) was made responsible for natural history and minerals; the German historian Gerhard Friedrich Müller (1705–1783) for history and ethnography; and the French astronomer Louis de l'Isle de la Croyère (1690–1741), the younger brother of Joseph-Nicolas Delisle,[1] for astronomical and cartographic studies (Black 1983). As well as two painters and other participants, the Academy component included several students, for example Stepan Krasheninnikov, of whom more below.

The various expedition components left St Petersburg at different points in 1733, partly because of the problems of obtaining supplies and completing necessary paperwork, and because of the difficulties of housing and provisioning such a large party of people at stopping points along the route. As had happened on the First Expedition, the land and river routes they followed proved difficult. Eventually the three components reassembled at Yakutsk in September 1736. An important achievement of this part of the expedition, however, was the charting of much of the north coast (Frost 2003, 72–3, 76–7). Thus, after two failed attempts, Dmitrii Ovtsyn finally succeeded in 1737 in sailing by sloop down the Gulf of Ob' to the sea and then east along the coast to the mouth of the Enisei. In 1735–6 the survey of the coast from the mouth of the Lena westwards to that of the Enisei was begun by V. M. Pronchishchev; after his death in 1736 the task was only completed in 1741–2 by Khariton Laptev, travelling partly overland. A party from this expedition under Semen Chelyuskin surveyed the bulk of the Taimyr Peninsula, reaching the cape now named after him (the northernmost point of Eurasia) at some point in 1742. Meanwhile Khariton Laptev's cousin, Dmitrii Laptev, surveyed the sea coast from the mouth of the Lena eastwards to that of the Kolyma, thereafter travelling overland to Anadyr'. All these expeditions faced the problem of sea ice, and thus the coastal surveys were completed partly by land.

Not until much later, in the late-eighteenth and early-nineteenth centuries, was the remaining gap in the survey of the north coast, from the mouth of the Kolyma eastwards to Cape Dezhnev, finally closed. This was the accomplishment of the expeditions of James Cook, Joseph Billings and Ferdinand von Wrangel, the last two in the service of the Russian state.

Another signal achievement of the Second Kamchatka Expedition was the Russian discovery of Alaska (Hintzsche and Nickol 1996). Although the North American continent had first been sighted from the west in 1732 by Ivan Fedorov and Mikhail Gvozdev in a campaign directed at the suppression of the Chukchi people, it was not until some ten years later that the continent's geographical relationship with eastern Asia became clear. Owing to various delays and difficulties, Bering arrived in Okhotsk only in August 1737, and only three years later in 1740 was the construction of two ships, the *St Peter* (to be commanded by Bering) and the *St Paul* (to be commanded by Chirikov), completed. The ships left Okhotsk for Kamchatka in September of that year, founding the city of Petropavlovsk (named after the two ships) on Kamchatka's Pacific coast towards the end of the year. In early June 1741 they left Petropavlovsk bound for America, but later that month the two ships were separated in a storm. They nevertheless separately sighted Alaska in the middle of July and made landings on the mainland or on nearby islands. Chirikov decided to return to Kamchatka, which he reached in October. Bering meanwhile was shipwrecked off what is now Bering Island near Kamchatka in early November and died the following month. His party, which had been depleted by further deaths, overwintered on the island and then built a smaller vessel to take them back to Kamchatka, where they arrived in late August 1742.

Frost makes the point that the accomplishments of the Second Kamchatka Expedition became internationally known only gradually, partly because of the Russian government's policy of secrecy. However, the educated world eventually became aware that its achievements included a much more accurate understanding of the geography of the North Pacific (as reflected in Müller's map of 1754) as well as a fuller understanding of the flora, fauna and ethnography of eastern Siberia (Frost 2003, 232). The latter was in part the result of studies undertaken by Gmelin and Müller. But also significant was the work of two of their younger colleagues, Stepan Krasheninnikov and Georg Wilhelm Steller, to which we now turn.

Stepan Krasheninnikov (1711–1755) and his 'Description of the Land of Kamchatka'

Relatively little is known about Krasheninnikov's early life (Fradkin 1974; Polevoi 1994). Born in Moscow the son of a soldier, he was educated at the Slavic-Greek-Latin Academy. Evidently showing signs of early promise, Krasheninnikov was selected as one of a group of students to take part in the Second Kamchatka Expedition, and was sent to the Academy of Sciences in St Petersburg to study botany, zoology and minerals. But he also soon evinced an interest in history and ethnography. He was subsequently appointed as 'student' to the Academic detachment of the Second Kamchatka Expedition under the supervision of Gmelin and Müller, accompanying Gmelin in his journey across Siberia and making various observations on the way. They reached Yakutsk in autumn 1736 where Gmelin and Müller, reluctant to undertake the hazardous journey to Kamchatka at this point, decided to send Krasheninnikov ahead to arrange housing and to make various preparations for themselves and the Academic contingent before the arrival of the main group. The professors also issued him with an extensive set of instructions, including the requirement to undertake his own research in the meantime (Polevoi 1994, 5). Having left Yakutsk in early July 1737, Krasheninnikov reached Okhotsk on the Pacific coast in August. Here, while waiting for a ship to take him across to Kamchatka, he undertook extensive research into the local meteorology, flora and fauna, including questioning the locals. He also made a study of the local 'Lamut' (Even) language. Various items of interest were sent back to St Petersburg for the *Kunstkammer*.

Eventually in October Krasheninnikov boarded ship for Kamchatka, rather late in the year for such a dangerous trip. Perhaps unsurprisingly he was subsequently shipwrecked on the coast of Kamchatka, having lost most of his possessions en route, but was fortunate enough to save many of his books and scientific instruments. He then established himself at Bol'sheretsk *ostrog* on the south-west coast of Kamchatka from where, in a series of trips across and up the peninsula, he undertook numerous studies of the local environment and peoples (Polevoi 1994, 5–10). In many ways, then, Krasheninnikov followed in the footsteps of Messerschmidt, as a naturalist engaged in encyclopedic studies of a largely unknown land, writing reports on his findings and sending material collections back to his superiors in eastern Siberia or St Petersburg.

In 1740 Krasheninnikov was joined in Kamchatka by Steller and de L'Isle de la Croyère. Professors Gmelin and Müller had decided meanwhile to remain in Siberia. Early in the following year, before he departed with Bering on his voyage to America, Steller decided to send Krasheninnikov to Yakutsk to talk to Gmelin and Müller about problems in the payment of their salaries. In the event Krasheninnikov had to travel to Irkutsk to speak to the professors. He was detained by them in Irkutsk and was unable to return to Kamchatka. He subsequently travelled back to St Petersburg with the two men, arriving in February 1743.

Krasheninnikov's remaining career was to work as a member of the Academy of Sciences, being appointed adjunct in 1745 and professor of natural history in 1750 (one of the few Russians to become a full member of the Academy in the eighteenth century). His book, *Opisanie zemli Kamchatki* ('Description of the Land of Kamchatka'), containing an account of his scientific studies on the peninsula, was published in 1755, the year of his death (Krasheninnikov, 1755). In view of the lack of information available on the North

Pacific at the time, it quickly attracted international attention and several foreign editions soon appeared (Polevoi 1994, 16–17). The first to be published was the English translation by James Grieve, which appeared under the title *The History of Kamtschatka and the Kurilski Islands with the Countries Adjacent*, published in Gloucester (Krasheninnikov 1764). The quotations that follow are taken from this edition (Shaw, 2010).

The *History* is divided into four parts. Part one is a general geographical description of Kamchatka. It also contains a description of the nearby American coast, which Steller had visited in 1741–2 with Bering. Part two concerns natural history and is a typically encyclopedic treatment of what we would today call the physical geography of the territory (for example the climate, volcanoes and hot springs, vegetation, fauna and other features). Part three is devoted to 'The Natives of Kamtschatka and their Customs and Manners'. Finally, part four approaches most closely what would now be understood as a history, with an account of the Russian conquest of the region and changing relations with the indigenous peoples, of present-day settlement, of the way of life of the local Cossack communities, and of routes across eastern Siberia to Kamchatka, including a discussion of Krasheninnikov's own journey there.

What perhaps strikes the modern reader of Krasheninnikov's book is its strongly utilitarian orientation, as virtually every plant and animal is described in terms of the use to which it is put by the locals. Thus chapter 5 of part two, 'Of Trees and Plants', begins as follows:

> The most useful wood is the larch, and the white poplar, which serves for building their houses and forts; and they are fit not only for building such boats as the inhabitants use, but even for the building of ships. The larch-tree indeed, only grows upon the river Kamtschatka, and such other rivers as fall into it: in other places they make use of the white poplar. (Krasheninnikov 1973, 81)

Not least among the traits of the locals to interest the naturalist are their food and medicines:

> Their principal nourishment is from the nuts of the *slantza*, which grows everywhere, both in hills and dales … The greatest virtues of these nuts is, that they are a good remedy against the scurvy, as all our seamen can witness: for in the most severe scurvy this is, as one may say, almost their only medicine. (Krasheninnikov 1973, 82)

There follows a detailed discussion of a series of other plants, mainly used for food and medicine. Among these is one called the *saranne*, which was used as a substitute for grain. Another, the 'sweet plant', was used to distil 'brandy' or spirits (in Russian: *vino*). Krasheninnikov provides a detailed description of the method of distillation, as well as some alarming comments on the effects of imbibing it:

> Mr Steller made the following remarks upon this brandy: first, that it is very piercing, and contains a good deal of a sharp acid, which coagulates the blood and makes it black; secondly, that a small quantity of it makes people drunk and quite senseless and causes their faces to turn black; thirdly, that if a person drinks a few drams of it, he is plagued the whole night with disagreeable dreams, and next day is uneasy and disturbed, as if terrified with the apprehension of the greatest misfortune and, what is very extraordinary, he has seen some people the day after they have been drunk with this spirit, from one draught of cold water, become again so drunk that they could not stand upon their feet ... Many of the Kamtschadales, who desire to have children, will not eat this herb, green or dry, imagining that it impairs the generative faculties. (Krasheninnikov 1973, 87)

The section on food concludes with the following observation:

> These are the principal plants which they make use of in their kitchens ... However, [Mr Steller] tells us the natives have obtained such a knowledge of plants, and of their use both in food and medicine, that he is surprised; and that one shall not find so much knowledge of this sort among any barbarous nation, not even, perhaps, amongst the most civilized. They give a name to every one of their plants, and know all their properties, and the different degrees of virtue which they derive from the various soils and expositions in which they grow; and so accurate are they in these distinctions, and also in the proper time of gathering the several fruits and other produce, that it is truly wonderful. Hence the Kamtschadales have this advantage over other peoples that they can find food and medicine everywhere; and, by their knowledge and experience, are in little danger from the noxious plants. (Krasheninnikov 1973, 91)

Although it is sometimes suggested that the eighteenth-century Enlightenment insistence on the need to bring all scientific knowledge within the bounds of a single 'map' or synthesis led to the dismissal or discounting of local knowledge systems, here we find just the opposite – not only the careful analysis of an indigenous knowledge system based on a practical understanding of nature, but a sense of wonder at how dependable and all-encompassing this system was. Here in effect was a rejection of the Enlightenment idea that rationality was based purely on the European scientific outlook, and the acceptance of the significance of local experience and environmental expertise. Both Steller and Krasheninnikov clearly felt they had much to learn from both the indigenous peoples and Russian locals.

The book's next chapter turns to consider 'the Land Animals':

> The principal riches of Kamtschatka consist in the great number of wild beasts: among which are foxes, sables, stone foxes, hares, marmottas, ermines, weasels, wolves, reindeer wild and tame, and stone rams. Their fox skins in the beauty, length and thickness of their hair equal, if not excel, all the foxes of Siberia. (Krasheninnikov 1973, 95)

Not surprisingly, Krasheninnikov has much to say about that most valuable fur-bearing creature, the sable. Among other things he comments on its hunting, complete with moralistic observation:

> The sables are still in much greater plenty here than in any other country ... And if the people of Kamtschatka were as industrious in hunting as those about the Lena, they could sell a great many more than they; but such is their natural laziness, that they never kill more than they must pay in tribute, and what will pay their debts. (Krasheninnikov 1973, 97)

With regard to what Grieve translated as 'rats' but Krasheninnikov calls 'mice' in the Russian original, the latter notes that there are three kinds in Kamchatka, and makes some brief remarks on their behaviour and eating habits. He also comments interestingly on their migration habits:

> The [rats] change their habitations like the wandering tartars, and sometimes for a certain number of years they all leave Kamtschatka, and go to some other place. This retirement is very alarming to the Kamtschadales, who think it forebodes a rainy season and a bad year for the chase; but when the creatures return, they confidently

expect a fine one and good hunting; so that, as soon as they begin to reappear, expresses are sent to all parts to carry the good news. (Krasheninnikov 1973, 105)

Krasheninnikov was assured by some of the inhabitants that certain 'rats', on leaving their nests, cover their stores of food with poisonous herbs to protect them against other 'rats' and that, if they lose their entire stock of winter provisions, 'they strangle themselves for vexation, squeezing their necks between the forked branches of shrubs.' However, in a remarkable spirit of scientific scepticism, he goes on: 'Although all these circumstances are related by the most serious of the Kamtschadales, yet we must not implicitly rely on their authority, before the facts are better enquired into' (Krasheninnikov, 1973, 106).

As noted earlier, part three of the book is devoted to the 'Natives of Kamtschatka and their Customs and Manners'. This is a superb anthropological discussion ranging from the geographical distribution of the different peoples (Kamchadales or Itelmens, Koryaks, and Kurils or Ainu), through their histories, habitations, dress and other characteristics, to their religious practices, illnesses and so on. Short separate accounts are given of the Koryaks and Kuril peoples where these differed from the Kamchadales. As was the case with Ides and other eighteenth-century European travellers, however, Krasheninnikov found it impossible to refrain from moralistic comment. He tells us, for example, that the manner of living of the locals was 'nasty' and their actions 'stupid'. This opinion was shared by Grieve, who in the introductory 'Advertisement' to his translation (likely written by him) we are informed that:

> The third part of this work has been most considerably abridged, as in treating of the manners, customs and religion of this barbarous nation, it was loaded with absurd practices, idle ceremonies, and unaccountable superstitions. Sufficient examples have been retained to show the precise state of an unpolished, credulous and grossly ignorant people. (Krasheninnikov 1973, Advertisement, 3)

Georg Wilhelm Steller (1709–1746), his travel journals and his *Description of the Land of Kamchatka*

The German naturalist Georg Wilhelm Steller, who was Krasheninnikov's superior in Kamchatka, also made a seminal contribution to the study of the peninsula, though he arrived there later. The scholarship on Steller is immense, not least because of the extended joint project between the University of Halle and the Russian Academy of Sciences to recover, translate and publish his written archive. This project, led by Wieland Hintzsche, began in 1992.[2] Here only a brief account of Steller's life and work can be given together with some sense of the nature of his contribution to Russian geographical endeavour (Kuentzel-Witt 2019).

Steller was born in 1709 at Bad Windsheim near Nuremberg in northern Bavaria and was educated at the University of Wittenberg, where he studied theology. He then transferred to Halle where he studied natural history, botany and medicine (Kolchinskii, 2009). Finding himself unable to find a permanent university position in the German lands, he decided, like many promising German students at this time, to seek his fortune in Russia, arriving in St Petersburg in 1734. He subsequently applied to join the Second Kamchatka Expedition and was appointed adjunct of the Academy of Sciences and assistant to Professors Gmelin and Müller. In the meantime he had married the widow of Daniel Messerschmidt. Leaving St Petersburg in December 1737, Steller reached Eniseisk, where Gmelin and Müller were awaiting him, a year later (he had spent three months in Solikamsk in the Urals waiting for his supplies and putting the local botanical garden in order, and was further delayed by severe illness in Tomsk). In Eniseisk the two professors issued him with an extensive list of instructions and sent him off in March 1739 to resume his journey to Kamchatka via Irkutsk. Unfortunately there were further delays on the way due to a lack of provisions and transport and to bureaucratic difficulties with the local administrations. While waiting he spent much time making extensive natural-historical and ethnographic studies in the Transbaikal region. Such studies were meticulously recorded in his travel journals and other manuscripts, as indeed were all the studies he had undertaken since his departure from St Petersburg. Finally in March 1740 Steller was able to leave Irkutsk, sailing down the Lena to arrive in Yakutsk and then, by travelling overland, to reach Okhotsk on the Pacific coast in August, where he first met Bering. Finally, in September, he arrived in Kamchatka and established himself at Bol'sheretsk *ostrog*, immediately commencing his studies of the local area and making a trip to Avacha Bay on the east coast. He was also able to oversee the work of the student Stepan Krasheninnikov, who had been on Kamchatka since 1737.

In February 1741, after making a trip to the south, Steller received a letter from Bering inviting him on a voyage to America (Steller 1988). He joined the *St Peter*, which set sail on 4 June from the new settlement of Petropavlovsk on Avacha Bay. This voyage has been briefly discussed above, but for Steller the experience was somewhat marred by the difficulties incurred in trying to reconcile the venture's exploratory and purely scientific goals. This led to heated disputes between Steller and the ship's officers. Thus he was allowed only a few hours to study and collect plant and animal samples and also human artefacts on Kayak Island, just off the Alaskan coast (Frost 2003, 150–64). Fortunately he was allowed by Bering to participate in a meeting with indigenous Americans (Aleuts) on the Shumagin Islands (Frost 2003, 188–98). But together with the rest of the crew Steller experienced the misfortunes of the remainder of the voyage – the shipwreck on Bering Island, Bering's death, and the overwintering. During that winter Steller wrote the first description of the now extinct sea cow, as well as descriptions of the sea otter, fur seal and sea lion, in 'De bestiis marinis', published by the Academy of Sciences some years after his death (Steller 1751).

Returning to Kamchatka in August 1742, Steller spent two more years there travelling widely and undertaking an extensive series of studies. Finally, having heard that the expedition had been officially terminated in 1743, he sailed to the mainland in August 1744 and spent the ensuing winter in Yakutsk. Unfortunately he was accused in Irkutsk of having stirred up rebellion among the Kamchadal people and was put on trial. Eventually he was found not guilty and freed to resume his journey west. Reaching Solikamsk he once more spent a period working in the botanic garden and making studies of the local area. The authorities in St Petersburg, however, had not heard of Steller's exoneration and ordered that he once more be returned to Irkutsk to stand trial. Happily, on the way back to Irkutsk he and his party were overtaken by an official courier who informed him that he was free. By this time, however, his health had begun to deteriorate and he died in Tyumen' in western Siberia in November 1746. His scientific collection was subsequently sent to the Academy of Sciences.

Gmelin's and Müller's instructions to Steller supplemented those he had already received from the Academy of Sciences in St Petersburg. These new instructions, which are dated 18 February 1739 and consist of 50 points, have recently been published in English by two American scholars, Margritt Engel and Karen Willmore (Steller 2020, 9–23), along with their edition of his travel journal.[3] Thus instruction 1 orders Steller to 'investigate and describe – en route as well as on Kamchatka – everything concerning natural as well as political history, and in all places where it seems appropriate [to] carry out meteorological observations as well as those concerning the nature of the earth'. Instruction 2 specifies what his underlings are to do: the painter Berckhan is 'to draw and paint everything noteworthy in natural and political history', the student Gorlanov to help with observations and correspondence, the prospector Samoilov to look for ores, the huntsman Gilyashev to shoot animals and birds (for the scientific collections), and the servitor Klimovskoi 'to interpret in the Yakut language and communicate with other native peoples and interview them about their faith, customs and way of life'. What is envisaged here, then, is a typical eighteenth-century encyclopedic investigation of nature and peoples in eastern Siberia and Kamchatka, areas that were little known at the time and that had certainly not been subject to rigorous scientific study. It was, in other words, a more extensive and ambitious version of the work undertaken by Messerschmidt some fifteen or more years before – a mixture of pure and applied scientific studies.

The travel journal from Irkutsk to Kamchatka is a day-by-day account of all Steller regarded as 'noteworthy in natural and political history' (in other words, in nature and ethnography). It was first published in German (Steller 1774) but was translated into Russian only in the twentieth century (see Aleksandrovskaya 1989, 223). Here Steller describes in detail the plants and animals he observes, with some interesting asides. Thus on 22 May 1740, as he travels along the Lena, he notes that:

> Opposite three rock pillars, I encountered the beautiful marsh cinquefoil, also the greater rock jasmine. (Steller 2020,104)

Next day:

> I went botanizing along the cliffs for about ten kilometres and discovered two large caves; in the rock I found veins of grayish-white marble, widening all the way to the foot of the mountain and stretching to the river's bank. The ice had polished the marble such that an artist could not have done a better job of it. (104)

On 6 June he:

> learned that the best sable and squirrel pelts are to be found in rocky regions, the blackest in larch and Siberian pine forests, and those of lesser quality in Scots pine, Siberian spruce and Japanese white birch forests – on account of the food that these animals get from buds and cones ... I noticed from the last day of May on, insects were within eight days as numerous in these parts as

at home in Russia in July. On May 1 and 2, I found large weevils, lice and mosquitoes, which shows that the long days shorten their maturation dates by a lot. (110–11)

On 26 July, Steller records what may be the first observation of permafrost:

> Not far from our camp that night, I saw a curious phenomenon in the woods. A stream flowed between two mountains separated from each other by half a kilometre. On both sides the cut banks were made up of ice up to two feet thick. On top of the ice were soil and muskeg and very tall larch trees. I gathered that this ice has never thawed and has been lying here since times immemorial and represents solid ground. (141)

He also has some sharp observations to make about the local inhabitants. On 13 March he notes that:

> As a general rule about Siberia, it can be noted that people in poor and bad places are much more industrious and of a better mind-set than in rich places and those of abundance. There is no house in these parts where hemp and burlap are not spun and woven for shirts and pants; young and old are intent on saving themselves from poverty as much as possible. Whereas in Irkutsk the womenfolk – as soon as the tea and cabbage soup have been prepared – can be found lying together on the stove like sausages in a frying pan, smoking their asses so they don't rot and fall apart from all the moving and whoring. (91)

Unlike the travel journals, Steller's *Description of the Land of Kamchatka* is a systematic examination of the peninsula's physical and human geography. It consists of general overviews of Kamchatka's peoples and physical characteristics followed by 37 systematic chapters on specific topics. Thus chapters 1 to 18 focus on the region's physical characteristics (water, mountains, weather, minerals, flora, and fauna including marine and land animals, fish, insects and birds). Chapters 19–37 consider Kamchatka's inhabitants, particularly the Kamchadals – their history, religion, general character, physical appearance, clothing and way of life. The Russian editor of the 2011 edition argues that the book's ethnographic part is more valuable than the physical, largely on the grounds that many of Steller's conjectures on the physical geography (for example, on the origin of volcanoes and earthquakes) have since been disproved whereas the ethnography describes a way of life since irretrievably lost (Steller 2011, 15–23). Particularly memorable are the chapters on the weather (climate), vegetation, fauna and peoples. Steller's high opinion of the Kamchadals has been mentioned in the above section on Krasheninnikov. 'Of no other peoples in Siberia and Russia', he writes, 'can one have more hope that within a short time their representatives will be converted into good Christians and become the best Russian subjects' (Steller 2011, 81). He thus evidently shared the colonial outlook of the Kamchadals' imperial masters and mistresses in St Petersburg.

Building on the example of Messerschmidt in the time of Peter the Great, therefore, Krasheninnikov and Steller developed the encyclopedic study of areas of Siberia and the Far East as an inherent part of Russian geographical endeavour. More particularly they illustrated the scientific value to be derived from the intensive study of one restricted area – namely in this case Kamchatka. It was an example that would be followed by future generations of Russia regional geographers.

Geographical writings and publications in the post-Petrine period

Unlike previous periods in Russia history, the post-Petrine era was noted for the widespread writing, publication and dissemination of geographical texts, including the translation of foreign geographical works. The educated Russian public enthused about the scientific (including geographical) discoveries of the day, which were popularized through periodical publications such as the appendices to the St Petersburg *Vedomosti* ('Gazette'), calendars, and the Academy of Sciences' *Monthly Compositions* (Lebedev 1957, 19–23; Leckey 2022). In addition there were scientific and specialist publications. Here we shall briefly consider four of the latter, written by Ivan Kirilovich Kirilov, Vasilii Nikitich Tatishchev, Philipp Johann von Strahlenberg and Petr Ivanovich Rychkov.

Ivan Kirilov's *Tsvetushchee sostoyanie Vserossiiskogo gosudarstva* ('Flourishing Condition of the All-Russian State') was completed in 1727 but not published until 1831 (Kirilov 1831 and 1977). It was the first general survey of Russia compiled on the basis of information provided by government departments, including questionnaire returns (Aleksandrovskaya 1989, 210). Kirilov divides Russia into its provinces (*gubernii*) and sub-provinces (*provintsii*). Within each province and sub-province, information is given on such matters as the location of towns, their fortifications and administrative personnel, military forces and dispositions, institutions like monasteries, factories, mills and schools, post stations, sources of government income, merchants and trade, mines and so on. The accent is thus on what might loosely be called the political, administrative and commercial geography and sources of wealth, though omitting estates and rural life. Towards the end, lengthy statistical tables summarize data on provincial characteristics (total number of monasteries, factories and so on), government income and expenditure, and military dispositions. There is little or nothing on the physical environment, and the book therefore cannot be regarded as a full geographical survey. It seems possible that Kirilov's work was also meant to serve as a kind of handbook for government officials, though why it remained unpublished for so long is unknown.[4]

In 1950, on the two-hundredth anniversary of Vasilii Tatishchev's death, the Soviet geographical publishing house published a volume of Tatishchev's geographical essays entitled *Izbrannye trudy po geografii Rossii* ('Selected Works on the Geography of Russia') (Tatishchev 1950). In his introductory essay, the scholar and specialist on Siberia, Aleksandr Ignatievich Andreev, explains that, although Tatishchev is widely celebrated as a historian on account of his *Istoriya Rossiiskaya s samykh drevneishikh vremen* ('Russian History from the Most Ancient Times'), published in five volumes between 1768 and 1848, his geographical work is little known because most of it remained unpublished (Andreev 1950). The 1950 volume contains nine essays by Tatishchev, only two of which were eventually published in the nineteenth century, long after his death. Perhaps one reason for this long neglect was that little of Tatishchev's substantive geographical work was actually finished, since as an important state official he was constantly called away to work on various government projects.

A 1736 essay entitled 'A general geographical description of the whole of Siberia' is an important work in the 1950 volume. The main text is preceded by an outline plan from which it is clear that this is just part of what was meant to be a substantial volume consisting of 45 chapters. The subjects of the latter range from Siberia's historical names, borders and size to its physical geography (for example the weather, hydrology, relief, elements of soil and rocks, minerals, vegetation and fauna) and its ethnography. The ethnographic material was evidently meant to be a considerable contribution since it was planned to describe 26 different peoples (though not the Russians) in considerable detail and to address 17 different aspects of their ways of life in each case. The remaining chapters were to address such matters as local administration and economy, the administration of the church, handicrafts, mills and factories, towns and so on. In the event it is impossible to say what the completed volume might have looked like since only 9 of the projected 45 chapters were written, plus parts of two others. Though unpublished in the eighteenth century, it is a significant indicator of the character of Russian geographical thought in the period.

A basic problem faced by Tatishchev was a lack of information. A questionnaire consisting of 92 questions was sent out in 1734 to provincial officials, who were slow to respond and often did so in an unsatisfactory manner. Tatishchev meanwhile sent his unfinished text to the Cabinet, which approved the enterprise and instructed its provincial governors and officials to respond appropriately. Responses began to arrive from early in 1735. Tatishchev based his work on these, on the text by Strahlenberg (see below) and a few other sources. In the meantime he revised and extended his questionnaire so that in the end it comprised 198 questions. This is contained in his 'Proposal for the composition of a history and geography of Russia', which was presented to the Academy of Sciences in 1737 (Tatishchev, 1950, 77–97). As a result additional material began slowly to accumulate. Reading through Tatishchev's revised questionnaire, however, one is struck by its wildly ambitious nature, demanding enormous amounts of detail on a huge range of issues. It was surely beyond the capacity of the skeletal provincial administration to respond satisfactorily. Material from this questionnaire was used by Tatishchev in subsequent essays, again largely unfinished. These suggest that Tatishchev's concept of geography consisted of an encyclopedic study of basic geographical material, both environmental and human, organized in systematic fashion.

The most important geographical work by Tatishchev published in the eighteenth century is his *Leksikon rossiiskoi istoricheskoi, geograficheskoi, politicheskoi i grazhdanskoi* ('Russian Historical, Geographical, Political and Civil Lexicon') (Tatishchev 1793), though this did not appear until long after the author's death. This will be considered in chapter five along with other eighteenth-century geographical dictionaries.

Philipp Johann von Strahlenberg, known also as Tabbert (1676–1747), published *Das Nord- und Östliche Theil von Europa und Asia* ('The Northern and Eastern Part of Europe and Asia') in Stockholm in 1730 (Strahlenberg 1730). Strahlenberg was born in Stralsund in Germany, then a Swedish possession, and joined the Swedish army in 1694 (Novlyanskaya 1966). Captured by the

Russians at the Battle of Poltava in 1709, he was obliged to live in Tobol'sk in west Siberia as a prisoner-of-war until the end of the Great Northern War in 1721, after which he returned to Sweden. As noted in the previous chapter, Strahlenberg spent his captivity studying the geography and ethnography of the region. It was also here that he met Daniel Messerschmidt and accompanied him on the first part of his expedition to the east.

Strahlenberg's book is quite eclectic, containing information relating not only to the physical and human geography of Russia but also to its history, politics, languages and much else. In some ways its title – 'The Northern and Eastern Part of Europe and Asia' – is quite misleading, since the book discusses not only Siberia and the northern parts of European Russia but Russia as a whole. Its full title is 'The Northern and Eastern Part of Europe and Asia: In so far that this Encompasses the Whole Russian Empire with Great Tatary ...' (it continues for several more lines). In view of the general dearth of factual material on Russia available in Europe at the time, Strahlenberg's book quickly attracted an international following and was soon translated into English, French and Spanish (see, for example, Strahlenberg 1738).

The introductory part of the work explains the many difficulties attending its composition and also the drawing of its accompanying map. Much attention is paid to boundaries, names and their origins, languages and similar issues. The author considers the exact position of the border between Europe and Asia (Tatishchev was later to claim that its delineation was originally his idea). Strahlenberg assures us that there are many differences in flora, fauna and minerals across the divide. He subdivides the empire into its provinces and the latter are grouped together into geographical zones according to climate, as was to become traditional. Prominent rivers and canals are described. The author then casts his net wider to encompass such issues as the old and new rulers of Russia and their residential cities, the dynastic history of the Romanovs, the reign and significance of Peter the Great, the tsars' titles, religion in Russia, church governance, state revenues, the armed forces and prominent families. Finally, and following the form of a geographical dictionary, an alphabetical list of the more important 'commercial centres, mines, minerals, flora, natural features, curiosities, antiquities, manufactories, mills and similar things in the Russian Empire' is given (Strahlenberg 1730, 308). Among other things, Strahlenberg specialized in eastern languages (he refers to all the eastern peoples as 'Tatars') and provides a dictionary of Kalmyk-Mongolian terms with a German translation (Strahlenberg 1730, 137–56). He is much taken with hieroglyphs and provides many illustrations of such symbols and alphabetical scripts. Symbols inscribed on ancient monuments and stones also fascinate him, as do archaeological remains.

A notable point in the book is where Strahlenberg recalls his meeting with Messerschmidt, with whom he evidently became quite close. As noted already, he accompanied the German doctor on the first part of the latter's journey from Tobol'sk. Strahlenberg regrets that they were unable to spend more time together in view of his recall to Sweden. He records that Messerschmidt handed over a number of items to be conveyed to Blumentrost in St Petersburg (Strahlenberg 1730, 409–11; 1738, 289).

In summary, then, Strahlenberg's book is an encyclopedic account of many aspects of the history, geography and political life of Russia in the early-eighteenth century. Being a foreigner himself, Strahlenberg may well have been writing for an international audience, hence the breadth of the book's coverage. Certainly it attracted a wide European readership. In Russia itself, however, its readership may well have been limited before its translation into Russian and publication in 1797 (Strahlenberg 1797).

Petr Ivanovich Rychkov (1712–1777) published his *Topografiya Orenburgskaya* ('Topography of Orenburg Province') in 1762 and thereby set a precedent that was later to be followed in many other Russian provinces (Rychkov 1762). As we have seen, the scientific studies of Krasheninnikov and Steller on Kamchatka were undertaken in connection with the Second Kamchatka Expedition in the far reaches of the northern Pacific. But the post-Petrine period also witnessed the beginnings of a new kind of geographical study – the intensive investigation of an individual region closer to the Russian heartland. In the eighteenth century this kind of work was often referred to as a topographical survey. Following classical precedent, a 'topography' was a description of an individual region or part of a country, in contrast to the country as a whole.

Petr Rychkov was born in the northern Russian town of Vologda, the son of a merchant (Mil'kov 1953; Efremov 1995). The family, which was of limited means, moved to Moscow when Rychkov was about eight years old. He received only a modest education but apparently showed early promise, especially in maths and languages. Eventually he started work as a bookkeeper in the port of St Petersburg. Here he attracted the attention of Kirilov, who was responsible for much of the cartographic activity being undertaken in Russia at the time. In 1734 Kirilov appointed Rychkov as bookkeeper in the newly established Orenburg Expedition, responsible for the defence, settlement and study of the huge territory of that name in the southern Urals and northern fringes of Central Asia. Evidently a capable administrator, Rychkov's duties quickly expanded, becoming responsible, for example, for mapping and for the search for useful minerals and ores. On Kirilov's death in 1737 he was succeeded as head of the Expedition by Tatishchev who, even though he remained in the post for only a few years, evidently inspired Rychkov in the direction of science.

The Orenburg 'Topography' has an interesting background. Following the publication of the 1745 *Atlas Russicus* ('Academy Atlas'), the idea arose of composing a detailed atlas of the little-studied Orenburg territory, which had suffered from various uprisings, especially among the turbulent Bashkirs (Vulpius 2016). A geography department, headed by Andrei Dmitrievich Krasil'nikov, was opened in the territory's chancellery to facilitate the mapping of the region. The atlas was compiled between 1752 and 1755 and, when completed, consisted of a general map of the province, nine maps of its constituent units, and two general maps of Central Asia, Afghanistan and the Kazakh steppe (Leckey 2017, 184). The 'Topography' was designed to be a textual accompaniment to the atlas. Rychkov sent the text to the Academy of Sciences, assuring the Academy that both the atlas and the 'Topography' had been composed in accordance with its instructions. The 'Topography' was approved for publication and appeared (at first in several parts) between 1759 and 1762.

Rychkov's account is on the whole more systematic and ordered than Krasheninnikov's description of Kamchatka, with little in the way of personal reference (Shaw 2010). Like Krasheninnikov's description it is eclectic, embracing both the natural and human worlds, but it lacks Krasheninnikov's superbly detailed anthropological discussion of indigenous peoples. The work is divided into two parts. The first is a systematic discussion of the region as a whole, beginning with consideration of the official name of the territory, a description of its extent and boundaries, of its sub-provinces and districts, and of the various peoples who had lived there both in the past and in the contemporary period. Chapter 5 of part one is a physical geography and natural history of the territory, with descriptions among other things of its principal lakes and rivers, upland regions, caves (in which Rychkov had a particular interest), 'the ruins of old towns and buildings', 'cattle and beasts' and other fauna. The land animals, birds and fish are arranged in alphabetical order by type. Particularly notable is the extended discussion of weather and climate. Chapter 6 considers commerce, and in particular Orenburg's expanding trade relations with the peoples of the steppe and the Central Asian khanates. The chapter finishes by discussing the Orenburg territory's economic output and the role that played in trade.

Part two of the book is a systematic description of the territory's regional subdivisions, beginning with that of Orenburg itself. The accent is on major buildings in the towns and forts, commerce, taxes and similar matters, with asides on issues like Bashkir and Cossack uprisings, some random details on indigenous peoples and other issues including the building of the Trans-Kama fortified defence line.

A notable absence in Rychkov's book is a detailed discussion of the region's natural vegetation. Vegetation is described in general terms in the context of the varied landscapes of the region, but Rychkov was far less interested in individual plant species or the uses to which they were put than was Krasheninnikov. While Krasheninnikov was able to some extent to rely on Steller, Rychkov, without a university education, clearly suffered from a lack of botanical advice. Indeed, in the introduction to chapter 5 of part one, he notes that the necessary full description of 'all that the surface and interior parts of the land produces' would require 'a considerable knowledge of physics and of natural things' but that this would lead to a 'particular and not inconsiderable book'. For this reason he apologizes for leaving such detail to those 'skilled in physics' and for rendering only a shortened account (Rychkov 1999, 105). Similarly, early in part two, Rychkov laments the fact that the likes of Gmelin and Müller had been unable to study the region in detail because of a Bashkir uprising. He notes that he has done what he could, working in the provincial chancellery, but that many areas are poorly studied – there is a need for 'skilled and diligent people' – and in the meantime he hopes that a simple description will suffice (Rychkov 1999, 168–9).

What he does give us, however, clearly reflects both knowledge derived from his duties as a government official and what must have been a keen amateur interest in aspects of the physical environment, derived no doubt from his many travels in the region and his long residence there. Thus, in addition to his detailed discussion of weather, climate and physiography (according to Mil'kov, Rychkov was the first scholar to study karst features in Russia), there are lengthy accounts of local minerals and fauna. No doubt he was able to obtain much information in the course of his official duties, as he clearly did when it came to statistics on commerce and the like, and from discussion with the locals, but much also seems to derive from personal observation.

With regard to the local fauna, like Krasheninnikov, Rychkov demonstrates the same interest in their appearance and habits, and gives details regarding their habitats. Again a utilitarian interest is apparent. Thus the *babr* (Turanian tiger), we are told:

> ... is a kind of tiger, in appearance like a lynx or a cat. Its fur is yellowish with stripes, eyes extremely sharp, neck short, bones exceedingly firm. Many are to be found among the reeds near the Aral Sea and along the Syr Darya, which bring great harm to people happening to be there, and especially to camels and horses. They possess such speed and strength that they immediately kill not only horses but even the camels which they catch. Although not very tall, they are so long that the biggest grow to a *sazhen'* or more. They catch the young ones and they say that the old *babry* feed them for three years and that during this time they are so submissive that they can be caught without danger ... At Orenburg they fetch a tariff of thirteen rubles each for large, eight for medium and five for small skins. (Rychkov 1999, 143)

In a rather similar way, the *barsuk* (badger) is accorded this description:

> A steppe creature which lives in burrows under the ground, of which there are many in steppe places. The Kalmyks kill and eat them and esteem the meat very highly on account of the fat. But their skins are in very little use. (Rychkov 1999, 143)

With respect to bird life, Rychkov's discussion, though not bereft of utilitarian interest, again embraces the nature and habits of the birds being described. Thus, in the case of the *baba* (rose pelican), he tells us that this is:

> ... somewhat like a swan, but much bigger in size with white feathers. [They] usually live along large rivers; not a few live along the Yaik in the summer period ... they feed on fish which they catch in a surprising manner, namely – gathering together near a sandy place, they swim together towards the nearby bank and, when they are close, they join their wings and, thrusting them into the deep, make a semicircle and in this way, like a dragnet, they drive the fish towards one place and, having driven them towards the bank, they fall on them all and eat them. (Rychkov 1999, 152)

This description bears all the hallmarks of personal observation, not to say a certain fascination with the creatures concerned.

Conclusion

This chapter has demonstrated how Peter the Great's successors were able to build successfully on the foundations he laid, the political uncertainties of the period notwithstanding. One key achievement was the establishment of the Academy of Sciences, which quickly assumed a leading role in mapping, expeditionary work and other aspects of geographical endeavour. The leading members of the Academy were foreigners, especially Germans or Baltic Germans, the employment of foreign specialists being a characteristic hallmark of Russian policies to modernize. Another hallmark was the centralized control of science, which expedited progress and arguably aided the efficient employment of funds and other resources.

As a result, by the accession of Catherine the Great in 1762 Russian geographical endeavour had advanced well beyond the achievements of the Petrine period. In mapping, for example, the basis provided by Peter had been consolidated not only in areal coverage but also in the adoption of scientific, mathematical methodologies. In expeditionary work Russia was beginning to mount larger-scale and properly planned ventures involving many more people and wider spatial coverage. Furthermore, rather than being solely concerned with discovering new lands and peoples and with navigation and locational issues, attention was now being paid to a deeper, scientific study of already known regions, including relatively small-scale ones and those closer to the Russian heartland. The dissemination of geographical understanding, at least among the literate elite, was being furthered through publication of geographical literature, including semi-popular literature, and through the gradual proliferation of institutions of education and training.

The reign of Catherine the Great was to witness the further development of these trends, including both developments in the recording and mapping of smaller regions and districts and evidence of a growing interest in the global scale. This increasingly complex geographical endeavour will be examined in the next chapter.

Notes

1 Both versions of the family name were in use at the time, and the brothers have each become known under their respective spelling.
2 See for example Hintzsche and Nickol (1996).
3 Extracts from Steller 2020 are used by permission of the publisher, Indiana University Press.
4 In view of the amount of official data it contained, it may at first have been deemed secret and thus copied by hand for the use of government personnel only.

5
The era of Catherine the Great (1762–96): a new age of imperial expansion

> *From now until [June] I shall be making a tour of various provinces the length of the Volga, and perhaps at the moment when you least expect it, you will receive a letter from some little hut in Asia.*
> Catherine the Great to Voltaire, March 1767
> (Dixon 2009, 158)

If the post-Petrine period can be said to be when Peter the Great's reforms were fully applied to Russian geographical endeavour, the reign of Catherine the Great was when that endeavour may be said to have come of age. The reign marked an important stage in Russia's imperial expansion when, as a result of such episodes as two wars against Turkey (1768–74 and 1787–92), the full absorption into the empire of the previously semi-autonomous Cossack-controlled land of 'Little Russia' (Ukraine), the incorporation of Crimea (1783), and the three Partitions of Poland (1772, 1793 and 1795), new territories were added to the empire. In particular, the extensive steppelands of southern Ukraine and south European Russia, together with the Black Sea coast, were opened up to settlement by Ukrainians, Russians and other European peoples, and also to geographical study (Figure 5.1, and see Shaw 1989, 22). Thus the expeditions of the Academy of Sciences now embraced not only Russia's far-flung lands and overseas territories, seeking to expand its dominions into new regions and over new peoples, but also the inner spaces of the empire including the European steppe, carefully mapping their extent and character and inventorying their resources. All this supported Russia's new status as a major European power. Rigorous cadastral mapping not only demarcated the lands of individual settlements across European Russia but also promoted

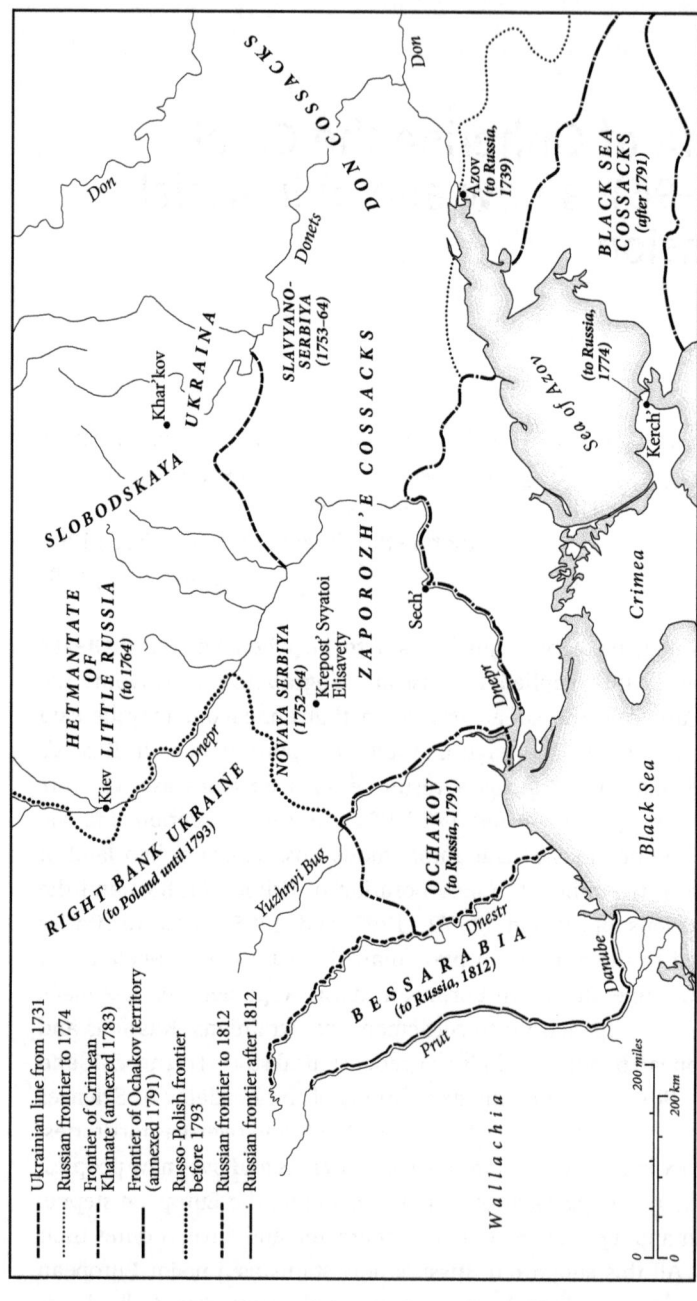

Figure 5.1 Late eighteenth and early nineteenth-century Russian expansion into Ukraine and the southern European steppe. The map indicates the important role played by organized Cossack groups. Reproduced with minor modifications from: Denis J B Shaw, 'The Settlement of European Russia during the Romanov Period', *Soviet Geography* 30 no 3, March, 207–23, Figure 4. By permission of Taylor and Francis. Map © D. J. B. Shaw, drawn by Martin Brown.

important advances in both large-scale and small-scale cartography. Frequent use of questionnaires directed towards officials of various kinds allowed the compilation of new regional or topographical surveys, supplemented by official statistics whenever possible. Russia was also influenced by the European fashion for encyclopedism, fostering the publication of geographical dictionaries and similar materials. The first overall and regional geographical surveys of Russia, describing both the empire's physical and human geographies, made their appearance. Furthermore, new institutions like Moscow University, founded under Empress Elizabeth in 1755 but slowly developing under Catherine, and the Free Economic Society, founded in 1765, began to make their contributions to geographical studies among others (Vucinich 1963, 131–5, 163–4; Leckey 2011). In other words, in this period Russian geographical endeavour achieved a range of method and approach never experienced before.

The Empress Catherine, who sponsored most of these initiatives, came to power as a result of a coup in 1762 during which her husband, Peter III, was deposed and then murdered. She herself was of German rather than Russian origin, having been born Princess Sophia of Anhalt Zerbst in Germany, and thus had no inherent right to the Russian throne. Nevertheless, following the coup, she ruled Russia for the next thirty-four years. Following the example set by Peter the Great, many of her geographical initiatives were adopted in furtherance of her policies to modernize Russia and to settle and develop her empire. Catherine prided herself on being an Enlightened ruler, an equal to other European rulers of the time and determined to use European methods to achieve her aims.

This chapter will survey a range of geographical activities that characterized the reign. First, consideration will be given to the great cadastral survey known as the General Survey, which eventually embraced most of European Russia and entailed various mapping activities at a variety of scales. Attention will then switch to the Academy of Sciences expeditions, particularly those of 1768–74 but not ignoring later ones. There will be a discussion of what we might call the Russian topographical tradition, building on the work of Petr Rychkov discussed in the previous chapter. The final part of the chapter will examine some of the geographical publications of Catherine's reign, including geographical dictionaries and general geographical surveys of Russia.

The General Survey and associated mapping activities

In her manifesto of 19 September 1765 Catherine ordered a cadastral survey to be undertaken across the Russian empire (Tsvetkov 1953; Madariaga 1981, 107–10). This huge undertaking, designed to resolve some of the landholding problems which had arisen since the previous century, soon became known as the *General'noe mezhevanie*, the 'General Survey'. The Survey was not completed until 1861, by which time it embraced 35 provinces of European Russia. It proved to be the most comprehensive geographical survey of Russia ever executed.

The need for such a survey arose out of changes in the status of landholding. Landholding had ceased to be the basis for noble service in the late-seventeenth century, while Peter the Great's reforms, such as the introduction of the Table of Ranks, the imposition of the poll tax, and the recruit levy, meant that the government was no longer interested in the amount of land held by the individual as the basis for taxation and service. Landholding documents became dated and no longer reflected the true situation on the ground. At the same time, the nobility lobbied for their landholdings to be legally documented so that poll-tax payers (merchants, townspeople, peasants) could be forced to surrender any plots of land that they had somehow acquired.[1] A struggle for land ensued, with many land plots being stolen, fomenting violent disorder in the countryside in the most extreme cases.

The General Survey was not the first attempt to solve this problem. Following Peter the Great's forest surveys discussed earlier, several unsuccessful surveys were tried. One of the most important was the survey of Ingermanland, the future St Petersburg province, situated on land recently conquered from the Swedes. This began in 1711–13 with the distribution of estates to military officers and officials and, after the end of the Great Northern War, the granting of further lands to Peter's associates and high-ranking public servants. Karimov studied the documents describing these land distributions and concluded that they owed more to Muscovite traditions than to Swedish practices (Karimov 2007, 81–5). Later, in the reign of Empress Elizabeth, there was an attempt to conduct a national land survey (1755–63) beginning with Moscow province. But this demanded that property owners show documentary proof of landholding rights, which was impractical in the circumstances (many documents having been lost over the years), and as a result the survey was widely resisted. It was, moreover, poorly organized and recorded (Karimov 2007, 80, 89–91).

Catherine's General Survey succeeded where earlier cadastral surveys had failed largely because it was conducted on a different basis

(German 1907; Milov 1965). Instead of demanding documentary proof, the Survey simply accepted the present-day pattern of landholding and land use as given (confirmed by questioning locals, including the peasants). Also, instead of attempting to demarcate between the landholdings of individual owners, an enormous task, it demarcated between the land of each settlement, or settlement together with its daughter settlements, and the lands of other settlements. The demarcation of estates or holdings belonging to individuals within each survey unit (*dacha*) was left to the agreement of the individuals concerned, with the incentive that where agreement could not be reached the land might be confiscated and sold to others.

To facilitate the conduct of the survey a new hierarchy of institutions was established. This was headed by the survey expedition attached to the Senate, below which were survey chancelleries at provincial level and survey offices for each district (*uezd*) or group of districts. These institutions employed geodesists or trained surveyors to undertake the actual surveys. The survey began with Moscow province, where a provincial chancellery was opened in 1766 together with two district offices. Later, as the survey extended into other provinces, the Moscow chancellery became the lead chancellery for all provinces. Thus, in keeping with Russian tradition, the survey was highly centralized and progressively standardized. A plan was drawn up for each *dacha* at a scale of 1:8,400, and then compiled into district plans at a scale of 1:42,000 (Postnikov 1989, 58). In 1782 the Kaluga survey chancellery published an atlas of the entire province with one map for the province as a whole at four versts per inch (1:10,500) and a map for each district at two versts per inch (1:21,000) (Tsvetkov 1953, 91). This initiative was approved by the Senate, which then ordered all surveyed provinces to compose atlases.

By the end of the eighteenth century surveys had been completed for 23 provinces of European Russia and begun for another nine, all of which were completed by the 1840s. Another three provinces (Vyatka, Perm' and Shenkursk district in Arkhangel'sk province) were also surveyed as part of the General Survey.

The General Survey thus provides a detailed cartographic representation of much of European Russia in the form of atlases, though the plans of the individual *dachi* were often lost or dispersed.[2] Apart from showing the location of many significant features, the survey atlases give a picture of the extent of agricultural and forested land in the case of 34 provinces. Even more valuable from a geographical viewpoint, however, are the economic notes (*ekonomicheskie primechaniya*) to the General Survey. These were studied in detail by L. V. Milov (1965). The point has already been made that Russian maps were often accompanied by textual descriptions, and the economic notes of the General Survey clearly follow in this tradition (though distinguished from earlier descriptions by the tabular form in which they present much of their data). The economic notes are of two types. First there are the 'economic notes to the general plans', which supplement the plans to each district. Second there are the so-called 'economic notes to the atlases' or 'short economic notes', a shortened version created primarily for the convenience of those working with the plans and economic notes on a day-to-day basis.

The present author has used the short economic notes to the atlases of Voronezh province, where the General Survey took place between 1777 and 1781 (see Shaw 1990b and Figure 5.2 below).[3] They are basically in tabular form accompanied by written addenda. Each survey unit is listed as a separate entry. Under each entry there first appears the name of the settlement together with its subsidiary settlements, although many units contain no settlements and are listed as individual pieces of land. Names of individual noble landowners are given in the same column or, in the cases of lower social categories (*odnodvortsy* or the like), they are indicated as a group. In the following columns are listed statistics for the number of houses or homesteads (*dvory*), the population according to the last revision or census, and the area of different categories of land use: land under settlement, arable, hay land, forest, unusable land, and the total land area. There then follow comments on such matters as mills and manufactories, churches, monasteries, noble residences, fairs and markets, land quality, the harvest, timber quality, and whether the dependent population were subject to labour service (*barshchina*) for their landlords or paid quitrent (*obrok*).

As a concrete example, we might take the large village (*sloboda*) of Pisarevka and its hamlets (*khutora*) of Titarev and Ploskaya Devitsa, situated in Boguchar district of south-eastern Voronezh province (the steppe part of the province).[4] This village (survey unit) belonged to Mariya Fedorovna Tatarchukovo, apart from some demarcated church land. The settlements consisted of 348 homesteads populated by 1,118 males and 1,231 females. The survey unit measured a total of 21,598 *desyatiny* and 369 square *sazheni* of land. Of this total, approximately 0.45 per cent was recorded as land under settlement, 84 per cent as arable, 10.2 per cent as hay land, 3.1 per cent as forest, and 1.9 per cent as unusable.

In the written addenda for this survey unit, we are told that there were two mills on the river, on the Asinov–Boguchar road, each with two millstones. There was a wooden church with a productive garden.

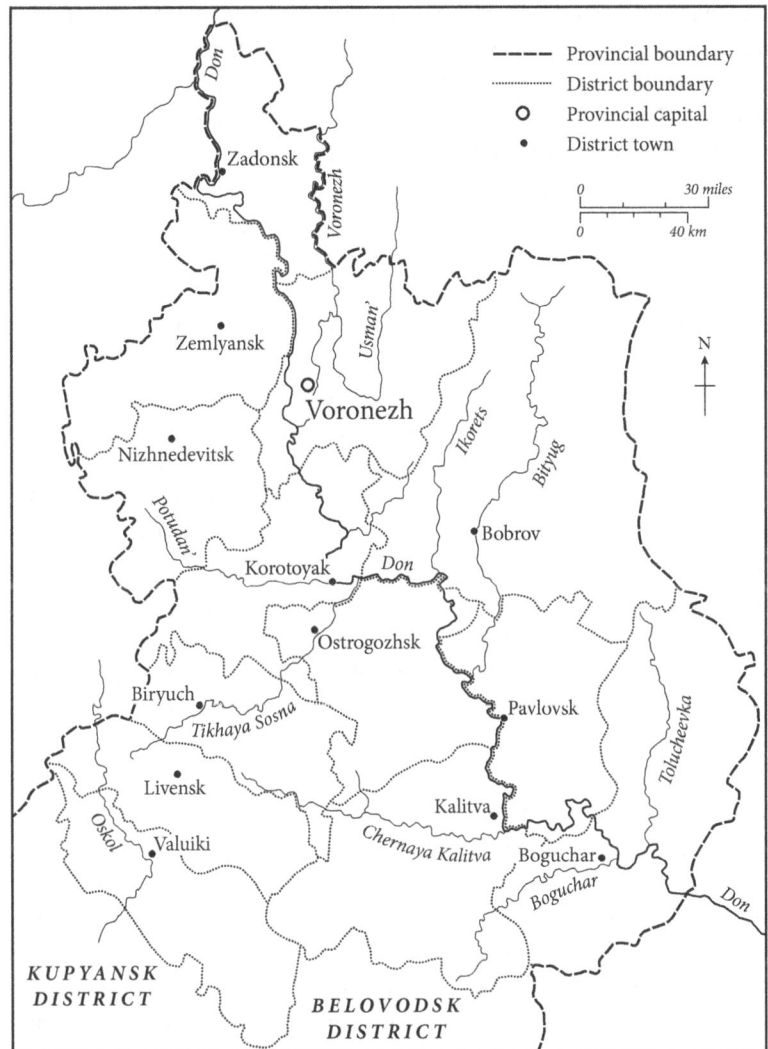

Figure 5.2 The province of Voronezh in the late eighteenth century. The map indicates the administrative geography of the province following the reform of 1779. The two southernmost districts, Kupyansk and Belovodsk, were subsequently hived off. Source: various. Map © D. J. B. Shaw, drawn by Martin Brown.

There was a stud farm where Russian horses were bred and a farm for breeding horned cattle of Kalmyk and *Cherkasy* varieties. Fairs were held each year on 7 January and 29 August, to which came merchants from various towns and nearby Cossack settlements (*stanitsy*) with cattle, horses and dried fish. The land is recorded as black earth (*chernozem*) and in places as stony, chalky or *solonets* (sodium rich). Harvests of grain and grass were poor. There was some forest with construction timber, between which there were groves of oak and aspen with small timber. The population of 'dependent Little Russians'[5] (*poddannye malorossiyane*) and peasants were subject to labour service.

Not all settlements belonged to members of the nobility, however. For example the hamlet of Monastyrshchina, together with five other hamlets in Boguchar district, was situated on former monastic land now secularized, which were populated by Economic peasants and Economic Little Russians, or former monastic dependants.[6] The hamlets contained 468 homesteads and the Revision population numbered 1,697 men and 1,520 women. In place of dues formerly paid to the monastery, the peasants now paid quitrent to the state. This survey unit surrounded several unpopulated parcels of land under separate ownership.

Often settlements were shared between noble landowners and a group or groups of other landowners. Typical was the village (*sloboda*) of Tolucheeva, again in Boguchar district, shared between 'state military inhabitants'[7] and a noble landowner, Il'ya Kirilovich Podovskii.[8] The village had nearly a thousand inhabitants and 144 homesteads, a wooden church and land that is described as 'grey sandy'. Nevertheless the harvests of grain and grass are described as 'medium'. Its forested land had construction timber of oak and aspen with some timber for fuel.

The situation in Zadonsk district, in the northernmost part of Voronezh province (in the forest steppe zone) was rather different. Whereas Boguchar district was still undergoing settlement at the time of the General Survey, the settlement of Zadonsk had begun in the late-sixteenth century. By the 1780s population density in Zadonsk was about four times that in Boguchar. A feature of this district was that individual settlements were often smaller than those in Boguchar, and were frequently shared between several noble landowners and others. Thus the villages of Ushkiny and Verkhnee Kazach'e (forming one survey unit between them), with a population of 585, belonged to eleven noble landowners and several *odnodvortsy*. Over half of its land was forested with small timber. There was an abandoned iron mill on the river, the district's land is described as silty and sandy, and its harvests as medium.[9]

In summary the General Survey's cartographic materials and accompanying economic notes present a highly detailed picture of the geography of much of European Russia in the second half of the eighteenth century and the first part of the nineteenth. Such materials were for the most part stored in the archive of the Senate's survey chancellery, and only those for Kaluga province, together with a single district of Tula province, were published. This raises the question of the extent to which such materials entered the public realm. Although they were undoubtedly consulted by officials of the survey chancelleries and offices to resolve questions of landownership and similar issues, they remained largely inaccessible to others. They are also quite difficult to use, partly because the data they record are to some extent impressionistic or subjective, such as that on soil quality, harvest yield and forest type. Milov has examined the land use data recorded in the economic notes and shown that classification of land into such categories as 'arable', 'hay land' and forest is misleading and oversimplifies what was in fact a very complex reality on the ground (Milov 1965, 160–75).[10] Nevertheless such materials contributed much to the state's knowledge of local geographies in Russia, and were used in the composition of topographical maps and for solving many local administrative problems, such as determining the locations of settlements and boundaries (Postnikov 1989, 70–1). Yet their overall importance for the educated public's understanding of local geographies was probably limited at the time.

Questionnaire surveys and topographical descriptions

Although the General Survey made an important contribution to knowledge of local geographies in Russia, topographical descriptions of provinces and districts – and the questionnaire surveys upon which they were often based – probably contributed more to public awareness. In seventeenth-century Europe, questionnaires were regularly distributed by antiquarians, natural historians, geographers, political economists and social reformers to collect information from locals, such as members of the gentry and clergy. As Fox writes, the idea of statistical enquiries was well established by the following century (Fox 2010). In Russia, however, this form of research came much later, no doubt in part because of a lack of educated people at local level (as noted earlier, the Russian parish clergy were often poorly educated). One of the first examples of a questionnaire survey in Russia was that distributed by Peter the Great's Senate in 1724, acting no doubt under the influence of Bruce and Tatishchev, who were keen to promote a geographical survey of Russia. This asked for information about the natural environment, natural resources, local history, geographical locations and other matters. Some of the returns were used by Kirilov in his *Tsvetushchee sostoyanie Vserossiiskogo gosudarstva* ('Flourishing Condition of the All-Russian

State') (Kirilov 1977; Shaw 1996, 168). As we have seen, some years later, in 1734, Tatishchev distributed a second edition of this questionnaire, which he sent to the survey chancelleries in the Urals and Siberia. The returns provided the basis for his 'General geographical description of the whole of Siberia'. The final edition of the questionnaire came out in 1737 and consisted of 198 detailed questions. These were sent to the geodesists in various parts of Russia (Aleksandrovskaya 1989, 99–100, 224).

Tatishchev's questionnaires set a precedent for many others distributed during the rest of the eighteenth century. Among the most notable was the so-called 'Academic questionnaire', composed under the auspices of the Academy of Sciences by Mikhail Vasil'evich Lomonosov in 1759 and consisting of 30 questions soliciting information on both the physical and human geography of each region, designed to provide the basis for a new atlas and written description of Russia. Returns from this exercise provided the main source for Hartwig Ludwig Christian Bacmeister's *Topograficheskie izvestiya* ('Topographical Information'), published between 1771 and 1774. Unfortunately, its coverage was restricted to Moscow and Novgorod provinces only (Bacmeister 1771–4). Aleksandrovskaya notes that as the century advanced more and more agencies sent out questionnaires, often with narrow ends in view, and the original aims of scholars like Tatishchev to work towards a comprehensive geographical description of Russia were gradually forgotten. The Free Economic Society, for example, founded in 1765 'for the promotion of agriculture and household management', used questionnaires from the moment of its establishment. Its focus was essentially on the economic conditions, and particularly on the agriculture, of the regions it considered (Aleksandrovskaya 1989, 102–3; Leckey 2011, 42). The Society appended a 65-point questionnaire to the first issue of its *Trudy* ('Works') published in 1766. This sought information on such issues as soil quality, the kinds of grain sown, dates of sowing and harvesting, the keeping of livestock, the extent and maintenance of forests, fishing and other activities. Over the next decade the Society published the full responses from 17 provinces located in various regions of European Russia.

Closely connected to questionnaire surveys were the topographical descriptions of individual provinces and districts that began to appear in the second half of the eighteenth century. A precedent was set by Petr Rychkov's *Topografiya Orenburgskoi gubernii* ('Topography of Orenburg Province') which was examined in Chapter 4. An exhaustive investigation of the topographical descriptions was undertaken by

N. L. Rubinshtein, who listed some sixty manuscripts that he had discovered in various national archives (plus associated manuscript atlases, where they existed) and others found in local archives. In addition he provided a list of 15 descriptions published in the eighteenth or early-nineteenth centuries (Rubinshtein, 1953). A further discussion of such material, together with a more general account of sources for the historico-geographical study of eighteenth- and early-nineteenth-century Russia, was published by V. M. Kabuzan (Kabuzan, 1963), who divided his topographical descriptions into three: those composed prior to Catherine's provincial reforms of 1775–85; those composed between Catherine's reforms and Tsar Paul's reforms of 1797; and those composed after Paul's reforms and into the early nineteenth century. Kabuzan's division reflects the changes to the provincial boundaries over this period.

Initially topographical descriptions seem to have been composed in a fairly disorganized way by local survey chancelleries using questionnaire returns as a basis. In 1777 some of the early descriptions were examined by the Senate, which expressed the wish that topographical descriptions be composed for all the empire's provinces (*Opisanie Tobol'skogo* 1982, 10). With the redrawing of provincial boundaries by the reform of 1775–85, the composition of topographical descriptions became compulsory. The Academy of Sciences established a topographical committee to further this work. A standardized questionnaire was composed, which was used for many of the topographical descriptions composed in the 1780s. In the case of Tobol'sk province in west Siberia for example, the description of 1790 consists of 16 questions related to the province's towns, 20 to each district, and 25 to the province as a whole (*Opisanie Tobol'skogo* 1982, 20–36, 243–6). Questions concerning the towns asked about a range of issues, including their geographical locations, local relief, history, landownership, important buildings, populations and economic life. A number of these questions were repeated in the case of the districts, which also had to answer questions on soils and agriculture, cultivation methods, lakes and rivers, local landmarks and land use (taking data from the General Survey if available for that district). In addition there were more specific questions, such as those relating to notable uses of trees and other vegetation (for example, for dyes and medicines), significant fauna (mammals, birds, insects, amphibians), unusual customs and ways of life, and the processing of mineral and metals. Although the questions demonstrated an interest in the natural environment, their main focus was the human geography.

The *Opisanie Tobol'skogo namestnichestva* ('Description of Tobol'sk Province') covered a huge slice of territory extending from the Urals to the upper parts of the western tributaries of the Enisei. It follows the above standardized questionnaire very closely. Thus there is a chapter for the province as a whole followed by chapters for all 16 of the province's towns, each accompanied by a separate chapter for the surrounding districts. Each chapter is subdivided into paragraphs numbered according to the question being addressed. This makes for rather repetitive, not to say tedious, reading. The description is nevertheless factually comprehensive.

Not all the topographical descriptions of this period are as rigid, however. That for Kaluga province, south-west of Moscow, written by Petr Aleksandrovich Soimonov (1737–1800) and published in 1785, takes the same form in general terms, but the chapters are very much shorter, covering much the same ground as the Tobol'sk description but in a more informal and discursive manner. There are no references to the questions being addressed. The main text is followed by a series of maps for the province and its districts (*Topograficheskoe opisanie Kaluzhskogo* 1785).

It is instructive to consider the Russian topographical descriptions in the light of the European descriptions being composed in the seventeenth and eighteenth centuries (though the latter generally cover much smaller geographical areas and were not composed under the aegis of a central authority) (Fox 2010). In England one of the most celebrated is the *Natural History of Wiltshire*, written by the antiquary and natural historian John Aubrey between 1651 and 1691, though published much later (Aubrey 1847). Aubrey divided his work into two parts, the first dealing with the physical and human geographies of the county, including weather, medicinal springs, geology ('minerals and fossils, stones'), flora, fauna, the human population and basic social statistics. By present-day standards, the second part is more idiosyncratic, containing not only a discussion of the local wool and cloth industry but also of local worthies and aristocrats, horse racing, hawking, 'accidents or remarkable occurrences', gentlemen's country seats and so on.[11] Part one, therefore, more closely approaches what would now be understood as a topographical study, though the personal nature of Aubrey's account – his use of anecdotes and his wide circle of local acquaintances and informants – is striking throughout. He seems to write as much to entertain as to inform.

Much closer to the Russian topographical descriptions both conceptually and temporally is Sir John Sinclair's *Statistical Account of Scotland* (Sinclair 1973–83). This was published in 20 volumes between 1791 and 1799, based on returns by parish ministers to a questionnaire of 160 questions. The overall aim was to achieve better government for the country. Sinclair divided his questionnaire into four parts: the first 40 questions focused on natural history, climate, resources, topography and the like; questions 41–100 addressed population and related issues; the next 16 questions enquired about agriculture and industry; and the final 44 consisted of questions on various issues including language, wage levels and other matters (Withers 2007, 200–1). The material is presented parish by parish and is more impersonal than that of Aubrey, but is by no means entirely standardized – much depends on the character of the parish and what is of interest there. In the case of the parish of Portpatrick on the coast of south-west Scotland, for example, much attention is paid to its harbour and its attendant commerce. Similarly in the case of Jedburgh in south-east Scotland close to the English border, the reader is advised about the healthiness of the climate, the longevity of certain residents and how a local scheme for inoculating the poor has preserved numerous lives against the threat of smallpox. Sinclair appears to have worked up the material provided by the ministers rather than simply reproducing their answers, making for an interesting and informative account.

From the comparative point of view the few Russian topographical descriptions of the 1780s and 1790s that the present author has been able to examine are disappointing. Compared with Rychkov's richly detailed description of the fauna of Orenburg province discussed in Chapter 4, for example, the later topographies represent a definite step backwards. Thus the answer to question 17 on the fauna of Tara district in Tobol'sk province simply reads as follows: 'Animals: sables, martens, rabbits, hares, ermine, otters, wolverines, beavers, elk, wolves, bears. Birds: ducks, black grouse, sand grouse, wood grouse, partridge, geese, cranes, white storks, swans. Reptiles: snakes, frogs, lizards, grass snakes, mice [sic], moles [sic]. Insects: mosquitoes, midges, spiders, horseflies'. No other information or comment is provided. One can only conclude that the officials in the survey chancelleries were ignorant of zoology, and perhaps not much interested.

Altogether, it seems likely that what the authorities expected from the topographical descriptions was not scientifically based commentaries on the geographies of provinces and districts (as were clearly expected in the case of the expeditions discussed below), but rather broad inventories of the geographies and resources of the empire's regions. The people employed for this exercise (namely local geodesists, probably unskilled in zoology, botany and geology) were most likely incapable of producing anything else. The result was descriptions that may have met the needs of government for quick reference and similar purposes, but largely lacked the spontaneity and human interest of contemporary and earlier European topographies.

The Academy of Sciences expeditions, 1768–74

The Academy of Sciences expeditions launched before the reign of Catherine II were mainly directed at the far-flung reaches of the Russian empire such as Siberia and the Far East. After Catherine II's accession, however, they also focused on regions closer to home such as the lower Volga, the Urals, the European north, the southern lands of Ukraine, the north Caucasus and, after its annexation in 1783, Crimea. Priding herself on being enlightened, Catherine was a keen supporter of the Academy and desired to learn about her new southern territories and to foster their settlement and development.[12] The expeditions have been described, perhaps with some exaggeration, as 'the greatest single undertaking of the Academy during the entire monarchical era' (Vucinich 1963, 150).

The exact origins of the 1768–74 expeditions are somewhat obscure, although they appear to have been conceived in connection with an expedition to study the transit of Venus in 1769. Most scholars have pointed to the famed German naturalist, Peter Simon Pallas (1741–1811), as the expeditions' organiser. Pallas had arrived in St Petersburg from Germany in 1767. The main purpose of the expeditions is made clear in the instructions issued to all their leaders: to study things of use to the state and to the dissemination of science. The leaders were exhorted not to pass through places 'uselessly' and to leave nothing of importance uninvestigated.

In terms of organization, there were in fact two expeditions, known as the Orenburg and Astrakhan' expeditions respectively, consisting altogether of five detachments (Gnucheva 1940, 95–115; Moon 2010, 211). The first detachment of the Orenburg expedition, led by Pallas, visited the mid-Volga region and the Urals on the way to Siberia, reaching as far east as Lake Baikal before returning by way of the lower Volga. The second detachment, under the leadership of the Russian Ivan Ivanovich Lepekhin (1740–1802), travelled down the Volga to Astrakhan' and then by way of the Urals to west Siberia. It returned to St Petersburg by way of the north of European Russia. The Orenburg expedition's third detachment, which was led by the Swedish naturalist Johann Peter Falck (1727–1774), a student of Linnaeus, visited the Volga, the

Urals and parts of the north Caucasus. The German Samuel Gottlieb Gmelin (1744–1774), nephew of Johann Georg Gmelin, a leader of the Second Kamchatka Expedition (see Chapter 4), headed one of the two detachments of the Astrakhan' expedition. This travelled down the river Don to Azov and then to Tsaritsyn on the Volga before proceeding to Astrakhan', the Caspian Sea, the Caucasus and Persia. The other detachment came under the leadership of Johann Anton Güldenstädt (1745–1781), a Baltic German who hailed from Riga. Güldenstädt took his detachment down the Don and then across to the Volga, down the latter and on across the Caucasus range to reach Georgia. His return journey took him across the north Caucasus steppe to reach Taganrog and then through southern Ukraine, or 'New Russia' as it was then called, to Moscow and St Petersburg.

The instructions issued to the expedition leaders were carefully studied by Fradkin (Fradkin 1950; Fradkin 1953, 44–7, 209–12). According to him, the instructions were widely discussed within the Academy which also sought the advice of other bodies such as the Free Economic Society, the Mining College, the Commerce College and the Medical College. According to Moon (2010, 212), they were strongly influenced by ideas deriving from German cameralism – and in particular the need to manage the economy centrally for the benefit of the state (see Chapter 6). The naturalists were enjoined to pay particular attention to nine issues during their travels: (1) to the nature of the lands and waters they saw on the way; (2) to land that was unsettled or unused, and the uses to which it might be put; (3) to the economy of each populated place, its disadvantages and advantages, how its agriculture might be improved and what tillage tools were used (giving descriptions and making drawings or models); (4) to the particular illnesses which were common in each place, including livestock plagues, what treatments were used or might be used, and how the peasants and indigenes treated such complaints; (5) to the spread and improvement of livestock farms, especially those producing wool, to beekeeping and silk production; (6) to methods of fishing and hunting, wherever possible making models of traps and hunting gear; (7) to useful types of land, salts, coal, ores of metals important in trade and lacking in Russia, and to mineral waters; (8) to mines, copper, salt and saltpetre works and other useful manufactories and mills; and (9) to the identification of plants useful in medicine, the economy and trade, especially those valued by foreigners, or completely new ones that might give rise to trade. Special emphasis was thus placed on the practical utility of the expeditions' findings.

In addition, the instructions listed other desirable objectives: for example that the travellers should keep an eye out for all phenomena that would add to the understanding of the local area, such as the weather, heat and severe cold and, in those places where the detachments spent some time, should describe the ways of life of the local inhabitants, their legends, and any remnants of the past. The naturalists were also enjoined to enhance their science and the imperial cabinet of curiosities (*Kunstkammer*) by describing, drawing or collecting (and wherever possible sending to the Academy) all notable objects and specimens, such as animals, birds, fish, insects, plants, minerals and ancient objects that were either rare or not to be found in the imperial cabinet. The leaders were instructed to overwinter in some 'suitable place', in which they were, as far as possible, to continue their research in the local area, for example looking out for minerals, factories, caves, antiquities and so on. But they were to leave their winter quarters as soon as conditions permitted. Strict instructions were given regarding the keeping of daily travel diaries, the sending of reports and accounts to the Academy and the spending of allocated funds. All the expeditions were accompanied by Russian students for whom the expedition was seen as an important part of their education.

On the whole these instructions were followed by all the expedition leaders. Here we shall focus on the expedition of Ivan Lepekhin, the only Russian expedition leader and one who is less well known than some of the others.

The expedition of Ivan Ivanovich Lepekhin (1768–72)

> *Whoever travels for only one purpose, for one known objective, having achieved this, is satisfied; but to travel to see the endless works of nature, observing, collecting and describing them, is to be wide awake in body and soul. It was in this continuous spirit of vigilance that Lepekhin spent a whole six years.*
> Nikolai Yakovlevich Ozeretskovskii 1822 (Fradkin 1953, 56)

Relatively little is known about the early life of Ivan Lepekhin. He was born in St Petersburg in 1740, the son of a soldier. He was admitted to the Academy's gymnasium in 1751 and then to the university, where he studied chemistry and the humanities. Showing great promise, however, and drawn to natural history, he was permitted to move to Strasbourg University, where he studied natural history and medicine. He graduated doctor of medicine in May 1767 and returned to St Petersburg in the autumn. He was quickly appointed an adjunct of the Academy (and a professor in 1771) and leader of one of the expeditions departing in 1768. The reason for his rapid rise seems likely to have been the fact that there were few Russians qualified to take on this responsible role. The route of Lepekhin's 1768–72 expedition, which departed St Petersburg in June 1768 and returned in December 1772, has been outlined above. He was accompanied by several students, the most prominent being Nikolai Yakovlevich Ozeretskovskii (1750–1827), later to be noted for his expeditions to the upper Volga and the European Russian north. Lepekhin's four-and-a-half-year expedition was followed by a shorter one in 1773, this time to Belorossiya (Belarus). During the rest of his career he was largely engaged in administrative activities, notably as editor of the Academy's scientific-popular journal *Novye ezhemesyachnye sochineniya* ('New Monthly Compositions'), as director of the Academy's botanical garden, and as inspector of its gymnasium.

Lepekhin's most important publication was his *Dnevnye zapiski puteshestviya … Ivana Lepekhina po raznym provintsiyam Rossiiskogo gosudarstva* ('Daily Notes of the Journey of … Dr Ivan Lepekhin through Various Provinces of the Russian State'), published in four volumes between 1771 and 1805 (Lepekhin, 1771–1805). The first three volumes were translated into German in 1774–83. As the title suggests, the 'Daily Notes' are a day-by-day account of Lepekhin's journey recording both natural-historical and ethnographic observations, very much in the spirit of Messerschmidt.

Perhaps the easiest way to summarize this work is to quote Fradkin. The 'Daily Notes', he tells us, describe in detail:

> plants, animals, birds, insects, fish; they speak of the farming, the industries, the way of life of the people, their customs, beliefs, language. Here and there the author of the *Notes* also speaks of himself. Reading the book we can imagine him on the expedition: how he travelled thousands of versts from village to village in a covered wagon, how he examined a geological outcrop somewhere on a steep river bank, how he wandered in a meadow collecting plants, how he chatted with passers-by about livestock diseases, about folk legends [*narodnye primety*], about daily peasant tasks.
>
> We read a description of the route taken by Ivan Lepekhin in the first year of his journey. We are presented with old Russian villages, country roads, lively Russian towns at the end of the eighteenth century. We travel with Lepekhin to Vladimir surrounded by cherry

orchards, to celebrated Murom with its leather and soap works, to the provincial towns of Nizhnii Novgorod province – Arzamas and Alatyr', to the Volga town of Simbirsk. This was only the beginning of a thousand-*verst* journey. The pages of the *Notes* also speak of the Caspian steppe, the Ural mountains, the Arkhangel'sk region, and the islands of the White Sea. (Fradkin 1953, 55–6; Lukina 1965)

During the course of his discussion of Lepekhin's expedition, Fradkin uses his 'Daily Notes', supplemented by his reports and accounts sent to the Academy of Sciences, most of which are now housed in the Academy's archive in St Petersburg. Only a few episodes recorded in these sources can be noted here.

In the summer of 1768, for example, soon after the beginning of his journey, Lepekhin and his group visited Vladimir, situated to the east of Moscow. On the outskirts of this town they came across a deep ravine in which young elms and birches were growing. The bright summer sunshine revealed pretty insects, among which was a kind of ladybird 'not yet described by anyone'. The predominant vegetation included so-called 'tsar grass' and broom. Lepekhin also noted the presence of the 'composite' (*sostavnoi*) Siberian pea 'which, according to Mister Linnaeus, grows only in Siberia' (Fradkin 1953, 59). Being trained in medicine and botany, Lepekhin was particularly interested in the medicinal use of plants (which had been the avowed purpose of the Messerschmidt expedition). Such knowledge derived not only from educated people but also from questioning local peasants and the like. According to Fradkin, among the academicians and participants of the Orenburg expedition, 'only Lepekhin, an educated and gifted naturalist and also a simple Russian, was close to the people's way of life' (Fradkin 1953, 60). But this also gave rise to difficulties, such as when he allowed his youthful and impatient temperament to propel him into arguments with the locals about the best means of curing particular medical complaints.

Lepekhin continued his journey into Nizhnii Novgorod province and then, crossing the Volga, reached the river Cheremshan, where he visited villages populated by Mordva, Chuvash and Tatar peoples. Here he acquainted himself with their agriculture, handicrafts, customs and rituals and wrote an 'excellent' account of the peoples of the Cheremshan – 'a superb example of eighteenth-century ethnography' (Fradkin 1953, 65). He spent the winter of 1768–9 in the Volga town of Simbirsk, where Pallas and his detachment were also overwintering. Lepekhin fished in the Volga to ascertain what fish lived there and to observe the way of life of the local fishermen. From mid-December he investigated the nearby fauna, especially mink, desman and birds – red duck and tit. During this winter Lepekhin and his companions were entertained by stoats and a weasel that they kept in iron cages in their hut. The travellers seem to have been impressed by their savagery and agility (Fradkin 1953, 69).

As noted already, Lepekhin was obliged to send to the Academy on a regular basis specimens and materials he had collected. For example in one of his reports, sent in the winter of 1768–9, he recorded a list of materials sent by cart from Simbirsk to St Petersburg in five chests: 309 insects of various kinds, 405 types of grass or herb, 30 kinds of bird, 16 animals, 4 animal traps, 77 minerals, a packet with old Tatar coins, 4 animal heads, 2 fish, daily records, accounts of money spent on travel and minor expenditure … a Mongol astrology, a small Russian book of home cures, an enumeration of insects, animals, minerals, birds, fish, and drawings of things recorded in the 'Daily Notes' (Fradkin 1953, 68).

In May 1769 Lepekhin left Simbirsk and travelled down the Volga, partly by boat, to Astrakhan' and Gur'ev-gorodok. There was a side visit to see the saline Lake El'ton and its saltworks. Crossing the salt desert between the Volga delta and the mouth of the Yaik (Ural) river close to the shore of the Caspian Sea, perhaps the most difficult part of the entire journey, the party was almost overwhelmed by the saline environment. Lepekhin took note of the salt-loving vegetation and the fauna, most notably the saiga antelope, and birds. They then travelled up the Yaik to Orenburg and thence to Tabynsk on the river Belaya in the Urals, where they overwintered.

The summer of 1770 was spent visiting the Urals ironworks and also, following in the footsteps of Rychkov, the caves of the region, including the famous ice caverns at Kungur. According to Fradkin, Lepekhin's ideas concerning the origin of caves, namely that they are the product of the dissolution of limestone by water, were not only well ahead of their time but also one of the principal findings of his expedition (Fradkin 1953, 153–5).

The winter of 1770–71 was spent at Tyumen' in west Siberia. From here he was expected to return to St Petersburg, but instead Lepekhin, wishing to seek greater independence from Pallas, travelled north-west to Arkhangel'sk to study nature and people in the European north. He was the first Russian naturalist (barring the Orenburg expedition's students) to do so. Travelling through territories inhabited by the Komi, whose way of life and especially land cleared for agriculture (*podseka*) he carefully studied, Lepekhin arrived in Arkhangel'sk in late August. From here he attempted to leave by boat to study the fisheries of the White Sea but was soon forced back by autumn storms. Not until the following year was he able to pursue his studies of the coast of the White Sea and Kola Peninsula, the Solovetskii Islands and the Kanin Peninsula. He returned to St Petersburg in December 1772, having added descriptions of the unfamiliar landscapes and peoples of the European north to his 'Daily Notes'.

Lepekhin thus gave a comprehensive account of his journey through many natural regions of European Russia, an account that followed the eighteenth-century encyclopedist tradition of recording the most notable features of both the natural and human environment. Though essentially empirical, the account occasionally advances conjectures regarding the causes of phenomena, thus helping to lay the foundations for the theoretical sciences of the future. It advanced understanding of both some of the more populated parts of Russia as well as parts of its periphery. Together with the other Academy of Sciences expeditions of the 1768–74 period, it constituted a substantive contribution to the geographical understanding of Russia.

Later expeditions, geographical publications and the dissemination of geographical knowledge

Although by far the most important time for expeditionary activity under Catherine the Great, the years 1768–74 were by no means the only period when such ventures occurred. Later expeditions included one by Vasilii Zuev, a pupil of Pallas. Having led an independent expedition down the River Ob' and south-westwards along the coast of the Arctic Ocean to the Kara Gulf (now known as Baidaratskaya Bay) in 1771, he conducted an Academy of Sciences expedition to the south, including New Russia, in 1781–2. Joseph Billings and Gavriil Andreevich Sarychev led a nine-year expedition to north-east Siberia between 1785 and 1794, exploring the region of the Lena and Kolyma rivers, the Chukotka peninsula, the Aleutians and mainland Alaska. Lepekhin's student Nikolai Ozeretskovskii studied lakes Ladoga and Onega in 1785 followed by visits to Lake Il'men' (1805) and to Lake Seliger and the upper Volga (1814). Pallas's second expedition occurred in 1793–5 when he travelled down the Volga to Tsaritsyn, on to the Caspian Sea, the Caucasus, Crimea and then back to St Petersburg via the river Dnepr (see Pallas 1801). Of all the naturalists at work in Russia in the latter half of the eighteenth century, Pallas was perhaps the most gifted and well known. As Vucinich writes: 'Pallas's star generated most light and its rays reached furthest' (Vucinich 1963, 154). Pallas's scientific work has been discussed by many others.[13]

The second half of the eighteenth century coincided with a period of intense interest in geography on the part of the educated Russian public. There was a similar rise in enthusiasm for geography in other European states at this time.[14] In Russia, geographical knowledge was spread through such periodicals as the 'New Monthly Compositions', a semi-popular Academy of Sciences publication initiated and edited from 1755 to 1764 by the German historian Gerhard Friedrich Müller (Black 1986, 123–58; Leckey 2022). This journal published essays and reports on many of the most notable expeditions and discoveries of the day.[15]

Also important to the spread of geographical understanding was the work of Moscow University, founded in 1755 (Aleksandrovskaya 1989, 145–50). As Aleksandrovskaya writes, although geography (broadly defined) had no clear subject content or administrative section, it was taught almost from the first moment of the university's foundation. Thus geography was being taught in the 1750s and 1760s by D. V. Savich, who also taught physics – at this stage the subject was closely aligned with the natural sciences. Another important teacher of geography was the botanist P. D. Veniaminov, who studied the flora of central European Russia and made a collection of the plants of the region. M. A. Afonin, the university's first professor of natural history, was a pioneer of soil science, emphasizing the practical uses of soil and the need to study its regional variations. Afonin was also an advocate of forest conservation. From 1789 the department of physics was headed by P. I. Strakhov, a pioneer in meteorology. Other university teachers of geography were much closer to history. They included Kh. A. Chebotarev, who taught geography at the university's gymnasium from 1776 and then in the university's department of history in the years 1780–1815. Another important figure was N. E. Cherepanov, professor of history, statistics and geography, whose textbook *Geografichesko-istoricheskoe uchenie* ('Geographical-Historical Studies', 1792–3) had a significant influence on the teaching of geography. In the last third of the eighteenth century Russian geography became more differentiated, and much of it distanced itself from natural history under the influence of German cameralism. This new approach to geography tended to be taught by historians like Johann Gottfried Reichel, who arrived in Russia from Germany in 1757. Reichel taught courses in history, statistics and geography. Another cameralist arrival from Germany was Johann Heim, a native of Braunschweig, who taught courses on classics, history and geography from 1784. At the time of the university reform in 1805 Heim was appointed head of the new department of world history, statistics and geography, and then became rector of the university.

Moscow University's work in spreading geographical understanding, however, did not end with the teaching of students and associated activities like the writing of textbooks. An important role was also played by the university's printing house, which opened in 1756 (the ancestor of today's Moscow University Press). This published some of the most significant work of the day including Tatishchev's history, Polunin's geographical dictionary, and others. The printing house achieved prominence under the ten-year leadership of Nikolai Novikov (1779–89), during which it published more than seven hundred titles. Another significant institution was the university library, also opened in 1756 and accessible to the public. In Aleksandrovskaya's words, the 'public accessibility of one the largest libraries in Russia strengthened the university's ties with society and promoted the spread of scientific understanding across the country' (Aleksandrovskaya 1989, 149).

The great expansion of published geographical literature in Catherine's reign can be divided into five types (not counting the semi-popular publications noted above). The first are the travel accounts and diaries of the various expedition leaders. Lepekhin's 'Daily Notes' is of this type, as is Pallas's account of his 1793–5 expedition to southern European Russia (Pallas 1801). Perhaps most famous is his *Reise durch verschiedene Provinzen des Russischen Reichs* (Pallas 1771–6). The original German text was subsequently translated into Russian, French and English (appearing as *Travels Through the Southern Provinces of the Russian Empire* in 1812). The second type consists of geographical lexicons and dictionaries, to be considered below. Third are thematic publications such as Johann Georgi's *Geographische-physikalische und naturhistorische Beschreibung des russischen Reichs* ('Physico-Geographical and Natural-Historical Description of the Russian Empire') (Georgi 1797–1802) and a three-volume ethnography subsequently translated into French and German (Georgi 1776–7). Also of this type are Pallas's two volumes on Russian flora and three volumes on Russian fauna (Pallas 1784–8, 1811–31). A fourth group comprise general geographies of the Russian empire, notably that of Sergei Pleshcheev discussed below, plus a handful of textbooks. And finally there are regional descriptions such as the topographical descriptions already described, Pallas's *Kratkoe fizicheskoe i topograficheskoe opisanie Tavricheskoi oblasti* ('Short Physical and Topographical Description of Tauride Province') (Pallas 1795) and Güldenstädt's *Geograficheskoe i statisticheskoe opisanie Gruzii i Kavkaza* ('Geographical and Statistical Description of Georgia and the Caucasus') (Güldenstädt 1809). The remainder of this chapter is devoted to a consideration of Sergei Pleshcheev's *Obozrenie Rossiiskoi imperii* (*Survey of the Russian Empire*, Pleshcheev 1790, 1792) and of Fedor Polunin's and Lev Maksimovich's geographical dictionaries (Polunin 1773; Maksimovich 1788–9).

Sergei Pleshcheev's *Survey of the Russian Empire*

Sergei Ivanovich Pleshcheev (1752–1802) served as a soldier and then learnt naval affairs as a cadet on British ships sailing along the coasts of North America. He returned to Russia, served in the Russian navy and became tutor to the Imperial family. His *Obozrenie Rossiiskoi imperii* (Pleshcheev 1790), published in English as *Survey of the Russian Empire* (Pleshcheev 1792), was probably the first to give a full geographical account of Russia, and proved sufficiently popular to be reissued in several editions.[16] It was also translated into German and French.

The book is divided into three parts. Part one (pages 3–38 in the 1790 edition) is a general geographical survey of the country. Outline information is given on such topics as the boundaries, position, surface characteristics and climate of Russia (the nearest we get to a physical geography), the country's products and trade, and its various peoples. In other words, it is a listing of facts rather than an attempt at explanation. At the same time it is testimony to the fact that by this time scholars were beginning to assemble a general understanding of the geography of at least the European part of Russia, with some comprehension of what was eventually to become known as geographical or natural zonation. Something of this is apparent from the following quotation taken from the early part of the book:

> That part of Russia which lies on this side of the Oural [Ural] mountains presents a very extensive plain verging westward by an easy descent. The vast extent of this plain has a great variety of different climates, soils and products. The northern part of it is very woody, marshy and but little fit for cultivation, and has a sensible declivity towards the White and the Frozen Seas. The other part

of this vast plain includes the whole extent along the river Volga, as far as the deserts extending by the Caspian and the Azov Seas, and constitutes the finest part of Russia, which in general is very rich and fruitful, being more arable and meadow land than wood, marshes or barren deserts. The most remarkable for superior quality and taste of every kind of fruit and produce is that part which extends towards Voronezh, Tambov, Penza and Simbirsk as far as the deserts. It has everywhere a most admirable rich soil, consisting of black earth, richly impregnated with saltpetre. But that part which begins between the Azov and the Caspian Seas, and extends near the shores of the latter, and between the Volga and Oural, and as far as the river Emba, is nothing but a desert, level, high, dry, barren and full of salt lakes. (Pleshcheev 1792, 5–6)

Pleshcheev also has a reasonable but not entirely satisfactory grasp of the division between European Russia and the empire's eastern territories:

> Russia, by nature, is divided into two great parts by a range of mountains called Oural which, through the whole breadth of it, form one continual uninterrupted barrier, dividing Siberia from the remaining Russia. (Pleshcheev 1792, 5)

With regard to Siberia, however, the author's understanding of the region's geography is hazier and more inaccurate. Thus, while sketching out the character of the west Siberian Plain and the mountainous region to its east, he suggests that between the Ob' and 'Enissey' there is more woodland than open ground, and, the other side of the Enisei:

> is entirely covered with impervious woods as far as the lake Baical [Baikal], but the soil is fruitful everywhere; and whenever the trouble has been taken of clearing it of the wood, and of draining it of unnecessary water, it proves to be very rich and fit for cultivation … (Pleshcheev 1792, 7–8)

The reality is that most of Russia's eastern regions, apart from a triangular region of forest-steppe and steppe situated to the southwest, are entirely unsuited to cultivation. But the author does at least display an accurate grasp of one key feature of the region's geography:

> Proceeding on farther towards the east, the climate of Siberia becomes by degrees more and more severe, the summer grows

shorter, the winter longer, and the frosts prove more severe. (Pleshcheev 1792, 8)

The book's second part, which occupies by far its greatest portion (pages 39–177), is a regional treatment of geographical material organized province by province. The provinces are grouped together into three 'belts' according to climate, vegetation and human activity – namely northern, middle and southern belts. The reason for this reliance on provincial boundaries is that scholars at this time lacked sufficient data for a more sophisticated regionalization. Thus Pleshcheev tells us that the northern belt extends from 57° to the northern extremity of the empire and embraces 15 provinces. Likewise the middle belt extends between 57° and 50°, while the southern belt lies south of 50°. Pleshcheev allocates only three or four pages to each province, giving brief information about its position and boundaries, its towns and their distances from the provincial capital (or, in the case of the latter, from Moscow), notable places, rivers and water bodies, population and the economy. Some attempt is made to describe the character of the soil and agriculture in each province.

Part three is an alphabetical index of the place names and notable characteristics appearing in the book.

Pleshcheev's book thus serves essentially as a geographical reference book rather than as a volume to read from cover to cover. In this it was rather typical of the eighteenth century (Withers 2007). Thus the Scot William Guthrie's *New Geographical, Historical and Commercial Grammar*, first published in 1770 and covering the geography of the entire world country by country (countries being grouped together into continents), examines a rather similar if not altogether uniform list of topics for each country (Guthrie 1795). Much the same can be said of the American Jedediah Morse's *The American Geography*, first published in 1789. Explicitly written to express an American perception of the geography of the United States (in reaction to the perceptions of Europeans), Morse's book first considers 'astronomical geography', then the geography of the country as a whole, before discussing each US state separately (the thirteen newly independent states plus Maine and the 'western territory', as far as the Mississippi). Finally it turns to the rest of the world (Morse 1789). It may tell us something about the Russian geographical outlook at this time that Pleshcheev's survey contains no discussion of the world beyond Russia.

The geographical dictionaries of Vasilii Tatishchev, Fedor Polunin and Lev Maksimovich

Although the idea of the encyclopedia (an ordered presentation of knowledge) probably dates back to the classical period (White 1968), the eighteenth century was the period when this literary form reached its apogee throughout Europe. To many scholars this is related to the 'ferment of knowledge' of the period – that sudden explosion of facts and ideas that was the consequence of the Scientific Revolution and the great geographical discoveries (Rousseau and Porter 1980). The desire to name, order and classify knowledge, the hallmark of the encyclopedia or dictionary, reflected the need to make sense of what had begun to seem like a disordered world (Yeo 2001, 2003). The literary products of this need were commonly referred to as encyclopedias, dictionaries, directories, grammars or lexicons. Perhaps the most celebrated example of this genre is the French *Encyclopédie*, published between 1751 and 1772 (*Encyclopédie* 1751–72).

The ordering principle governing the various entries in encyclopedias or dictionaries varied. In the case of the above-mentioned *New Geographical, Historical and Commercial Grammar*, Guthrie ordered the entries by country, within a higher-level grouping into continents. There is no suggestion of an alphabetical order between countries, and the length of each entry seems to have been dependent, among other things, on its assumed importance for the British, or more specifically Scottish, reader. The idea of an alphabetical ordering of entries, however, was already common in dictionaries and the like by the late-seventeenth century. Apart from its inherent convenience, this was a way of evading the issue of the interrelationships between different branches of knowledge (Yeo 2003).

An early example of the geographical dictionary in Russia is the already mentioned *Leksikon rossiiskoi* ('Russian Lexicon') by Vasilii Tatishchev, unfinished at the time of his death in 1750 and finally published only in 1793 (Tatishchev 1793). This is an alphabetical dictionary, beginning with the letter 'A' and proceeding only as far as 'K', where it ends. Many of the entries concern specific locations or geographical features, mainly but not exclusively in Russia, such as towns, rivers, lakes and so on. A few entries explain civil and military terms of the Petrine era: heraldmaster, duke, guild, gymnasium, geodesist. There is little in the way of entries on physical geography, such as forest or marsh, and nothing on maps, but 'globe' is defined. The term 'climate' is explained in the traditional way, following the definition given by

Varenius (see Chapter 3). Lengthy entries are provided for geography, and for mathematical and physical geography, almost certainly because of the novelty of such pursuits in the Petrine and post-Petrine periods.[17] In entries on other words, Tatishchev seeks to explain both geographical terminology as well as the location and character of different places and landscape features.

The same cannot be said for some of the other eighteenth-century geographical dictionaries. Thus the important *Geograficheskii leksikon Rossiiskogo gosudarstva* ('Geographical Lexicon of the Russian State'), written by Fedor Polunin and published in 1773, is an alphabetical dictionary describing specific geographical features across Russia but lacking Tatishchev's entries on general geographical terminology (Polunin 1773), thus making it more of a gazetteer. The work was edited by Gerhard Friedrich Müller. According to Aleksandrovskaya it contains 1,537 entries, of which 379 are on settlements (Aleksandrovskaya 1989, 219). Perhaps the best indication of its contents is given by Polunin himself on the title page, where he states that this is a dictionary 'describing in alphabetical order the rivers, lakes, seas, mountains, towns, forts, important monasteries, winter tribute gathering places, mineral works and other notable places of the enormous Russian empire …'. Detailed historical and contemporary information is given for the most significant towns, rivers and so on, with indications of location and other matters. The dictionary uses information gathered from Russian- and German-language geographical sources, including materials of the Second Kamchatka Expedition but, perhaps not surprisingly, it lacks data from the still-ongoing Academy of Sciences expeditions of 1768–74. Little is known about Polunin personally, though he appears to have died in 1787. It seems he was educated at the Cadet Corps School in St Petersburg and served in the military from 1747. He was later appointed *voevoda* (governor) of the town of Vereya, near Moscow.

The third significant Russian geographical dictionary of the eighteenth century, Lev Maksimovich's nine-volume *Novyi i polnyi geograficheskii slovar' Rossiiskogo gosudarstva* ('New and Full Geographical Dictionary of the Russian State'), is also an alphabetical dictionary (Maksimovich 1788–9). Aleksandrovskaya suggests that this is essentially a reworking of Polunin's text taking into account the new provincial boundaries of 1775–85, but it is in fact far more than this (Aleksandrovskaya 1989, 94). Not only does it contain many more entries, making it about five times longer than Polunin's work, but it also expands its field of vision to cover Russia's many ethnic groups. A lot of historical and geographical information is given on the more important settlements, including precise geographical coordinates in many cases. However, unlike Tatishchev's *Lexicon*, it lacks explanation of geographical terminology. Maksimovich was born in 1754 and died before 1816. He was educated at Pereyaslav seminary, the Kiev Academy and then at Moscow University, where he studied languages, and later taught at the gymnasium and the University. He became a senior administrator at the Moscow archive of the College of Foreign Affairs. The dictionary was published by the University printing house.

Conclusion

The introduction to this chapter claimed that the reign of Catherine the Great was the period when Russian geographical endeavour came of age – in other words, when the geographical initiatives introduced by Peter the Great achieved their full fruition. In terms of 'how people came to know the world', Catherine's reign witnessed a remarkable expansion in both the range and methods of geographical study. Some of these produced a more accurate, scientific vision of the world than others. In mapping, for example, greater precision was being achieved through the adoption of more exact determinations of coordinates (the chronometer, developed in the 1760s, finally allowed accurate calculation of longitude) and the gradual introduction of triangulation. In cadastral survey, the General Survey, with its precise demarcation of the lands of different settlements (though not of individual landholders), its detailed listings of the major characteristics of each survey unit (major land uses, soils, harvests, revision populations, individual noble landholders, mills, and so on) and its accompanying maps and atlases, provided an unparalleled insight into local geographies, albeit at the cost of some compromises (for example, the impressionistic character of some land-use designations). Similarly the detailed findings of expeditions like the Academy of Sciences expeditions of 1768–74 made a substantial contribution to Russian science. Elsewhere geographical achievement was more limited – witness the distribution of questionnaires to local officials of variable education, and the dull, standardized nature of many of the resulting topographical descriptions. The latter do at least cover many provinces of the Russian empire, though lacking the interest and local insight of many of their European equivalents. The next chapter will consider to what extent Russians were able to address the gaps in their knowledge of Russia's geography, and to begin to consider the world beyond, during the remaining years of Russia's 'long eighteenth century'.

Notes

1 A law of 1746 prohibited the acquisition of settled land by poll-tax payers apart from merchants, who were allowed to buy serf villages to provide labour for their mills and factories.
2 Nevertheless the Survey department of Rossiiskii gosudarstvennyi arkhiv drevnikh aktov (the Russian State Archive of Ancient Acts) (hereafter RGADA) apparently houses some 600,000 *dacha* plans (Milov, 1965, 33).
3 RGADA f. 1355.
4 RGADA f. 1355 d. 228 ll. 3–4.
5 'Little Russia' was the common Russian term for Ukraine at the time. 'Dependent Little Russians' were enserfed Ukrainian peasants.
6 RGADA f. 1355 d. 228 l. 5. Church land was secularized by Catherine in 1764. The former monastic peasants were henceforth known as Economic peasants or, if Ukrainian, as Economic Little Russians.
7 'Military inhabitants' (*voiskovye obyvateli*) was the term used in the eighteenth century for the former *Cherkasy* (Cossacks).
8 RGADA f. 1355 d. 228 l. 27.
9 RGADA f. 1355 d. 249 l. 2. The fact that settlements to the south tended to be bigger than those to the north is probably related to the relative abundance of wells and water sources in the forest-steppe lands to the north compared to the drier southern steppe where, in the eighteenth century, wealthier noble landowners were often invited to take up landed estates and to establish large settlements together with their serfs. In the militarily precarious situation of the previous century, it was often safer for less wealthy landowners to establish their settlements together with their neighbours both for reasons of defence and for the sharing of agricultural tasks.
10 For example, some of the 'unusable' land may well have been occasionally used for grazing.
11 Authors of the time commonly promoted the socially superior in the hope or recognition of their patronage.
12 Famously, in 1787, under the influence of her favourite Prince Grigorii Potemkin, Catherine herself travelled south to view her new domains in New Russia (southern Ukraine). See Dixon (2009, 286–8). For the role of the expeditions of the 1760s–80s in contributing to the rise of a modern concept of 'state resources', see Bekasova (2010).
13 See, for example, the extensive reference list in Sytin (2014).
14 For the situation in Britain, see Stock (2019, 36–7).
15 For details on the chequered history of popular publishing by the Academy of Sciences, see Schulze (1985, 321–2).
16 Kirilov's *Flourishing Condition (Tsvetushchee sostoyanie)*, published in 1727 and discussed in Chapter 4, does not consider the physical environment.
17 For a discussion of the novelty of geographical and related pursuits at the time, see Cracraft (2004, 204–12).

6
Widening horizons: geographical endeavour at the end of the 'long eighteenth century' (1796–1825)

> *During the time that I was serving in the English navy in the revolutionary war of 1793 to 1799, my attention was particularly excited by the importance of the English trade with the East Indies and China. It appeared to me by no means impossible for Russia to participate in the trade by sea.*
>
> Adam von Krusenstern, 1813

Catherine died in November 1796 to be succeeded by her son, Paul. Relations between mother and son had not been good. Paul, born in 1754, had been excluded from the Russian throne by his mother's usurpation, and once he succeeded her, he proved determined to reverse many of her policies. Even so some important reforms were enacted during his reign. Although assessments of Paul's character differ, there can be little doubt that his autocratic temperament led to the creation of many personal enemies. He was finally overthrown and murdered in a palace coup in March 1801.

Paul's successor was his son Alexander I, a man of very different stamp. Veering between a vague liberalism on the one hand and reaction on the other, Alexander's elusive and contradictory character has long mystified scholars. Unlike his father and grandfather, however, he was to die of natural causes, in December 1825.

Paul's and Alexander's policies towards science were markedly different. Paul, like his mother in her later years, had been frightened by the threat posed by the French Revolution; he had forbidden the import of Western books and prevented Russian students from studying abroad. He also starved scientific institutions like the Academy of Sciences and the Free Economic Society of funds. Many of these measures were reversed by Alexander on his accession. Acting under liberal influences, the new tsar embarked on a series of educational reforms, opening a new Ministry of Education in 1802, granting additional funding to the Academy of Sciences and the Free Economic Society, founding new educational institutions like universities, and increasing the network of schools, including higher professional schools. The new universities included Dorpat[1] and Vil'na/Vilnius (1802), Khar'kov and Kazan' (1804) and the re-establishment of St Petersburg (1819). Moscow University was granted a new charter in 1804, opening its doors to students from all social classes. This soon became a model for other universities. The Academy of Sciences was granted a new, more liberal, charter in 1803 and developed the range and specialization of its activities. It remained the foremost scientific and research institution in Russia, though an increasing role in this regard was now being played by the universities. Also contributing to scientific endeavour were new societies like the Society of Naturalists (1805) and the Mineralogical Society (1817), and also museums such as the Asiatic Museum (1818) and the Botanical Museum (1824). Other institutions were to follow, although geography did not make a formal appearance until the establishment of the Russian Geographical Society (1845) and the opening of the first university departments of geography in the 1880s (Oldfield and Shaw 2016, 35–7). The basis for the new natural sciences was thus gradually expanding.

The period between the accession of Tsar Paul in 1796 and the death of Alexander I in 1825, or the end of what is often called Russia's 'long eighteenth century', was marked by many new demands on the empire's resources arising from the turbulence and military threats posed by revolution and war across much of Europe. This chapter will first discuss the development of cartography between the late-eighteenth century and the first quarter of the nineteenth, since better maps were an urgent necessity in a situation of domestic and international instability. The period is noted for reforms in the administration of the mapping enterprise, the development of military mapping, and the adoption of more accurate mapping methods, such as triangulation.[2] Consideration will then be given to Evgenii Bolkhovitinov's *Istoricheskoe, geograficheskoe i ekonomicheskoe opisanie Voronezhskoi gubernii* ('Geographical, Historical and Economic Survey of Voronezh Province'), a work that might be considered Russia's first example of a local geography and history, or what the Germans call a *Landeskunde*. Attention will subsequently switch to the new statistical approaches to geographical endeavour that began to appear in this period, together with some significant publications of the time. Finally there will be a consideration of the ways in which Russians began to pay more attention to the world beyond Russia as the new century dawned, notably in the first Russian round-the-world voyage of Adam von Krusenstern.

Cartographical endeavour in the late-eighteenth and early-nineteenth centuries

The importance of the project to map the empire as fully and accurately as possible had become particularly apparent in the latter part of the eighteenth century. The huge Pugachev peasant revolt in 1773–5 goaded Catherine II into a sweeping reform of provincial administration in order to strengthen government control of the regions, streamline military recruitment and taxation at the local level, and promote regional economic development (Madariaga 1981, 277–307). All this demanded new maps and the collection of a mass of data about the new provinces and districts (Bagrow 1975; Postnikov 1989, 69–95; Seegel 2012, 65–88). The process continued under Catherine's successor Paul, who launched a second provincial reform in 1797 aimed at yet further government control over the countryside at the expense of the local nobility.

The materials available for mapping were now much richer than those at the command of the Petrine geodesists. These included not only the 1745 *Academy Atlas*, the many large-scale maps and atlases associated with the General Survey and the cartographic materials produced by the Academy expeditions of 1768–74, but also new sources such as the more accurate lists of astronomically calculated coordinates drawn up by the expeditions of Ivan Ivanovich Islen'ev (1768–73) and Petr Borisovich Inokhodtsev (1781–5). During the period 1766–86, the Geography Department of the Academy of Sciences produced 148 maps, of which 58 were published as part of various scientific texts. According to Postnikov, of 90 maps distinguished by their scientific accuracy and detail, no fewer than 67 were the work of just three experienced cartographers, Jakob Friedrich Schmidt (33), John Truscott (24) and Ivan Ivanovich Islen'ev (10) (Postnikov, 1989, 69).

The mapping activity of this period was characterized by three features. First, there was a concerted effort to map Russia at a large scale through the production of new maps and atlases. This movement was stimulated by the administrative reforms of Catherine and Paul, which meant that the new provincial boundaries had to be redrawn on the basis of more accurate surveys. Second, there was a gradual militarization of mapping, as it was realized that maps produced by the Geography Department were unsatisfactory for military use. Fears over security loomed large as the international situation deteriorated with the French Revolution and the rise of Napoleon Bonaparte. Third, there was a renewed emphasis on mathematical accuracy, with the gradual triangulation of Russia's provinces, a process that began in the late-eighteenth century and continued until the middle of the nineteenth (Seegel 2012, 68–71).

The period witnessed the production of numerous maps and atlases. In 1776, for example, to celebrate its fiftieth anniversary the Academy of Sciences published a general map of Russia at a scale of 1:7,227,000. This was drawn by Schmidt and Truscott. Ten years later a new 3-page map of Russia at a scale of 1:5,250,000 was drawn by the same cartographers plus Friedrich von Schubert. This new edition was necessitated by Catherine's provincial reform of 1775–85. Arguably more important, however, was the work of Alexander Wilbrecht (A. M. Vil'brekht) (1756–1823), who worked in the Academy of Sciences Geography Department. In 1786 Catherine established a new institution known as the Geography Department of Her Imperial Majesty's Cabinet, which employed Wilbrecht and was tasked with composing new maps and an atlas of the Russian empire. The latter was published in 1792, entitled the *Rossiiskii atlas, iz soroka chetyrekh kart sostoyashchii* ('Russian Atlas Consisting of 44 Maps'). It depicted Russia's new provincial boundaries following Catherine's reform. Paul's reforms soon necessitated a new edition of the 1792 atlas, however, which came out in 1800.

Another notable publication was the *Podrobnaya karta Rossiiskoi imperii i blizlezhashchikh zagranichnykh vladenii* ('Detailed Map of the Russian Empire and Nearby Foreign Domains'), published in 1805 at a scale of 1:840,000. Also known as the '100-page Atlas' it actually contained 107 pages as a result of the last-minute addition of seven maps of north European Russia (*Podrobnaya karta* 1805). The *Karmannoi pochtovoi atlas vsei Rossiiskoi imperii razdelennoi na gubernii s pokazaniem glavnykh pochtovykh dorog* ('Pocket Postal Atlas of the Whole Russian Empire') was another significant production of the period (*Karmannoi pochtovoi atlas* 1808).

Meanwhile Russia's mapping project had been undergoing reorganization. In March 1797 the expanded Geography Department of the Cabinet had been transferred from the Cabinet to the Senate, and in 1800 was renamed His Imperial Majesty's Map Depot. This became responsible for archiving maps of all kinds and gradually assumed the role of Russia's chief mapping agency. In 1810 it was transferred again, this time being placed under the aegis of the War Ministry; two years later it was renamed the Military-Topographical Depot. Finally in 1816 it became part of the army's General Staff. But as the government's own mapping activity grew, the Academy of Sciences' Geography Department correspondingly diminished, and it was abolished in 1800 (its engraving section finally closing in 1805). The Department had been losing significance since the mid-1780s as a producer of general maps because of the growing role of the Cabinet and then the Map Depot. But its overall contribution to Russian mapping had been very considerable – between 1726 and 1805 it had published 324 maps, including atlases and general maps of the empire (Postnikov 1989, 70).

The reorganization of mapping was closely connected to the need for maps useful for military purposes, a need that became increasingly apparent in the second half of the eighteenth century. Traditionally the military relied on provincial and district survey offices to provide the maps and information needed for conducting military manoeuvres, defending frontiers and so on but, especially during the Napoleonic campaign of 1812–14, it was found that the maps provided lacked both the scale and the information needed by the army. Until the early-nineteenth century the army had no mapping department of its own. Only through the establishment of a specialized military-topographical service and the training of a cadre of military cartographers could this problem be resolved. Rather like the British Ordnance Survey, therefore, Russian mapping became increasingly associated with the military.

In addition to the production of new maps and atlases and the militarization of mapping, the period witnessed an increased adoption of triangulation based on astronomically determined locations as the basis of mapping. Although the Russian origins of this method date from the late-eighteenth and the beginning of the nineteenth century, with the triangular surveys of Finland and other western provinces, Postnikov states that the triangulation of Vil'na province in 1816–21 under the supervision of the military geodesist and astronomer Carl Friedrich Tenner was the beginning of the systematic triangulation of Russia. On the foundation of this astronomical-geodesic work, in 1819–29 Tenner conducted Russia's 'first continuous plane-table survey with a basis in triangulation' (Postnikov,1989, 108). This was followed by the triangular surveys of many other provinces (Seegel 2012, 68–71).

The period may therefore be said to have witnessed the beginning of modern mapping in Russia. But it was only the beginning. It was well into the twentieth century before Russia could be said to have been properly mapped (Shaw and Oldfield 2015, 44).

Evgenii Bolkhovitinov's 'Historical, Geographical and Economic Description of Voronezh Province' (1800)

Evgenii Bolkhovitinov (baptized Efimii Alekseevich Bolkhovitinov) (1767–1837) was an example of an Orthodox priest with strong academic leanings. Born into the family of a parish priest in Voronezh, he studied at the Voronezh theological seminary and then from 1785 at the Moscow Slavic-Greek-Latin Academy and Moscow University, specializing in philosophy, theology and languages, notably Greek and French. He then taught at the Voronezh seminary for several years and began work on several publications, including a history of Russia and the above-mentioned description of Voronezh province. In 1800, having lost both his wife and children, he became prefect of the Alexander Nevsky Academy in St Petersburg, where he taught philosophy and oratory, and became a monk. In 1802 he was appointed Archimandrite of Sergievskii Monastery and then successively Bishop of several dioceses including Staraya Russa (Novgorod), Vologda and Kaluga. In 1816 he was elevated to the position of Archbishop of Pskov and in 1822 to the Archbishopric of Kiev, becoming Metropolitan of Kiev and Galicia in the same year.

During all this time Bolkhovitinov continued with a wide range of academic studies, including history, church history, archaeology, palaeography, Russian secular writers and other subjects (Shmurlo 1888a, 1888b). In view of his evident erudition he was voted a member of the Russian Academy in 1806 and a Corresponding Member of the Academy of Sciences in 1826.

Bolkhovitinov's *Istoricheskoe, geograficheskoe i ekonomicheskoe opisanie Voronezhskoi gubernii* ('Historical, Geographical and Economic Description of Voronezh Province'), which he published at the comparatively early age of 33 (Bolkhovitinov 1800), is regarded by Rubinshtein as a late example of the eighteenth-century topographical tradition, but he suggests that it probably derives from the personal initiative of the author himself rather than in response to that of the Academy of Sciences or the Free Economic Society (Rubinshtein 1953, 79). For this reason it is perhaps best regarded as an early example of the local historical or area studies (*kraevedenie*) that were to become prominent later in the nineteenth century (Johnson, 2006). Certainly, though it does resemble in certain respects the earlier topographical descriptions, it also strongly reflects Bolkhovitinov's personal interests in history, church history, archaeology and related subjects. It illustrates the way in which at least part of Russian society was now embracing an educated outlook, thus contributing to the modernization and arguably to the strengthening of the realm.

The first 19 of the volume's 218 pages are devoted to a general chronological history of Voronezh province, beginning with the ancient Scythians described by Herodotus in his celebrated *Histories*. Numerous sources are cited, many of them well known. Bolkhovitinov cites the Nestor Chronicle, which suggests that the town of Voronezh already existed in 1177, whereas the modern view is that it was founded only in 1585–6 (Zagorovskii 1969, 21). For the eighteenth century he discusses Peter the Great's celebrated shipbuilding activities at Voronezh (see Chapter 3) and describes in considerable detail the provincial reforms of Peter, Catherine and Paul. There follows a survey of the province's characteristics in the contemporary period and in the recent past: population numbers and social divisions, land use (according to the recently completed General Survey), settlements, economic activities, and other matters. The use of official statistics is notable in lists and tables, provided no doubt by provincial governor A. B. Sontsov, whose help and encouragement are acknowledged. Little is said about the natural environment.

The rest of the book is laid out systematically in much the same way as earlier topographical descriptions, with each town being described followed by its district (*uezd*). Reflecting Bolkhovitinov's historical inclinations is the long discussion devoted to the history of the town of Voronezh, based in part on original sources. The author notes that, after a fire in 1773, the town was accorded a new regular plan, and the ensuing provincial reform led to the construction of many public buildings and fine new merchants' dwellings, thus greatly improving the town's appearance.[3] The remainder of the section on the town of Voronezh concerns the contemporary town, containing such details as its cathedrals, churches and monasteries, its public and private buildings, its principal institutions (seminary, printing house, theatre and others), main streets, suburbs and trade. A list of governors recorded in the documents since 1590 is provided. Finally, there is a table on the official post.

The discussion of Voronezh district that follows Bolkhovitinov's introduction is rather idiosyncratic, focusing on things that most interested him. First, he briefly gives various statistical details, such as the size of the population before the provincial reform, the number of settlements, and details on the monastery, churches, houses of the nobility, mills, manufactories and dwellings. There follows a lengthy description of the Tolshevskii Spaso-Preobrazhenskii Convent, situated some forty versts north-east of Voronezh. Bolkhovitinov then considers the former town and fort of Tavrov, situated south of Voronezh close to its confluence with the Don and associated with Peter the Great's shipbuilding activities. A long discussion follows of the village of Kostenki to the south of Voronezh on the Don. What interests the author is the name of this settlement, which derives from the word 'bones', a result of the large number of mammoth bones discovered here on the banks of the Don. Bolkhovitinov speculates about the origins of the bones and provides a long quote relating to them from Samuel Gmelin, who visited the region in 1768–9 (Gmelin 1770–4). Archaeology, or rather in this case palaeontology, was one of Bolkhovitinov's primary interests. He concludes his section on Voronezh district with a short description of the former town of Orlov, including its important horse fair, and a list of the district's principal rivers. Thus the author confines himself to giving only brief details about the fundamental geographical facts of the district, but is expansive on the history and issues of personal interest. He tells us almost nothing about the natural environment or agriculture.

The remainder of the book takes the same form: a description of each district centre followed by that of its district, though much shorter than those for Voronezh and its district outlined above. Thus Pavlovsk, situated some 150 versts south-west of Voronezh on the Don and founded as a fort by Peter the Great in 1709, is accorded a brief history followed by a discussion of the town's major buildings, and particulars regarding its population, land use, trade and crafts. The author informs us that Pavlovsk is celebrated for its cultivation of watermelons, which were famous across Ukraine and even in Moscow. On account of the fineness of its sheep's wool, moreover, the women of Pavlovsk commonly knitted stockings and mittens, which also found a wide market.

The usual statistical details are also provided for Pavlovsk district, together with a short description of the most significant trading settlements. The district was particularly noted for the Shipov forest, an oak forest that was a rather unusual feature of the forest-steppe environment. Bolkhovitinov informs us that timber from this sizeable forest had been much used in the past for shipbuilding and for fortifications, beginning with the reign of Peter the Great. But the best construction timber had now been exhausted, and part of the forest had been given into private ownership.

Following discussion of the province's other towns and districts, Bolkhovitinov's survey is concluded with a series of appendices on ecclesiastical matters: a history of Voronezh diocese, a list of the presently existing monasteries in the diocese, a list of those now closed,[4] and an account of past bishops. These appendices thus once again reflect the author's interests in church affairs.

The reasons why Bolkhovitinov chose to write his historical and geographical description of Voronezh province can only be guessed at but must presumably include an interest in the region of his birth. The work is the product of much hard labour, but it is as a compendium of facts rather than of selective interpretation that it is most memorable. As a work of geography the book clearly falls in the Russian topographical tradition but also reflects the author's personal interests, especially in church history. As we have seen, it seems likely to have been the product of the author's personal initiative rather than that of a central agency, although he does make much use of official statistics. His limited interest in (and perhaps understanding of) the natural environment is very apparent. Nevertheless, the work seems to reflect the growing interest in local studies, which was becoming ever more apparent at the time.

The new statistical geography (from the late-eighteenth century)

As was the case in many European countries, in the late-eighteenth century Russia fell under the influence of new, statistical approaches to the understanding of the world, and especially of the human world (Pearson 1978). The German word *Statistik*, coined from late Latin and first publicly aired in 1672, was understood, at least in the German lands, to be a 'science dealing with the facts of a state' (Woolf 1989, 590). The link with the state was particularly apparent in absolutist states like Prussia and France, which had long traditions of state intervention in economic and political development. Especially in such cases as Prussia and other parts of the Holy Roman Empire, which lacked overseas colonies, resources for development were mainly to be found in the home territories. As Woolf asserts, in such states 'statistics meant the ordered and (usually but never exclusively) numerical description of the state'. In practice, statistical survey meant a search for and description of all sources of wealth, starting with the human population and embracing all terrestrial, mineral, floral and faunal resources as well as agriculture, manufacturing and trade. In the words of Smith-Peter, 'statistics was a way to extend the reach of the sovereign by increasing his knowledge of his own lands' (Smith-Peter 2007, 48).

Because of its close links with the state, the use of statistics in the German lands, involving the widespread collection of data of all kinds, became a central activity of the state administration (the *Kammer*). This reliance on official statistics became known as 'cameralism'. According to Raeff, the purpose of cameral statistics was 'to maximize the country's productive potential, increase its wealth and power, and promote its material well-being' (Raeff 1983, 28, 31). It was thus tied to policy (or 'police' in the English usage of the time) as governments issued directives (*Polizeiordnungen*) instructing the population and its officials in such matters as behaviour and economic and social activity. The cameralist state thus became a 'regulated state'. In Russia such regulation dated back to at least the time of Peter the Great (Ptukha 1945; Shaw 1999b). Indeed, as argued in Chapter 3 above, Peter initiated a whole series of data-collecting exercises, which were continued by his successors. By the late-eighteenth and early-nineteenth centuries cameralism dominated Russian statistics and had an important influence on policymaking. This was in part the product of the close Russo-German connections that characterized the eighteenth century, especially in science (Osipov 1995; Dahlmann and Smagina 2015). It was also the result of the activities of certain key individuals, notably Anton Friedrich Büsching (1724–1793) and August Ludwig von Schlözer (1735–1809).

Büsching was educated at the University of Halle, after which he was appointed tutor to the family of the departing Prussian ambassador to St Petersburg. Returning to Germany soon afterwards, he was appointed professor of philosophy at Göttingen University, and then in 1761 accepted a post as pastor to the German congregation in St Petersburg, where he founded a famous school. From 1765 he supervised another school in Berlin and edited two journals. His vast published output included works on geography and history, education, religion and biography. He played an important role in developing the cameralist tradition, building on the earlier work of Georg Achenwald (1719–1772) (Woolf 1989, 590). His most important geographical work was his *Neue Erdbeschreibung* ('New Earth Description') published in several parts between 1754 and 1761. The first four parts concerned Europe while the fifth (published in 1768) was on Asia. Portions of this expansive work were subsequently published in Russian and other European languages.

Schlözer was educated at Wittenberg and Göttingen and subsequently went with Gerhard Friedrich Müller to St Petersburg as Müller's literary assistant and family tutor. He was appointed adjunct to the Academy of Sciences in 1762 and ordinary member three years later. Leaving Russia in 1767, Schlözer returned to Göttingen where in 1769 he was appointed ordinary professor. Like Büsching, his academic interests were vast, especially in the fields of history (he was particularly noted for his work on global history), politics and statistics. With regard to the latter, and like Büsching, he made important contributions to cameralist statistics. His attempted description of Russia (*Neuverändertes Russland*) was published in parts in Riga between 1767 and 1773 but, according to Aleksandrovskaya, failed to achieve any kind of coherence (Aleksandrovskaya 1989, 227).

In addition to the influence of Büsching and Schlözer, other German scholars who worked for a period in Russia also brought a cameralist approach to geographical studies. Among the most notable were Johann Gottfried Reichel, Johann Heim, August Wilhelm Hupel, Heinrich Friedrich von Storch, and Benedikt Franz Johann von Hermann. Like their forebears, these scholars were characterized by their dependence on official statistics rather than on their work in the field. They in turn influenced the work of the Russians. Evdokim Filippovich Zyablovskii (1764–1846) and Konstantin Ivanovich Arsen'ev (1789–1865) were two such Russians whose work merits consideration.

Zyablovskii graduated from Sevsk theological seminary and was then appointed as a teacher at Kolyvan' in Siberia. Here he wrote a description of the region. In 1797 he became professor of geography and history, and subsequently of statistics, at the St Petersburg institution that became the Pedagogical Institute in 1804 and St Petersburg University in 1819. He served as rector of the university (1821–5) and as dean of the historico-philological faculty (1828–33). Zyablovskii wrote several statistical works, including *Rossiiskaya statistika* ('Russian Statistics', from 1831), *Kurs vseobshchei geografii* ('A Course in General Geography', 1818–19) and *Geografiya Rossiiskoi imperii* ('A Geography of the Russian Empire', 1831 and 1837). His general approach was that of a staunch conservative and a strong proponent of cameralism. Below we will consider the second edition of his 'Russian Statistics', published in 1842.[5]

Zyablovskii's 'Russian Statistics' may be taken as a typical example of the statistical or cameralist approach to geography that characterized the first half of the nineteenth century (Zyablovskii 1842). Aleksandrovskaya argues that this approach, deriving from a number of initiatives rooted in the previous century, formed the basis for a future economic geography (Aleksandrovskaya 1989, 91–8). Although this is no doubt correct, it is important to note the differences between this kind of approach and earlier approaches typified by the Russian topographical tradition. First, in the statistical approach there was much less interest in physical geography and the natural environment – such as the detailed listings of rivers and other natural phenomena. Second, since cameralism was wedded to the state and its activities, cameralist works often described the institutions of the state and their functions in considerable detail. This is not what we would expect in economico-geographical accounts. It is as though the cameralists saw their purpose as not only describing for the benefit of the ruler the nature of the territory over which he or she ruled, but also the instruments which could be used to exploit or transform that territory.

The book is split into two parts, with two chapters in part one. The first chapter concerns the land and the peoples of Russia, thus falling very much within the Russian topographical tradition. The section on the land constitutes a brief discussion of the country's physical geography, including its natural products. The latter include products of the plant world (both natural and cultivated), of animals (wild and domestic) and of minerals (building materials, salt, coal, metals, ores and others). The accent throughout is on those features of the Russian environment that are useful to society and the state. The chapter then moves on to a short survey of the peoples of Russia, such as their overall numbers, ethnic groupings, religions and so on. The statistics are based on census data and only a simplified picture is given. A notable difference from earlier ethnographic accounts is that little is said about the ways of life of the peoples concerned.

Chapter two is where Zyablovskii's account entirely departs from the Russian topographical tradition, being a survey of the realm of state structure and administration. It is in fact rather longer than the first chapter, embracing the state's legal foundations including its basic laws, its absolutist nature, social ranks and titles, and both the higher state organs and the lower administration. It includes such details as the strength of the armed forces, the state's finances, foreign affairs and other matters. The chapter also contains details of scientific societies and institutions, and of relations and treaties with other European states. This chapter, therefore, is a general survey of the Russian state, useful for anyone enquiring into the state's capacity for achieving its policy objectives.

Part two is where 'Russian Statistics' approximates most closely to what would now be called an economic geography. The first section ('division one') concerns human industries based on the vegetable, animal and mineral kingdoms whose raw materials were discussed in part one. Thus production based on the vegetable kingdom includes grain farming, forestry, the cultivation of plants for making fabrics (for example flax, hemp), fruit and vegetable gardening, the raising of plants for dyes, medicinal plants, spices and mushrooms. A similarly comprehensive approach is taken towards production based on animals and that on minerals. In summary, what we are presented with is a full account of primary production in Russia, with careful attention paid to those regions where such productive activities are possible, as well as indications, especially for activities based on the vegetable and animal kingdoms, where such activities are not possible (due to considerations of climate, soil types and so on).

The remaining 'divisions' of part two of the book concern secondary production (factories, mills), trade and exchange (internal and external trade), the general economic situation, and such matters as public welfare and education (educational and training institutions, numbers of students, scientific societies, libraries and so on).

In order to provide a fuller picture of Zyablovskii's statistical approach, we can examine the section on grain farming in more detail. The author tells us that in terms of national well-being this is the most important source of state wealth but, because of the variability in climate and soil quality, it is conducted in some belts with excellent results, in others with moderate or little success, while elsewhere again it is a hopeless enterprise. Since at this stage relatively little was known about the detailed geography of climate and soils (this was to come later in the nineteenth century, see Oldfield and Shaw 2016), the practice was to describe such variability by latitudinal belts and, within each belt, by provinces. The best belt for grain farming, says Zyablovskii, is that between 50° and 55° North, to the west of the Urals. Here the soil is in general fertile ('black') with little need for additional fertilizing, summers are pleasant and frosts moderate. Hence this belt is the country's main granary and its inhabitants are the best grain farmers. The region produces so much grain that, after local provisioning, a considerable portion can be sent to northern and southern provinces or abroad. The belt between 55° and 60° North, which includes Moscow, parts of St Petersburg and the Baltic provinces, is then described, including details of the relief, climate and soils. Here production is inferior to the belt further south and deteriorates eastwards towards the Urals. It is even poorer north of 60° North, an area that embraces Finland and north European Russia, characterized by an abundance of sandy and marshy soils and frequent summer frosts. Looking south in European Russia (south of 50° North down to the southern border), including New Russia, Crimea and the North Caucasus, the author informs us that parts are fertile and productive whereas others are semi-arid and suffer local shortfalls in production. Details are given on particular provinces such as Orenburg and Astrakhan'. Finally, the author turns to Siberia east of the Urals: the best grain-growing regions here stretch from the southern branches of the Urals and the Kirgiz steppe eastwards to Lake Baikal and north to 56° North. In general, although this part of Siberia is best for grain farming in terms of climate, it is not always suitable because of poor soil quality. Some areas in Tobol'sk province, however, grow enough grain to ship down the Ob' to provision some of the northern regions and also send grain over the Urals to Perm' province. Other Siberian grain-producing regions are described and average yields given.

Having thus discussed the geography of grain farming in Russia, Zyablovskii turns to more general aspects of this activity. Here he clearly benefits from the relatively recent research and publications of the Free Economic Society and other organizations. Thus he comments on how the land is worked and on the tools used, showing how average yields vary across Russia as a result of both environmental and social factors. He compares the predominant use of the three-field system in Russia with the more variegated rotation systems that characterize western European countries, very much to the advantage of the latter. He makes various recommendations about how Russian agriculture might be improved. He also discusses the new agricultural societies that have appeared in recent years and the contribution they might make to agricultural improvement. He makes considerable use of official statistics throughout.

Zyablovskii gives a similar detailed account of all other sources of national wealth in Russia. His approach is therefore very different from that adopted by the topographical descriptions of the previous century, which are focused much more on the general physical and human geography of each province without detailed discussion of economic activity and resources. Zyablovskii's account is therefore more centred and very much in keeping with the interventionist spirit of cameralism. In essence it provides a detailed, statistically based description of the geography of the Russian empire, a pioneering venture at the time.

Konstantin Arsen'ev, the other major contributor to statistical geography in this period, was born the son of a village priest in the northern province of Kostroma and attended the Kostroma Ecclesiastical Seminary from 1799 (Pertsik, 1996). As one of the brightest students in his class he was sent in 1806 to the St Petersburg Pedagogical Institute, where he studied German and French. Graduating in 1810 he was then appointed teacher of Latin and geography at the institute. In 1817 he became adjunct professor of geography and statistics at the Pedagogical Institute, which two years later was to become St Petersburg University. Initially he had been assistant to Zyablovskii, but they soon fell out as a result of their contrasting views of the purpose of statistics (Smith-Peter 2007, 50–1). Zyablovskii, as we have seen, was an ardent cameralist, believing that the sole purpose of statistics was to foster the power of the state. For Arsen'ev, by contrast, it was the well-being of the people that mattered primarily, and only through that the well-being of the state. Following the ideas of Adam Smith, he considered that only a free and enterprising people could flourish to the advantage of the state. Hence he considered serfdom to be a burden and a barrier to economic development.

Needless to say, Arsen'ev's views were considered dangerously radical at the time and in 1821 he, his academic colleague and former mentor Carl Theodor von Hermann and another colleague were tried for propagating liberal views and expelled from the university. However, Arsen'ev was saved from further punishment through the protection of Grand Duke Nikolai Pavlovich (soon to ascend the throne as Tsar Nicholas I). In 1828 Arsen'ev was appointed tutor in history and geography to the heir to the throne, the future Alexander II (who eventually abolished serfdom in Russia in 1861, arguably in part influenced by his childhood tutor). Under Nicholas I, despite the latter's reactionary inclinations, Arsen'ev flourished, becoming a corresponding member of the Academy of Sciences in 1826 and a full member ten years later.[6] From 1835 until his retirement in 1853 he was head of the statistical division of the Council of the Ministry of Internal Affairs. This body organized the collection and analysis of a broad range of statistical data and made policy recommendations accordingly. In 1843 Arsen'ev became a leading member of the Ministry's Provisional Statistical Committee, where he was able to influence the statistical training of a future generation of bureaucrats. He was also one of the founders of the Russian Geographical Society (1845), which published some excellent statistical work under his influence.

Arsen'ev published numerous geographical and statistical works, the most significant of which were his *Obozrenie fizicheskogo sostoyaniya Rossii* ('Survey of the Physical Condition of Russia', 1818), *Nachertanie statistiki rossiiskogo gosudarstva* ('Outline of the Statistics of the Russian State', 1818, 1819), *Kratkaya vseobshchaya geografiya* ('Short General Geography', 1818–19) and *Statisticheskie ocherki Rossii* ('Statistical Notes on Russia', 1848) (Arsen'ev 1818a, 1818b, 1818–19, 1819, 1848). The 'Short General Geography' achieved a wide circulation as a school textbook, being reissued in twenty editions between 1818 and 1849 (Pertsik 1996, 109).

Arsen'ev's 'Outline of the Statistics of the Russian State' was written in the spirit of Zyablovskii's 'Russian Statistics', but with certain important differences. The book was published in two parts in 1818 and 1819. A general introduction at the beginning of part one entitled

'A Geographical-statistical survey of the Russian state' discusses Russia's geographical position, principal geographical features and natural products. Part one itself, subtitled 'On the condition of the people' (thus underlining its Smithian rather than cameralist emphasis), first considers the population, including its size, dynamics and social and ethnic divisions. It then moves on to survey 'The national wealth'. Rather like Zyablovskii's discussion, this embraces all types of production from farming in all its forms, forestry, hunting and fishing, to mining, manufacturing, trade and so on. It concludes with a discussion of weights and measures and the Russian monetary system. The final section focuses on education: the principal educational institutions, scientific bodies, and the general level of education in Russia.

By far the most interesting part of Arsen'ev's book, and an important departure from Zyablovskii's approach, is where he comments critically on some of the most significant problems of the Russian economy. Thus, in his consideration of agriculture, he comments that:

> ... even in its present state, it is the most abundant source of wealth for the state, a sure spring bringing forth all kinds of occupations, that it has lately achieved important successes, but that it is far from attaining that perfection which could be reached in the future.

Following Smith, he moves on to comment on the burden of the 'unproductive classes' – those not directly involved in production – on the government and the economy (Smith-Peter 2007, 50). He cites four particular barriers to agricultural development: first, the excessive number of servants kept by the upper classes in their homes, thus excluding them from productive labour; second, too many healthy and strong peasants depart from the hard life of the countryside for the ease of the towns where they take on 'frivolous jobs that could easily be done by women or children', leaving the land unproductive, or at least less productive than it should be; third, the 'idle' life of a large part of the population of southern Russia, and especially of much of Siberia, that is suitable for agricultural development. Here Arsen'ev clearly has in mind the indigenous peoples who preferred to engage in herding or gathering on fertile land that could otherwise be put to arable use. He notes the 'positive' effects of some government schemes to settle nomadic peoples, introducing them to arable farming and converting them to Christianity. Needless to say, he fails to suggest what the indigenes themselves felt about such policies. Fourth, he cites the burden of serfdom on agriculture. Here Arsen'ev is at his boldest:

> The enserfment of the agriculturalists is a great obstacle to the improvement of agriculture. The man who is uncertain of receiving the full reward of his labour will by no means produce as much as he who is free from all such bonds of coercion.

He goes on to state that land cultivated by free labour will produce much more than land of the same quality cultivated by serfs. Centuries of experience, he claims, show that free labour and the free economy are the surest guarantee of the increase of private and social wealth and that there is no greater spur to economic well-being than full civic freedom. He cites the experience of foreign colonists in Russia as evidence (Arsen'ev 1818b, 101–7). It was the open expression of such views that was to lead to Arsen'ev's trial and expulsion from the university three years later.

Part two of the book, which was published as a separate volume in 1819, follows the cameralist spirit in focusing 'On the condition of the government'. Like the analogous section in Zyablovskii's work, this addresses Russia's fundamental laws, its government and administration, its finances and similar matters (Arsen'ev 1819).

Arsen'ev's longest work is his 'Statistical Notes on Russia', published in 1848. This follows the same lines as his 1818 work but is more detailed and, as a result of his important position in the Ministry of Internal Affairs, benefits from the author's access to a greater range of official statistics. A significant feature of the book is a general regionalization of the empire, whereby Russia is subdivided into ten regions, treating Siberia as a separate region (Arsen'ev 1848, 165 ff.). Each region is discussed in terms of its major environmental characteristics, with the accent on characteristics of the greatest human value. However, Arsen'ev's regionalization method, a novel procedure at the time, was subject to considerable criticism.[7] Some critics, for example, suggested that it was insufficiently quantitative, others that he had chosen the wrong variables. To some extent political differences were clearly influential. However, regionalization is always to some degree subjective, based upon what variables the author considers most important in defining his or her regions.

The new statistical geography of the late-eighteenth and early-nineteenth centuries, therefore, signals a marked change from the Russian topographical tradition. Gone is the importance accorded to general description to be replaced with the detailed (and often numerical) discussion of economic activities of all kinds. The central attention is focused on agriculture and the population as the major sources of national wealth. Also of prime interest, at least to the cameralists, is the state – its legal and institutional form and principal functions. Statistics are seen as close to geography, indeed as part of geography. This focus abets an interest in regionalization and thus points towards the economic geography of the future with an accent on how geographical studies might be used to foster not only the well-being of the state but also that of the people. The statistical approach greatly enhanced the state's knowledge of its local geographies and resources thus adding to possibilities for the empire's economic development and military capability.

Comparison of work in the statistico-geographical tradition in Russia with similar work in other European countries at the same period suggests how varied such work was, with greater or lesser emphasis on economic activities as against more general topographical and travel-related material (see, for example, Holsche 1788; Cooke c. 1826).

Shchekatov's 'Geographical Dictionary', 1801–9

Among the wide variety of geographical publications rolling off Russian printing presses in the first quarter of the nineteenth century, Afanasii Mikhailovich Shchekatov's *Geograficheskii slovar' Rossiiskogo gosudarstva* ('Geographical Dictionary of the Russian State') was among the most notable (Shchekatov 1801–9). This was published in seven volumes over eight years (see Figure 6.1), the first volume being co-edited with Lev Maksimovich and the remaining ones by Shchekatov alone, under a slightly different title. The dictionary is clearly a revision of those of Polunin and Maksimovich though many entries were rewritten or extended (see Chapter 5 above).

As is the case with other compilers of geographical dictionaries in this period, relatively little is known about Shchekatov personally except that he seems to have been born about 1753 and died in 1814. He was a writer, translator and geographer, the father of several children, and seems to have suffered loss of property as a result of the French occupation of Moscow in 1812.

As its title suggests, the dictionary is entirely focused on the Russian empire and contains no terminological or explanatory entries. Even neighbouring states like China (*Kitai* in Russian), in which Russians were intensely interested during this period, are given no entry. Instead, individual human-geographical features like particular towns, forts, monasteries, peoples, mills, provinces, archaeological remains, churches, and so on are listed. Similarly, on the physico-geographical side, particular geographical features – rivers (for example, the Volga and Neva), mountains, lakes, peninsulas, seas, forests and so on are named

ГЕОГРАФИЧЕСКІЙ
СЛОВАРЬ
РОССІЙСКАГО ГОСУДАРСТВА.

КАБАНЪ озеро, находящееся подлѣ Губернскаго города Казани, изъ котораго произтекаетъ рѣчка Булакъ. Имя сіе Сарматское, по Россійски означаетъ Синее.

КАБАНЕЙ, мѣстечко, Воронежской Губерніи, въ Острогожскомъ уѣздѣ, лежитъ на рѣчкѣ Красилнкѣ, выше Красилнска въ 35, а ниже Шултина въ 22 верстахъ.

КАБАНОВА, КАБАНОВСКАЯ защита, или КАБАНОВСКОЙ редутъ, въ Томской Губерніи, на правомъ берегу рѣки Иртыша, на Иртышской линіи, отдѣляющей Киргисъ-Кайсацкую степь отъ оныя Губерніи, въ Семипалатинскомъ уѣздѣ, разстояніемъ отъ Желѣзинской крѣпости въ 82, а отъ Омской крѣпости во 128 верстахъ.

КАБАНОВО городище, упоминаемое въ Большомъ Чертежѣ бывшимъ встарину на рѣкѣ Уды, впадающей къ Донецъ, отъ устья ея версты съ двѣ, на лѣвой сторонѣ, ниже городища Хорошаго въ 18, а Донецкаго въ 23 верстахъ, стоявшихъ по щой же рѣчкѣ Удамъ.

КАБАНСКОЙ островъ, Иркутской Губерніи, въ Верхнеудинскомъ уѣздѣ, лежитъ подъ 52° 4' Сѣверной широты, при рѣчкѣ Кабаньѣ, которая съ поверсты отсюда въ протокъ рѣки Селенги впадаетъ; въ сихъ мѣстахъ хлѣбопашество и скотоводство преизрядныя. Разстояніемъ отъ Верхнеудинска въ 95, Селенгинска, къ которому онъ прежъ сего принадлежалъ, въ 204, Тресковой слободы въ 18 верстахъ.

КАБАНЬЕ озеро, въ Тобольской Губерніи, на Ишимской степи, лежитъ отъ рѣки Ика къ Сѣверо-Востоку истеченія никуда не имѣющее. Озеро сіе, такъ какъ и другія, отъ Кабаньей крѣпости къ Ишиму лежащія озера, не велико и не солоно, хотя по близости онаго находящіяся еще другія мѣлкія озера, всѣ изобильны поваренною и горькою солью, и около ихъ есть солончаки. Оно изобилуетъ рыбою и водяною дичью, которая здѣсь, по причинѣ умѣренныхъ еще жителей, спокойно гнѣздится.

КАБАНЬЯ крѣпость, Тобольской Губерніи, въ Курганскомъ уѣздѣ, на Тобольской линіи, между крѣпостей Прѣсногорьковской и Прѣсновской, разстояніемъ отъ первой въ 48, а отъ послѣдней въ 46 верстахъ. Расположена на ровномъ мѣстѣ, между двухъ прѣсныхъ озеръ, изъ коихъ одно называется Литнымъ, а другое Кабаньимъ. Имя сіе, какъ сказываютъ, дано ей отъ множества кабановъ, водившихся въ прежнія времена около сихъ мѣстъ. Форштатъ сей крѣпости составляютъ не болѣе 75 обывательскихъ дворовъ, коихъ жители упражняются отчасти въ земледѣліи и скотоводствѣ.

КАБАРДА, прекрасная Область Горскихъ Черкесовъ, въ Кавказскихъ горахъ лежащая, отъ Астрахани къ Западу. Отдѣляется отъ Кавказской Губерніи рѣками Малкою и Терекомъ; къ Западу тою же рѣкою Малкою отъ Кубани и рѣкою Сунжею, отъ Восточной части Горской земли Кистетовъ.

Часть III. A

Figure 6.1 Introductory page of volume three of Afanasii Shchekatov's 'Geographical Dictionary of the Russian State', published by the University Printing House in Moscow in 1804. Source: author's collection.

with dimensions given where relevant. Clearly the compilers of dictionaries had learnt much from the maps, topographical surveys, expedition reports and similar materials published or archived in previous years. According to some scholars, Shchekatov had also enriched his knowledge through discussions with individuals and scholars from the localities described.

Some entries attract particular attention. Notable, for example, is the entry in volume 3 on 'the Cabinet of the Imperial Academy of Sciences in St Petersburg' (otherwise known as the *Kunstkammer,* though not so named here) (Shchekatov volume 3, 1804, 7). The entry explains that this institution has housed the imperial archive from the time of Catherine the Great and is now one of the richest collections of human artefacts and natural phenomena in Europe. The Cabinet was founded, we are told, by Peter the Great who purchased collections throughout Europe. Among its more recent collections, at the time of writing, were those of Messerschmidt and Gmelin.

Entries for particular peoples and cities are often extremely rich, containing enormous detail about the ways of life, histories and beliefs of the peoples concerned, and about the geographies of individual cities. The entry for Kazan' on the Volga may serve as an example (Shchekatov volume 3, 1804, 84–114). This entry occupies thirty pages. Having outlined the city's geographical position, including its geographical co-ordinates and distances from other cities, the entry goes on to discuss its history from medieval times as an independent Tatar khanate and its subsequent conquest by Ivan the Terrible in 1552. The major buildings are described, including its schools (and what is taught in them), plus the number of dwellings. The entry contains many details on the city's commercial life – on its trade, fairs and markets, manufactories, mills and so on. There are statistics on the city's population and its social categories. Finally, Kazan' district (*uezd*) is discussed in terms of its population, land use, agriculture, forestry, rivers (particularly as modes of communication), and trade.

Geographical dictionaries, therefore, served quite a different purpose from eighteenth-century topographical surveys, or the statistical geographies discussed earlier in this chapter. Rather than seeking to provide detailed statistical or economic information on a regional basis, or explanations of geographical terms, they are gazetteers – alphabetical lists of particular places with detailed information on the most significant features within them. In this respect Russian dictionaries had much in common with those of other European countries at this time (see, for example Salmon 1746; Muetzell 1821–5).

Russia and the wider world: the round-the-world voyage of Adam von Krusenstern (1803–6)

Down to the end of the eighteenth century Russian geographical endeavour had been largely concerned with the exploration and exploitation of Russia's own expanding territory. Russians had of course long been aware of the regions beyond their own borders. These represented geopolitical and trading opportunities – and occasional threats, depending on circumstances. But there was little in the way of systematic description of such territories. By the early nineteenth century, however, as Russians had largely completed the geographical survey of their own enormous lands, albeit superficially, and had embarked on expansion into North America, they evinced a broader interest in the wider world.[8] One important example of this developing interest will be discussed here: the round-the-world voyage of Adam von Krusenstern (1803–6), the first such voyage in Russian history.

Adam Johann von Krusenstern (1770–1846) was a Baltic German, born in Hagudi in what is now Estonia, to a family of Swedish aristocratic descent (Alekseev 1996).[9] He studied at the Naval Cadet Academy in St Petersburg from 1785 and joined the Russian navy in 1787, serving in the war against Sweden, evidently with some distinction. Partly as a result of this he received rapid promotion. As a naval cadet he was sent in 1793 to serve for a period in the British navy to broaden his experience, and visited North America, India and China. He returned to Russia in 1799. It soon became apparent that Krusenstern had learnt much from his experience and that he was a man of ideas. He prepared a memoir that he was determined to submit to the Russian authorities. In his own words:

> For several years past the very confined state of the active trade of Russia had occupied my thoughts ... During the time that I was serving in the English navy in the revolutionary war of 1793 to 1799, my attention was particularly excited by the importance of the English trade with the East Indies and with China. It appeared to me by no means impossible for Russia to participate in the trade by sea ... Most of the European nations which have any commerce by sea, had more or less share in the trade with these countries, so rich in all kinds of natural productions, and those which have particularly cultivated it, have always arrived at a high degree of wealth. (Krusenstern 1813a, vol. 1, xxiv–xxv)

Krusenstern went on to explain that first the Portuguese, then the Dutch and now the British had greatly profited from this trade, and that he could see no reason why the Russians should not do so as well. In Canton he had met a British commander who had sailed across the North Pacific from north-west America with a rich cargo of furs, which sold at a high price in that port. At present, Krusenstern asserted, Russian furs are sent across the rough and dangerous seas from Alaska and its islands to the difficult port of Okhotsk, from where they are transported overland to Kyakhta on the Chinese frontier. This roundabout journey could be obviated by a direct maritime link from Alaska to Canton. The main barrier, it seems, was a lack of skilled commanders among Russian merchant traders, and he suggested means whereby this shortage could be rectified. In the meantime he advocated sending an expedition consisting of two ships from the port of Kronstadt, situated in the Gulf of Finland just off St Petersburg, to Alaska:

> ... with every kind of material necessary for the construction and outfit of vessels ... with skilful shipwrights, workmen of all kinds, a teacher of navigation as well as with charts, books, nautical and astronomical instruments. (Krusenstern 1813a, vol. 1, xxvii)

The aim was that well-made ships could be constructed in Alaska to send furs directly to Canton. From there, he suggested, Chinese goods could be sent in the same vessels home to Russia together with other Asian commodities, thus avoiding the present need to pay 'large sums' to the British, Swedes and Danes for Chinese and East Indian wares. Furthermore, Russia could supply northern Germany and other European countries with such goods at cheaper rates than other states, since its costs were lower. In this way the Russian-American Company might soon outcompete Britain's East India Company and similar trading companies based elsewhere (Krusenstern 1813a, vol. 1, xxv–xxvi).

Krusenstern had considerable difficulty drawing the attention of the Russian authorities to his memoir, but eventually, through the good graces and support of Admiral Nikolai Mordvinov, minister of marine, and Count Nikolai Rumyantsev, minister of commerce and chancellor of the empire, it was submitted into the hands of the Tsar. Alexander approved the project and ordered that the expedition be commanded by Krusenstern.

The original purpose of the expedition, as envisaged by Krusenstern, was therefore trade-related, but as the government and the Academy of Sciences pondered its aims, they were notably broadened. Thus, also trade-related, was the instruction that Krusenstern convey the ambassador Nikolai Rezanov, one of the directors of the newly founded Russian-American Company,[10] to Japan to negotiate a trade treaty (Alekseev 1996, 87). The expedition was also instructed to explore the possibility of provisioning Russian America and the Russian Far East by sea as against the difficult overland route from European Russia and western Siberia.[11] Strategically, showing the Russian flag in the North Pacific regions was regarded as an important demonstration of Russian power and of Russia's determination to hold on to these territories in defiance of competitors like the British, the Americans and the Spanish.

The expedition also had important scientific aims. The ships were equipped with 'all the articles which are indispensable in so long a voyage', including medicines and 'a complete assortment of astronomical and other philosophical instruments' (Krusenstern 1813a, vol. 1, 7).[12] In addition there was a library of books, charts and the most up-to-date lunar tables (for determining longitude by astronomical observation). Apart from physicians and surgeons, accompanying the expedition was an astronomer (Dr Jean Gaspard Horner) and two naturalists (Drs Wilhelm Gottlieb Tilesius von Tilenau and Georg von Langsdorff). In addition, in Ambassador Rezanov's suite were a painter and Dr Theodor (Fedor) Brinkin, a physician and botanist.

Perhaps the major scientific purpose of the voyage was to survey and chart the coasts and islands of the North Pacific, including attempting to map the coast of the island of Sakhalin (which was rumoured to be a peninsula) and to plot the estuary of the river Amur. The presence of naturalists suggests that the study of vegetation and fauna was a significant aim, although Krusenstern's travel account tells us little about this. Also important was the study of the sea itself, marine science developing quickly in this period (Deacon 1971; Bekasova 2020). Meteorological data were recorded throughout the voyage.

The expedition consisted of two ships: the 450-ton *Nadezhda* (*Hope*), commanded by Krusenstern, the expedition leader, and the 350-ton *Neva*, commanded by Yurii Fedorovich Lisyanskii. Both vessels had been purchased in Britain. The expedition left the port of Kronstadt in August 1803 and proceeded to Copenhagen, constantly taking measurements of the depth and temperature of the sea on the way. In Copenhagen Krusenstern was forced to unload and reload his ship, since some of the food stowed away was found to be in danger of going bad. The resulting tedium was relieved, however, by visits from various educated gentlemen and a visit to Copenhagen Observatory whose director, Professor Thomas Bugge, was a natural historian. After this forced stay, Krusenstern proceeded to Falmouth in England and then to the Canaries. Crossing the Equator in November 1803, the expedition engaged in a fruitless search for Ascension Island before calling in at St Elizabeth Island off the coast of Brazil. Rounding Cape Horn in

March 1804 the two ships were separated in a storm. Krusenstern made for the Marquesas Islands where he was met by Lisyanskii, who had sailed via Easter Island. Having spent a short time on Nukahiwa, the largest of the Marquesas, the two ships sailed for Hawaii (at that time known as the Sandwich Islands, as named by James Cook on his third voyage). Here their hopes of obtaining ample provisions were disappointed, and soon the captains separated by agreement, Krusenstern heading for Kamchatka while Lisyanskii sailed to Kodiak Island off the coast of Alaska. Krusenstern reached Petropavlovsk in Kamchatka at the beginning of July 1804 and left for Japan towards the end of August. The *Nadezhda* dropped anchor in Nagasaki harbour at the end of September. There followed more than six months of fruitless negotiations with the Japanese over a trade treaty. The ship then returned to Petropavlovsk, having surveyed parts of the west coast of Japan and some portion of the south and east coast of Sakhalin on the way. Ambassador Rezanov and his suite left the ship in Petropavlovsk. Within a month Krusenstern left Petropavlovsk again for further hydrographic studies of the seas around Sakhalin and of the estuary of the Amur. Finally, at the end of September 1805, he left Petropavlovsk for the third and final time on the return voyage to Kronstadt. The *Nadezhda* reached Macao in China on 20 November 1805, where it was joined by the *Neva* at the beginning of December carrying a valuable cargo of furs from Russian America. The two ships left Macao at the end of January 1806. However, they were unexpectedly separated near the Cape of Good Hope and made their ways back to Kronstadt independently. The *Neva* reached Kronstadt on 22 July, the *Nadezhda* on 7 August 1806.

Krusenstern wrote a vivid account of the difficulties of navigating a sailing ship through only partially known seas at the beginning of the nineteenth century – the uncertain weather, the possibility of storms and the hazards of fog and ice, inaccurate sea charts, unexpected currents, the dangers of shoals and reefs, the difficulties of establishing one's exact location using chronometers that failed to agree with one another, the constant need for fresh water and adequate provisions, the possibility of disease (especially scurvy), the uncertain relations with indigenous peoples and with other states, and others. Much of Krusenstern's account concerns the detailed determination of his location and course, the mapping of coasts, the search for islands described in earlier accounts, encounters with indigenous peoples, and similar matters. Wherever possible he was able to correct the conclusions of earlier navigators. Unfortunately, however, he was unable to determine whether Sakhalin was an island (he favoured the idea, incorrectly, that it was in fact a peninsula) and the exact nature of the estuary of the Amur (see Bassin 1999, 35).[13]

Krusenstern provided some arresting accounts of the peoples he met on his voyage. Of all these, he appears to have had the lowest opinion of the Japanese:

> Everyone knows of the insulting jealousy which is observed towards strangers in Japan: we had no right to expect a more favourable treatment than other nations; yet, as we had an ambassador on board, who was sent merely with assurances of friendship, by the monarch of a powerful empire bordering upon these people so suspicious in their politics, we hoped not to be received unfavourably. (Krusenstern 1813a, vol. 1, 251)

In this, as we have seen, they were disappointed. Further on, he refers to the 'barbarous intolerance' of the Japanese, their 'mistrustful conduct' and concludes that they are 'a suspicious and haughty people' (Krusenstern 1813a, vol. 1, 256, 260, 272). Evidently, having spent so many months in Japan to no effect, Krusenstern's temper was thoroughly soured by the experience. The Japanese had for nearly two centuries banned all Europeans except the Dutch from residing in Nagasaki, where the VOC trading station was confined to a small island in the harbour.

Krusenstern gives a superb ethnographic account of the Polynesian inhabitants of Nukahiwa – from their personal 'beauty' and health, dress, houses, tools and furniture to their food, farming and fishing, arts of war, religious practices and belief in charms. Krusenstern had evidently arrived in the Marquesas full of positive feelings towards the inhabitants, based on the accounts of James Cook and George Forster. And the Russian expedition had been received with nothing but the friendliest behaviour. However, the commander was soon disabused of these warm feelings by the accounts of two Europeans who had lived on Nukahiwa for some years. Having recounted some grisly tales of the behaviour of the population, Krusenstern writes:

> From this description of the Nukahiwer, which perhaps may appear exaggerated, but really is not so, it is pretty evident that they have neither social institutions, religion nor humane feelings in any degree whatsoever, – in a word, that no traces of good qualities are to be found among them; that they undoubtedly belong to the very worst of mankind, and at any rate no one can quarrel with me for calling them savages.

He continues, with overstated generalization, that:

> Notwithstanding the favourable account in Captain Cook's voyages ... I cannot refrain from declaring the inhabitants of all the islands of this ocean to be savages ... as ranking generally, perhaps with a very trifling exception, with those men who are still one degree below the brute creation. In a word, they are all cannibals ... (Krusenstern 1813a, vol. 1, 182–3)

Thus this educated European does not hesitate to condemn all the indigenous peoples of the Pacific to the lowest possible moral status on the basis of very limited evidence indeed.

On his return to Russia Krusenstern published a series of scientific works related to his voyage. First, there was his travel account, the first part of which was published in 1809 and the second part a year later. This was quickly translated into English, French, Italian, German and other European languages, testifying to the widespread interest in round-the-world voyages at the time (for the English edition see Krusenstern 1813a). A third part, with essays by Horner, Tilesius, and Krusenstern together with other material appeared in 1812. This contained tables of data gathered on the *Nadezhda* during the voyage. Of particular value was the *Atlas k puteshestviyu vokrug sveta kapitana Krusenshterna* ('Atlas of the Voyage around the World of Captain Krusenstern'), published in Russian and German in St Petersburg in 1813 (Krusenstern 1813b). This depicted the North Pacific with coasts and islands as surveyed by Krusenstern plus a series of drawings of places visited by the expedition and of the animals, fish and inhabitants of Nukahiwa, Japan and elsewhere. The drawings were executed by Tilesius and Horner. His *Atlas Yuzhnogo Morya* ('Atlas of the Southern Sea') came out in two parts in 1823 and 1826 (Krusenstern 1823–6) together with an explanatory supplement. Further supplements followed. In addition to its cartographical endeavours, the voyage was noted for its contributions to oceanography, astronomy, hydrology, zoology, botany and ethnography.

Krusenstern's voyage became a model for other Russian oceanic ventures in the succeeding period – notably those of Vasilii Golovnin, Otto von Kotzebue, Fedor Litke (Friedrich Benjamin Graf von Lütke), Fabian Gottlieb von Bellingshausen and Friedrich Graf von Wrangel (Vrangel').[14] Bekasova has discussed the 1815–18 voyage of exploration to the Bering Strait region, a privately organized and funded venture sponsored by the above-mentioned Count Nikolai Rumyantsev together with Krusenstern, and commanded by Kotzebue (Bekasova 2020). Thus private initiative also played some part in these developments.

To what extent did Krusenstern fulfil the brief he was given? The careful charting of the islands and coasts of the North Pacific was clearly one important accomplishment, as evidenced by the atlases and published accounts of the voyage. Here, however, success was tempered by the failure to confirm Sakhalin's insularity and to survey the estuary of the Amur. As regards trade the picture was mixed, with the complete failure to come to a trade agreement with Japan but a definite possibility, in Krusenstern's view, of developing that with China. Lisyanskii's voyage from Alaska to Macao with a cargo of furs had shown the possibility of growing the maritime trade between Russian America and China. Even so the sheer difficulty of supplying and maintaining Russia's distant colony in America eventually forced it to sell the territory in 1867.[15]

Conclusion

In 1825, at the end of its 'long eighteenth century', Russia's geographical endeavour still retained many features inherited from the Petrine period. Thus the dominance of the state was still paramount in areas such as mapping, exploration, statistical survey and others. Some of the reactionary policies of Tsar Paul showed that this dominance was not always to the advantage of science or aspects of geographical endeavour. Alexander, however, pursued more positive policies, and during his reign and afterwards new knowledge of Russian geography was being created. Thus, in addition to the Petrine Academy of Sciences and the Catherinian Free Economic Society, new institutions such as universities and scientific societies were appearing and beginning to make their individual contributions to the understanding of Russian space. This culminated in the founding of the Russian Geographical Society in 1845, a pioneer in exploration, statistical survey and other geographical pursuits. New methods such as triangulation in cartography and statistical survey were beginning to add precision to the understanding of Russia's territory, greatly augmenting the knowledge of Russia's local geographies. Russia's launch as a maritime power, a project begun by Peter the Great, was now fomenting new scientific knowledge of the Northern Pacific and opening up new commercial possibilities. And much more was now being done to spread this knowledge through publication and education to broader sections of the population. In short, Alexander's reign laid the foundations for a new, more comprehensive and more scientific geography, one that was to come to full fruition later in the nineteenth century. In the meantime, Russian geographical endeavour had strengthened the security of the empire and advanced Russian understanding of itself and of its place in the world. Such accomplishments constituted a fitting tribute to Peter the Great's geographical project.

Notes

1. This was the reestablishment of a university originally founded in 1632. It is now the University of Tartu, in Estonia.
2. For the origins of triangulation in Russia, see Chapter 4 above.
3. Catherine the Great's Charter to the Towns, issued in 1785, stipulated that towns must be built according to an approved plan, thus extending the earlier work of the Commission for the Building of the Cities of St Petersburg and Moscow (1762), whose competence was extended to all Russian towns in 1768. See Blumenfeld (1944).
4. 'Apart from these monasteries in Voronezh diocese, there were another fifteen now closed. And so that their memory may not disappear altogether with time, we record them here, in so far as we can find historical information about them, especially since many of them were notable in their time' (Bolkhovitinov 1800, 178).
5. The earlier, 1832 edition, was unavailable to me at the time of writing. Zyablovskii's earlier work took a similar cameralist approach.
6. Despite his politically reactionary inclinations, Nicholas I was a proponent of science and technology; he built, for example, Russia's first railway. See Haywood (1969).
7. He had first discussed his method in his 1818 book (Arsen'ev 1818b, 22).
8. Russians had, however, long collected foreign maps depicting the globe as a whole. See Gol'denberg (1971), *Hundred Russian Maps and Atlases* (1991), and Postnikov (1996). For Russia's developing interest in the Northern Pacific and Arctic, see Jones, Kraikovskii and Lajus (2023).
9. See also Kopelev (2021).
10. The Russian-American Company, established in 1799 under Tsar Paul, was granted monopoly trading rights in Russian America and administered Russian settlements in the region.
11. For more on this issue, see Gibson (1976).
12. Thus Krusenstern mentions 'a reflecting circle … with flying nonius', sextants, artificial horizons, theodolite, azimuth compasses, nautical barometer, hygrometer, thermometers (including one for measuring the temperature of the sea underwater and a maximum–minimum thermometer), quadrants, telescopes, timepieces (chronometers) and other equipment.
13. Only in 1849 was the insularity of Sakhalin and the fact that the Amur emptied into the Seas of Okhotsk and Japan confirmed by the Russian navigator G. I. Nevel'skoi (Alekseev 1996, 91).
14. See Kopelev (2021). Fabian von Bellingshausen, who participated in Krusenstern's expedition, subsequently led an expedition to Antarctica – indeed he is widely regarded as the continent's discoverer. This expedition (1819–21) has been discussed by Bulkeley (2013), Tammiksaar (2016), and Tammiksaar and Kiik (2013).
15. The problem of supplying Russian America together with the difficulties of developing the market for Alaskan furs are explored by Gibson (1976).

7
Conclusion

> *The dramatic and dynamic drive eastward across the vast Eurasian plain by both private and government agents of Muscovy must rank among the great feats of human enterprise during the European age of exploration.*
> Henry Huttenbach, 1988

This book has considered what I have termed Russian geographical endeavour during the two centuries or so between the inauguration of the Romanov dynasty in 1613 and the end of the reign of Tsar Alexander I in 1825. In Western Europe this era, generally known as the early modern period, witnessed great change: cultural Renaissance, scientific discovery, and state- and empire-building. Despite its geographical location on the periphery of Europe and relative isolation until the end of the seventeenth century, Russia did not entirely miss out on such developments. Thus, already by the early-sixteenth century what had been a rather loose conglomeration of city states had amalgamated into a unified state under the leadership of the princes of Moscow. This process paralleled what was happening in other parts of Europe at the same time, or in some cases earlier (or indeed later). And in much the same way that many Western European states, especially those fringing the Atlantic, were building overseas empires in this period, Russia was also building an empire but, unlike them, that empire stretched eastwards over land across the enormous spaces of Siberia and the Far East. Only when Russian territorial expansion approached the Pacific coast and leaped over the Bering Strait to North America did it begin to assume some of the characteristics of a sea-based empire.

The book has argued that the period also witnessed a change in European attitudes towards geographical space. In medieval times the European understanding of the world's lands and peoples relied on a mixture of myth and empirical reality, the myths deriving in part from religious and classical legend and the empirical either from direct experience or from classical and related learning. The early modern era, by contrast, saw a new reliance on empirical observation and experiment. This change largely derived from the spatial problems that arose in the new era. Hence growing competition between European states meant that states were forced to militarize and centralize in order to facilitate access to the finance and resources needed for building armies, navies and other defensive and offensive capabilities. The need for defence and resources meant paying particular attention to the demarcation of frontiers and, whenever feasible, to the acquisition of new territories. Internally, states needed to eliminate the traditional autonomy of local elites, meaning that new regional and local boundaries had to be drawn to establish the authority of provincial and local government. This in turn encouraged the development of knowledge of local environments and resources. Also important was the establishment of new lines of communication to facilitate trade, commerce, administration and much else. Chapter 1 has outlined how all this necessitated or encouraged the development of geographical aids such as maps, exploratory expeditions, regional descriptions, cadastral surveys, spatial statistics and similar projects.

Throughout this book it has been apparent that in seeking to map, explore and describe its territories, Russia was motivated by the same factors that motivated Western European states. As they modernized and competed with one another, so Russia built up its military capabilities not merely for defence but also to expand its territorial dominions. In the early-seventeenth century, during the so-called Time of Troubles, Russia suffered at the hands of the Poles, who occupied Moscow for a short period. But as Russian power increased the tables were slowly turned, and later in the century Russia was able to annex part of Ukraine from the Polish-Lithuanian Commonwealth. Eventually, after a prolonged struggle, Catherine the Great's Russia participated in the Partitions of Poland-Lithuania, whereby it disappeared entirely from the European map. Meanwhile, earlier under Peter the Great, Russia had fought the long-lasting Great Northern War against Sweden, a formidable Baltic power at the time. Russia's victory in this war resulted in the acquisition of what became its Baltic provinces and also Ingermanland, thus securing Russia's access to the Baltic Sea. It was here that Peter built his new capital of St Petersburg. All this military activity was accompanied by, or resulted in, various kinds of geographical endeavour, including the mapping of the new territories, the demarcation of new frontiers, provincial subdivision, cadastral survey (as in Ingermanland) and the planning of the new capital.

Unlike many of the countries of Western Europe, Russia's open frontiers were permanently vulnerable to the threat of invasion. In our period, after the accession of the Romanov dynasty and in contrast to the previous era, the threat from the west was largely contained (with the major exception of the Napoleonic invasion of 1812). The threat from the southern nomadic peoples, however, was a very different matter, lasting in one form or another from the medieval period onwards. As we have seen, this entailed the Russian construction of extensive defensive systems crossing southern Ukraine, south European Russia, the North Caucasus, and the southern part of west Siberia and northern Kazakhstan. The development of defensive systems was accompanied by a gradual process of settlement and, as the defensive systems slowly moved southwards, the nomadic peoples were largely displaced. Finally, after a series of wars against the Turks, the whole of south European Russia and Ukraine was opened up to settlement by Russians, Ukrainians, Germans and others. Something similar happened in the North Caucasus and west Siberia, but this time against different opponents. The whole process of colonization was again usually accompanied by mapping, cadastral survey (without maps in the first instance) and similar measures.

As suggested in Chapter 1, the most dramatic movement of Russian explorers and adventurers in the early modern period was that to the east across Siberia towards the Pacific and beyond into North America. This was partly spontaneous – in the hunt for furs by Cossacks and others – and partly directed by agents of the state. The prospect of developing trade with China was also an important attraction. Ambassadors to China like Nikolai Spafarii in the 1670s were commonly ordered to describe their route across Siberia to the Chinese frontier and to map where possible. Later expeditions like that of Daniel Messerschmidt and the First and Second Kamchatka Expeditions added to the knowledge of these remote territories. Already in the pre-Petrine period it became possible to devise maps and atlases of the region, like the Godunov map of the 1660s, whilst Remezov's atlases dated from the end of the seventeenth century. Eventually Siberia made its contribution to the 1745 atlas, but it was to be many years before its vast territories were to be properly explored and mapped.

The Russian conquest of the already settled Caucasian and Central Asian regions occurred mainly in the nineteenth century and are for the most part beyond the scope of this book.

Russian geographical endeavour, as the book has suggested, gradually embraced not merely the peripheral parts of the empire but also its central parts. In the sixteenth century Russian geographical understanding of its own territories was patchy at best, with few property and regional maps. A major exception was the *Bol'shoi chertezh* ('Great Map') probably dating from the very end of that century and renewed in 1627. Although both the original and the second map were subsequently lost, they covered most of the empire as it then existed, as indicated by the textual accompaniment to the 1627 map known as the *Kniga bol'shomu chertezhu* ('Book of the Great Map'). Regional mapping greatly improved during the seventeenth century, many maps being drawn by foreigners, but the coverage was far from systematic or comprehensive, and the map projections lacked any mathematical basis. The most detailed geographical descriptions of individual districts were the cadastral surveys, but these had largely disappeared by the early 1630s. Apart from these, the authorities had to depend on the accounts and reports of ambassadors, travellers, local governors, expedition leaders, and Cossack hunters for an understanding of Russia's geography. Such understanding also depended on the reports and accounts of foreigners. It was through the latter especially, several of which were translated in this period, that Russian knowledge of the outside world also expanded, although the dissemination of such work was greatly hampered by problems of printing and publishing.

Under Peter the Great and his successors much of this was to change. It was Peter who began to hire foreign specialists like Henry Farquharson to instil in Russians the mathematical basis essential to modern mapping, to found institutions where such training might be given, and to send Russian students abroad to further their education. Peter began the systematic mapping of Russian provinces and inaugurated such ventures as atlases of the Don and the Baltic, and the modern mapping of the Caspian Sea. Peter also arranged for the publication of maps. Such cartographic initiatives bore later fruit in the publication of Ivan Kirilov's *Atlas Rossiiskoi Imperii* ('Atlas of the Russian Empire', 1734), the *Atlas Russicus* ('Academy Atlas', 1745) and many later maps and atlases. Under Peter there began the collection of a range of official statistics, which much later, under German influence, helped give rise to a new statistical approach to geography. This eventually resulted in detailed, statistical surveys of many parts of the empire. Peter revived the cadastral tradition on a new, more mathematical basis, and this was taken forward after his death, most notably in Catherine the Great's *General'noe mezhevanie* (General Survey). Russian geographical expeditions under Peter gradually assumed a scientific as well as a trade-related and strategic basis, meaning that they were as focused on nature, natural resources and the ways of life of the peoples they encountered as in such practical matters as routes, locations and opportunities for hunting and human exploitation. The expeditions were mainly aimed at regions peripheral to European Russia, such as Central Asia, Siberia and the Far East. This emphasis continued under Peter's successors, but now expeditions were also mounted to more central parts of the empire, most notably those of the Academy of Sciences in the period 1768–74. Eighteenth- and early-nineteenth-century expeditions gave rise to numerous publications, including those in the semi-popular output of the Academy of Sciences, which testify to the growing public interest in geographical issues. Indeed Peter's reforms to printing and publishing allowed for the publication of many textbooks and much academic material, including translations of foreign literature. Notable Petrine and post-Petrine Russian publications include Bernhard Varenius's *Geographia Generalis* ('General Geography'), Petr Rychkov's *Topografiya Orenburgskaya* ('Topography of Orenburg', which was followed by topographical descriptions of other Russian provinces), Krasheninnikov's *Opisanie zemli Kamchatki* (published in English as *History of Kamtschatka*), Pleshcheev's *Obozrenie Rossiiskoi imperii* (*Survey of the Russian Empire*), and the geographical dictionaries of Polunin, Maksimovich and Shchekatov. Numerous Russian publications were translated into foreign languages, mainly by European publishers, which together with published Russian maps greatly increased foreign understanding of the geography of Russia. The latter was augmented by the written or oral testimony of those foreigners who had worked in or travelled to Russia. Likewise Russian understanding of the geography of the globe was enhanced by reading foreign publications and maps. And although Russian geographical endeavour overwhelmingly focused on Russia and its near neighbours right to the end of our period, the round-the-world voyage of Adam von Krusenstern (1803–6) signalled the start of a period in which Russia's geographical horizons were to be considerably broadened.

Thus, as already stated, the motivations for Russians to engage in the exploration, mapping and survey of their own territories, and to discover their relationship to the outside world, were much the same as those that influenced other countries in the early modern period. And the measures employed were also similar. However, applying such measures to Russia was by no means easy. This book has discussed many of the barriers that hindered scientific progress in early modern Russia. One was the country's poverty, deriving in part from its relative geographical isolation from Europe and much of the rest of the world, leading to the weakness of its capitalist development. A harsh environment over most of the terrain abetted an unproductive agriculture, the basis of national wealth in this period. Difficulties of communication across the vast territory of Russia and lack of easy access to the world's oceans only added to the problems. State-building in Russia entailed the need to raise revenue from a thinly scattered population and to secure control over its huge territory characterized by relatively open frontiers and weak defences. Security of control was also complicated by the multinational and multicultural character of the empire.

Closely related to the Russia's environmental difficulties were a number of social factors. Despite policies designed to limit population movement, like the institution of serfdom, the population was in fact often mobile, making it difficult to secure for the state and landowning class the resources and revenue they required. In the opinion of many scholars and contemporary observers, serfdom (only abolished in 1861) was itself a barrier to economic development. And problems of control abetted a social lawlessness, which again hindered economic life.

Chapter 1 also discussed specific cultural barriers to scientific modernization in Russia. Down to the reign of Peter the Great, and even afterwards to some extent, Russia's strict Orthodox culture, related in part to its long isolation from the classical culture of the Latin world, and even to some degree from the more limited Romano-Greek classical culture of Byzantium, largely cocooned it in a culture of its own. The scientific outlook that was becoming established in Europe from the late-fifteenth century onwards was treated in Russia with grave suspicion as a danger to true religion. Only by the latter half of the seventeenth century did this situation begin to change, and only in the reign of Peter the Great was a concerted policy of scientific modernization adopted.

As a consequence of such problems, scientific development in Russia, and more specifically geographical endeavour, took on a number of characteristics that marked it out as different from geographical endeavour elsewhere. One was the widespread employment, especially in the early days, of educated foreigners. Since Russia prior to Peter lacked scientific specialists of its own, it had little choice but to pursue such a policy, especially before institutions like the School of Mathematics and Navigation, the Naval Academy and the Academy of Sciences were established. Peter himself, in his journeys abroad, was keen to employ scientific recruits for various purposes and employed representatives and foreign agents for the same purpose. Scientific specialists were recruited from many European countries but there was a preponderance of Germans, and especially of Baltic Germans who lived in the provinces annexed from Sweden in the Great Northern War. Indeed Germans predominated in the Academy of Sciences throughout the eighteenth century. Among the more famous of those who participated in various geographical ventures were Daniel Gottlieb Messerschmidt, Gerhard Friedrich Müller, Johann Georg Gmelin, Georg Wilhelm Steller, Peter Simon Pallas and Samuel Gottlieb Gmelin. In many ways, then, Russian geographical endeavour was an international undertaking, involving scholars from many parts of Europe but with a predominance of Russians and Germans. It is doubtful if this reliance on foreigners was replicated anywhere else.

A second way in which Russian geographical endeavour was distinctive was in its frequently (but by no means entirely) centralized character. Geographical expeditions, mapping projects, cadastral survey, translations, the collection of statistical data and other undertakings were commonly organized or initiated centrally, and publications, if not always initiated centrally, were at least centrally controlled. The centralization of much geographical endeavour was particularly characteristic of Peter the Great's reign, but became less rigid as time went on with the appearance of new institutions like the Academy of Sciences, the Free Economic Society and the universities (in all of which, however, there were continuing struggles for control between government and those desiring greater autonomy, as well as between those with more and less conservative inclinations). As the Russian scientific community expanded and the number of educated individuals grew, the scope for individual or private initiative increased, though such initiative was often also circumscribed by the activities of the state and its officials. The propensity of local officials, for example, to hinder the work of those undertaking expeditionary work has been noted at several points in this book. Also of note was the reluctance, or inability, of such officials to answer questionnaires or to give other forms of assistance to scientific travellers without formal permission or instructions to do so.

Closely related to the centralized character of much Russian geographical endeavour was the standardized approach taken towards a number of undertakings where this proved possible. In cadastral survey, for example, instructions were issued in both the seventeenth and eighteenth centuries specifying what form such surveys were to take. Catherine the Great's General Survey was perhaps the ultimate in state-controlled surveys, covering every type of landowner and eventually embracing most of European Russia. The Survey was conducted in accordance with a series of strict instructions issued by the centre.

Similarly, from the time of Peter the Great, mapping was done by appointed geodesists following the directions of the Academy of Sciences' Geography Department and its successor organizations. Official questionnaires such as that sent out by the Academy of Sciences' topographical committee in the 1780s, and the responses as reflected in the subsequent topographical descriptions of provinces and their districts, often follow a standardized pattern. As we have seen, the results were all too often dull and uninformative.

Perhaps the most distinctive feature of Russian geographical endeavour in the early modern period was that, unlike other European imperial states, there was no clear distinction between those activities that occurred predominantly in the home territory and those that took place mainly in the country's colonial possessions. Indeed, in the case of Russia it is difficult, if not impossible, to distinguish between the home territories and imperial possessions. The Urals provide no clear dividing line: who is to say that Russia's imperial possessions are those territories which lie east of the Urals (Bassin 1991)? Certain scholars have suggested that the most important location for European geographical endeavour in the eighteenth-century Enlightenment period was the Pacific, and that 'the ship was the Enlightenment's principal geographical instrument' (see for example Withers 2007, 89). This book argues that the vast landed spaces of Eurasia were also significant, and that here the overland expedition replaced the ship as the period's principal scientific instrument. Assessing the full implications of this difference for the global process of geographical exploration and survey remains a task for the future.

The geographical exploration and survey of the vast spaces of Eurasia, pioneered by Russians, Germans and others, forms an important chapter in the history of European imperialism and of European geographical endeavour. But it is a chapter all too frequently overlooked. If this book succeeds in drawing broader attention to this gap in our geographical and historical understanding of the early modern world, its principal purpose will have been served.

Glossary

(Plurals are in parentheses)

ataman (atamany): ataman or higher-ranking Cossack.
barshchina: labour service.
belomestnyi: 'white place'. *Belomestnyi (belomestsy)* atamans, Cossacks and other urban non-tax paying urban inhabitants who were free of certain obligations.
Cherkasy (pl.): Russian term for Ukrainian Cossacks, sometimes used for all Cossacks.
chernozem: black earth soil, noted for its fertility.
chertezh: sketch or map.
chertvert (*chetvert'*, *chetverti*): a land area equal to one half of a *desyatina*.
Cossacks: in origin, escaped peasants and others who survived in the steppe by emulating the freebooting lifestyle of nomadic peoples. Many later entered into various forms of military service to the tsars.
dacha (dachi): in the General Survey, a land unit or survey unit.
desyatina (desyatiny): a land measure equal to 1.092 hectares or 2.7 acres.
dorozhnik (dorozhniki): itinerary or road-book.
dozornaya kniga (dozornye knigi): provisional cadastral register.
dvor (dvory): household, house, homestead, courtyard, court.
gorod (goroda): town, or the fortified core of a town.
guberniya (gubernii): province.
khutor (khutora): an outlying landholding or small hamlet, often newly founded.
Kunstkammer: The Cabinet of Curiosities in St Petersburg, founded by Peter the Great.
lavka (lavki): shop.
obrok: quitrent, payable in cash or kind.
obrochnye lyudi: people obliged to pay quitrent for the use of certain resources.
odnodvortsy (pl.): in the eighteenth century, descendants of the seventeenth-century lower- and middle-class servitors, many of whom lived on the frontier.
ostrog (ostrogi): fort or fortified settlement.

pistsovaya kniga (pistovye knigi): cadastral register.
posad (posady): trading settlement or trading suburb of a town.
prikaz (prizaky): department of state (precursor to ministry).
provintsiya (provintsii): sub-province (subdivision of a *guberniya*) in this period.
pustosh' (pustoshi): land that was not inhabited though often worked; sometimes an abandoned plot of land.
raznochintsy: 'people of various ranks', or those who did not fit in to any of the accepted social categories.
rospis' (rospisi): inventory.
sazhen' (sazheni): unit of length equivalent to 2.13 metres or seven feet.
sloboda (slobody): settlement or urban quarter freed from certain impositions.
sokha: light or scratch plough; measure of tillable land or unit of tax assessment.
stanitsa (stanitsy): Cossack settlement.
strelets (strel'tsy): musketeer.
taiga: northern coniferous or boreal forest.
uezd (uezdy): district.
Ulozhenie: refers here to the 1649 Code of Laws.
verst (versta, versty): unit of length equal to 1.067 kilometres or 0.66 miles.
voevoda (voevody): military governor.
yasak: tribute.

References

Aleksandrovskaya, O. A. 1989. *Stanovlenie geograficheskoi nauki v Rossii v XVIII veke*. Moscow: Nauka.
Aleksandrovskaya, O. A. 1996. 'Vasilii Nikitich Tatishchev, 1686–1750'. In *Tvortsy otechestvennoi nauki: geografy*, 32–9. Moscow: Agar.
Alekseev, A. I. 1996. 'Ivan Fedorovich Kruzenshtern, 1770–1846'. In *Tvortsy otechestvennoi nauki: geografy*, 83–95. Moscow: Agar.
Alekseev, M. P. 2006. *Sibir' v izvestiyakh zapadno-Evropeiskikh puteshestvennikov i pisatelei*, 3rd edition. Novosibirsk: Nauka.
Anderson, M. S. 1978. *Peter the Great*. London: Thames and Hudson.
Anderson, M. S. 1987. *Europe in the Eighteenth Century*, 3rd edition. London: Longman.
Andreev, A. I. 1950. 'Trudy V. N. Tatishcheva po geografii Rossii'. In Tatishchev, V. N., *Izbrannye trudy po geografii Rossii*, 3–35. Moscow: Gosudarstvennoe izdatel'stvo geograficheskoi literatury.
Andreev, A. I. 1960. *Ocherki po istochnikovedeniyu Sibiri*, vol. 1: *XVII v.*, 2nd Edition. Moscow & Leningrad: Akademiya nauk SSSR.
Andrews, J. H. 1985. *Plantation Acres*. Newtownards: Ulster Historical Foundation.
Anuchin, D. N. 1949. 'Geografiya v Moskovskom universitete za pervye stoletiya ego sushchestvovaniya'. In *Izbrannye geograficheskie raboty*, 79–98. Moscow: Gosudarstvennoe izdatel'stvo geograficheskoi literatury.
Appleby, J. H. 2001. 'Farquharson, Delisle and the Royal Society', *Notes and Records of the Royal Society of London* 55/2: 191–204.
Arel, M. S. 2019. *English Trade and Adventure to Russia in the Early Modern Era: The Muscovy Company, 1603–1649*. Lanham, MD: Lexington Books.
Armstrong, T. 1965. *Russian Settlement in the North*. Cambridge: Cambridge University Press.
Arsen'ev, K. I. 1818a. *Obozrenie fizicheskogo sostoyaniya Rossii*. St Petersburg: Tip. Dep. nar. pros.
Arsen'ev, K. I. 1818b. *Nachertanie statistiki Rossiiskogo gosudarstva*, part 1. St Petersburg: Tipografiya Imperatorskoi vospitatel'nogo doma.
Arsen'ev, K. I. 1818–19. *Kratkaya vseobshchaya geografiya*. St Petersburg: Tipografiya Imperatorskoi vospitatel'nogo doma.
Arsen'ev, K. I. 1819. *Nachertanie statistiki Rossiiskogo gosudarstva*, part 2. St Petersburg: Tipografiya Imperatorskoi vospitatel'nogo doma.
Arsen'ev, K. I. 1848. *Statisticheskie ocherki Rossii*. St Petersburg: Tipografiya Imperatorskoi Akademii nauk.
Atkin, M. 1988. 'Russian expansion in the Caucasus to 1813'. In *Russian Colonial Expansion to 1917*, edited by M. Rywkin, 139–87. London: Mansell.
Atlas Russicus. 1745. Petropoli [St Petersburg]: Imperial Academy of Sciences.
Aubrey, J. 1847. *Natural History of Wiltshire: written between 1656 and 1691*, edited by John Britton. London: Wiltshire Topographical Society.
Avvakum, P. 1924. *The Life of the Archpriest Avvakum, by himself*, translated by Jane Harrison and Hope Mirlees. London: Hogarth Press.
Bacmeister, H. L. C. [Bakhmeister, Kh. L. K]. 1771–4. *Topograficheskie izvestiya sluzhashchie dlya polnogo geograficheskogo opisaniya Rossiiskoi imperii*. St Petersburg: Imperatorskaya Akademiya nauk.
Baddeley, J. F. 2010. *The Russian Conquest of the Caucasus*. Charleston, SC: Nabu Press.
Bagrow, L. 1955. 'The first map printed in Russia', *Imago Mundi* 12: 152–6.
Bagrow, L. 1975. *A History of Russian Cartography up to 1800*, edited by Henry W. Castner. Wolfe Island, ON: Walker Press.
Barber, P. 1997. 'Maps and monarchs in Europe, 1550–1800'. In *Royal and Republican Sovereignty in Early Modern Europe*, edited by R. Oresko, G. C. Gibbs and H. M. Scott, 75–124. Cambridge: Cambridge University Press.

Baron, S. H., trans. and ed. 1967. *The Travels of Olearius in Seventeenth-Century Russia*. Stanford: Stanford University Press.
Baron, S. H. 1992. 'B. A. Rybakov on the Jenkinson map of 1562'. In *New Perspectives on Muscovite History*, edited by L. Hughes, 3–13. London: Macmillan.
Bartlett, R. P. 1979. *Human Capital: The settlement of foreigners in Russia, 1762–1804*. Cambridge: Cambridge University Press.
Bassin, M. 1991. 'Russia between Europe and Asia: The ideological construction of geographical space', *Slavic Review* 50/1: 1–17.
Bassin, M. 1999. *Imperial Visions: Nationalist imagination and geographical expansion in the Russian Far East, 1840–1865*. Cambridge: Cambridge University Press.
Becker, S. 1988. 'Russia's Central Asian empire, 1885–1917'. In *Russian Colonial Expansion to 1917*, edited by M. Rywkin, 235–56. London: Mansell.
Behrisch, L. 1999. 'Social disciplining in early modern Russia'. In *Institutionen, Instrumente und Akteure sozialer Kontrolle und Disziplinierung im frühneuzeitlichen Europa*, edited by H. Schilling and L. B. Behrisch, 325–57. Frankfurt am Main: Klostermann.
Bekasova, A. V. 2010. 'Izuchenie Rossiiskoi imperii ekspeditsiyami 1760–1780kh gg.: "vzglyad" estestvoispytatelei i formirovanie predstavlenii o gosudarstvennykh bogatstvakh', *Istoriko-biologicheskie issledovaniya*, [Studies in the History of Biology] 2/4: 13–34.
Bekasova, A. V. 2020. 'Voyaging towards the Future: the Brig *Rurik* in the North Pacific and the emerging science of the sea', *British Journal for the History of Science* 53/4: 469–95.
Berg, L. S. 1924. *Otkrytie Kamchatki i Kamchatskie ekspeditsii Beringa*. Petrograd & Moscow: Gosudarstvennoe izdatel'stvo.
Berg, L. S. 1946. 'Pervye russkie karty Kaspiiskogo morya v svyazi s voprosom o kolebaniyakh urovnya etogo morya'. In *Ocherki po istorii russkikh geograficheskikh otkrytii*. Moscow & Leningrad: Izdatel'stvo Akademii nauk.
Berg, L. S. 1956. 'Iz istorii geograficheskogo obrazovaniya v Leningradskom universitete'. In *Izbrannye trudy*, by L. S. Berg, vol. 1, 377–86. Moscow: Izdatel'stvo Akademii nauk.
Bielski, M. 1597. *Kronika Polska M. Bielskiego*. Krakow: n.p.
Black, J. L. 1983. 'G.-F. Mueller and the Russian Academy of Sciences contingent in the Second Kamchatka Expedition, 1733–43', *Canadian Slavonic Papers* 25: 235–52.
Black, J. L. 1986. *G.-F. Müller and the Imperial Russian Academy*. Kingston & Montreal: McGill-Queen's University Press.
Blum, J. 1968. *Lord and Peasant in Russia: From the ninth to the nineteenth century*. New York: Atheneum.
Blumenfeld, H. 1944. 'Russian city planning in the eighteenth and early nineteenth centuries', *Journal of the American Society of Architectural Historians* 4/1: 22–33.
Boeck, B. J. 2008. 'When Peter I was forced to settle for less: Coerced labour and resistance in a failed Russian colony (1695–1711)', *Journal of Modern History* 80/3: 485–514.
Bolkhovitinov, E. 1800. *Istoricheskoe, geograficheskoe i ekonomicheskoe opisanie Voronezhskoi gubernii, sobrannoe iz istorii, arkhivnikh zapisok i skazanii*. Voronezh: Tipografiya gubernskogo pravleniya.
Borisenko, A. Yu. 2022. 'Filipp Iogann Tabbert fon Stralenberg: nauchnye izyskaniya shvedskogo voennoplennogo v Sibiri', *Arkheologiya, etnografiya i antropologiya Evrazii* 40/2: 111–18.
Bowen, M. 1981. *Empiricism and Geographical Thought: From Francis Bacon to Alexander von Humboldt*. Cambridge: Cambridge University Press.
Brotton, J. 2012. *A History of the World in Twelve Maps*. London: Allen Lane.
Brown, G. I. 1991. 'The evolution of the term "mixed mathematics"', *Journal of the History of Ideas* 52/1: 81–102.
Buisseret, D. (ed.). 1992. *Monarchs, Ministers and Maps: The emergence of cartography as a tool of government in early modern Europe*. Chicago: University of Chicago Press.
Bulkeley, R. 2013. 'Bellinghausen's first accounts of his Antarctic voyage of 1819–1821', *Polar Record* 49/1: 9–25.
Butler, W. E. 2021. 'Peter the Great as comparative lawyer'. In *Magic, Texts and Travel: Homage to a Scholar, Will Ryan*, edited by J. M. Hartley and D. J. B. Shaw, 214–26. London: Study Group on Eighteenth-Century Russia.
Charykov, N. 1878–81. 'Vvedenie'. In *Kosmografiya 1670 g.*, 1–92. St Petersburg: Tipografiya V. S. Balasheva.

Chekin, L. 2006. *Northern Eurasia in Medieval Cartography: Inventory, text, translation, commentary*. Turnhout: Brepols.
Chrissidis, Nikolaos A. 2004. 'A Jesuit Aristotle in seventeenth-century Russia: Cosmology and the planetary system in the Slavo-Greco-Latin Academy'. In *Modernizing Muscovy: Reform and Social Change in Seventeenth-Century Russia*, edited by J. Kotilaine and M. Poe, 391–416. London: Routledge Curzon.
Clark, W., Golinski, J. and Schaffer, S. (eds.). 1999. *The Sciences in Enlightened Europe*. Chicago: University of Chicago Press.
Cooke, C. c. 1826. *Topographical and Statistical Description of North Wales*. London: Sherwood, Gilbert and Piper.
Cracraft, J. 1997. *The Petrine Revolution in Russian Imagery*. Chicago: University of Chicago Press.
Cracraft, J. 2004. *The Petrine Revolution in Russian Culture*. Cambridge, MA: Belknap Press.
Cross, A. G. 2014. *In the Lands of the Romanovs: An annotated bibliography of first-hand English-language accounts of the Russian Empire (1613–1917)*. Cambridge: Open Book Publishers.
Cruys, C. c. 1703. *Nauwkeurige afbeelding vande Rivier Don*. Amsterdam: Hendrik Donker.
Dahlmann, D. and Smagina, G. I. (eds.). 2015. *Nemtsy v Rossii: nemetskii mir Sankt Peterburga. Sbornik statei*. St Petersburg: Izdanie 'Rostok'.
Daniels, R. L. 1973. *V. N. Tatishchev: Guardian of the Petrine Revolution*. Philadelphia: Franklin.
Deacon, M. 1971. *Scientists and the Sea, 1650–1900: A study of marine science*. London: Academic Press.
Dixon, S. 1999. *The Modernisation of Russia, 1676–1825*. Cambridge: Cambridge University Press.
Dixon, S. 2009. *Catherine the Great*. London: Profile Books.
Donnelly, A. 1975. 'Peter the Great and Central Asia', *Canadian Slavonic Papers* 17: 202–17.
Donnelly, A. 1988. 'The mobile steppe frontier: the Russian conquest of Bashkiria and Kazakhstan to 1850'. In *Russian Colonial Expansion to 1917*, edited by M. Rywkin, 188–207. London: Mansell.
Dukes, P. 1982. *The Making of Russian Absolutism, 1613–1801*. London: Longman.
Eaton, H. L. 1967. 'Cadasters and censuses of Muscovy', *Slavic Review* 26/1: 55–69.
Edney, M. H. 1997. *Mapping an Empire: The geographical construction of British India, 1765–1843*. Chicago: University of Chicago Press.
Efremov, A. V. 1995. *Petr Ivanovich Rychkov: istorik i prosvetitel'*. Kazan': Tatarskoe knizhnoe izdatel'stvo.
Encyclopédie, ou Dictionnaire raisonnés des sciences, des arts et des métiers (1751–72). Geneva: Pellet.
Esakov, V. A. 1983. *Geografiya v Moskovskom universitete: ocherki organizatsii prepodavaniya razvitiya geograficheskoi mysli (do 1917 g.)*. Moscow: Nauka.
Evteev, O. A. 1958. 'V. N. Tatishchev i russkie gosudarstvennye s'emki pervoi poloviny XVIII v. (po materialam fonda Senata TsGADA)', *Voprosy geografii* 42: 189–95.
Fedyukin, I. 2019. *The Enterprisers: The politics of school in early modern Russia*. Oxford: Oxford University Press.
Fel', S. E. 1950. 'Petrovskie geodezisty i ikh uchastie v sozdanii russkoi kartografii XVIII veka', *Voprosy geografii* 17: 5–22.
Fel', S. E. 1960. *Kartografiya Rossii XVIII veka*. Moscow: Izdatel'stvo geodezicheskoi literatury.
Filimon, A. N. 2003. *Yakov Bryus*. Moscow: Chistye vody.
Finnegan, D. A., 2008. 'The spatial turn: Geographical approaches in the history of science', *Journal of the History of Biology* 41: 369–88.
Fisher, R. H. 1981. *The Voyage of Semen Dezhnev in 1648: Bering's precursor*, London: Hakluyt Society.
Fox, A. 2010. 'Printed questionnaires, research networks and the discovery of the British Isles, 1650–1800', *Historical Journal* 53/3: 593–621.
Fradkin, N. G. 1950. 'Instruktsiya dlya Akademicheskikh ekspeditsii, 1768–1774', *Voprosy geografii* 17: 213–18.
Fradkin, N. G. 1953. *Akademik I. I. Lepekhin i ego puteshestviya po Rossii v 1768–1773*, 2nd edition. Moscow: Gosudarstvennoe izdatel'stvo geograficheskoi literatury.
Fradkin, N. G. 1974. *S. P. Krasheninnikov*. Moscow: Nauka.
Franklin, S. and Bowers, K. (eds.). 2017. *Information and Empire: Mechanisms of governance in Russia, 1600–1850*. Cambridge: Open Book Publishers.
Fraser, A. 1973. *Cromwell: Our Chief of Men*. London: Orion.

Frost, O. W. 2003. *Bering: The Russian discovery of America*. New Haven, CT: Yale University Press.
Geografiya, ili kratkoe zemnogo kruga opisanie (1710). Moscow, Moskovskaya tipografiya.
Georgi, J. G. 1776–7. *Opisanie vsekh v Rossiiskom gosudarstve obitayushchikh narodov, takzhe ikh zhiteiskikh obryadov, obyknovenii, odezhd, zhilishch, ukrashenii, zabav, veroispovedanii i drugikh dostopamyatnostei*, parts 1–3. St Petersburg: Tipografiya K. B. Myullera.
Georgi, J. G. 1797–1802. *Geographische-physikalische und naturhistorische Beschreibung des russischen Reichs*, 5 vols. Königsberg: Nicolovius.
German, I. E. 1907. *Istoriya russkogo mezhevaniya*. Moscow: V. Rikhter.
Gibson, J. R. 1976. *Imperial Russia in Frontier America: The changing geography of supply of Russian America, 1784–1867*. New York: Oxford University Press.
Giddens, A. 1985. *A Contemporary Critique of Historical Materialism*, vol. 2: *The Nation State and Violence*. Cambridge: Polity.
Glacken, C. J. 1967. *Traces on the Rhodian Shore: Nature and culture in Western thought from ancient times to the end of the eighteenth century*. Berkeley: University of California Press.
Glete, J. 2002. *War and the State in Early Modern Europe*. London: Routledge.
Gmelin, S. G. 1770–4. *Reise durch Russland zur Untersuchung der drey Natur Reiche*, 4 parts. St Petersburg: Imperatorskaya Akademiya nauk.
Gnucheva, V. F. 1940. *Materialy dlya istorii ekspeditsii Akademii nauk v XVIII i XIX vekakh: khronologicheskie obzory i opisanie arkhivnykh materialov*. Moscow: Izdatel'stvo Akademii nauk SSSR.
Gnucheva, V. F. 1946. *Geograficheskii departament Akademii nauk XVIII veka*. Moscow & Leningrad: Izdatel'stvo Akademii nauk.
Gol'denberg, L. A. 1965. *Semen Ul'yanovich Remezov, Sibirskii kartograf i geograf (1642–posle 1720)*. Moscow: Nauka.
Gol'denberg, L. A. 1971. *Russian Maps and Atlases as Historical Sources*, translated by James R. Gibson. Toronto: B. V. Gutsell Department of Geography, York University.
Gol'denberg, L. A. and Postnikov, A. V. 1985. 'Development of mapping methods in Russia in the eighteenth century', *Imago Mundi* 37: 63–80.
Goldstein, T. 1980. *Dawn of Modern Science*. Boston: Houghton Mifflin.
Golinski, J. 1998. *Making Natural Knowledge: Constructivism and the history of knowledge*. Cambridge: Cambridge University Press.
Goodman, D. and Russell, C. A. (eds.). 1991. *The Rise of Scientific Europe, 1500–1800*. Sevenoaks: Hodder and Stoughton.
Güldenstädt, J. A. [Gil'denshtedt, I. A.]. 1809. *Geograficheskoe i statisticheskoe opisanie Gruzii i Kavkaza: iz puteshestviya akademika I. A. Gil'denshtedta*. St Petersburg: Imperatorskaya Akademiya nauk.
Guthrie, W. 1795. *A New Geographical, Historical and Commercial Grammar and Present State of the Several Kingdoms of the World*. London: Vernor and Hood.
Hankins, T. L. 1985. *Science and the Enlightenment*. Cambridge: Cambridge University Press.
Hannam, J. 2009. *God's Philosophers: How the medieval world laid the foundations of modern science*. London: Icon.
Hans, N. 1950–1. 'The Moscow School of Mathematics and Navigation', *Slavonic and East European Review* 29: 532–6.
Harley, J. B. and Woodward, D. (eds.). 1987. *The History of Cartography*, vol. 1. Chicago: University of Chicago Press.
Hartley, J. M. 1999. *A Social History of the Russian Empire, 1650–1825*. London: Longman.
Hartley, J. M. 2014. *Siberia: A history of the people*. New Haven, CT: Yale University Press.
Hartley, J. M. 2021. *The Volga: A history of Russia's greatest river*. New Haven, CT: Yale University Press.
Harvey, P. D. A. 1987. 'Local and Regional Cartography in Medieval Europe'. In *The History of Cartography*, vol. 1, edited by J. B. Harley, and D. Woodward, D., 464–98. Chicago: University of Chicago Press.
Harvey, P. D. A. 1991, *Medieval Maps*. London: The British Library.
Haywood, R. M. 1969. *Beginnings of Railway Development in Russia in the Reign of Nicholas I, 1835–1842*. Durham, NC: Duke University Press.
Heesen, A. te 2000. 'Boxes in nature', *Studies in the History and Philosophy of Science* 31/3: 381–403.
Herf, J. 1984. *Reactionary Modernism: Technology, culture and politics in weimar and the Third Reich*. Cambridge: Cambridge University Press.

Hintzsche, W. and Nickol, T. (eds.). 1996. *Die Grosse Nordische Expedition. Georg Wilhelm Steller (1709–1746): ein Lutheraner erforscht Sibirien und Alaska*. Gotha: Perthes.

Holsche, A. C. 1788. *Historisch-topographisch-statistische Beschreibung der Grafschaft Tecklenburg*. Berlin and Frankfurt: The Author.

Hughes, L. 1998. *Russia in the Age of Peter the Great*. New Haven, CT: Yale University Press.

Hundred Russian Maps and Atlases of the Eighteenth and Nineteenth Century: Annotated Catalogue of the Exhibition for the 14th International Conference on the History of Cartography, June 1991. 1991. Leningrad: Library of the Academy of Sciences of the USSR.

Huttenbach, H. R. 1988. 'Muscovy's penetration of Siberia: the colonization process, 1555–1689'. In *Russian Colonial Expansion to 1917*, edited by M. Rywkin, 70–102. London: Mansell.

Ides, E. Y. 1704. *Driejaarige reize naar China, te lande gedaan door den Moskovischen afgezant E. Ysbrants Ides*. Amsterdam: Pieter de Coup.

Ides, E. Y. 1748. 'The Travels of his Excellency E. Ysbrants Ides, Ambassador from Peter the Great to the Emperor of China'. In *Navigantium atque Itinerantium Bibliotheca: Or, a complete collection of voyages and travels*, vol. 2, 918–60. London: John Harris.

Iofa, L. E. 1949. *Sovremenniki Lomonosova: I. K. Kirilov i V. N. Tatishchev*. Moscow: Gosudarstvennoe izdatel'stvo geograficheskoi literatury.

Johnson, E. D. 2006. *How St Petersburg Learnt to Study Itself: The Russian idea of Kraevedenie*. University Park: Pennsylvania State University Press.

Jones, R. T. 2014. *Empire of Extinction: Russians and the North Pacific's strange beasts of the sea, 1741–1861*. Oxford: Oxford University Press.

Jones, R. T., Kraikovskii, A. and Lajus, J. 2023. 'Russia: the first Arctic empire, 1000–1917'. In *The Cambridge History of the Polar Regions*, edited by A. Howkins and P. Roberts, 153–80. Cambridge: Cambridge University Press.

Kabuzan, V. M. 1963. 'Nekotorye materialy dlya izucheniya istoricheskoi geografii Rossii XVIII–nachala XIX v.', *Problemy istochnikovedeniya* 11: 153–95.

Kain, R. and Baigent, E. 1992. *The Cadastral Map in the Service of the State: A history of property mapping*. Chicago: University of Chicago Press.

Kandirbai, G. 2002. *Land and People: The Russian colonization of the Kazak steppe*. Berlin: Klaus Schwarz Verlag.

Karimov, A. E. 1999. 'Gosudarstvo, morskoi flot i lesa', *Voprosy istorii estestvoznaniya i tekhniki* 3: 30–42.

Karimov, A. E. 2007. *Dokuda topor i sokha khodili: ocherki istorii zemel'nogo i lesnogo kadastra XVI–nachala XX veka*. Moscow: Nauka.

Karmannoi pochtovoi atlas vsei Rossiiskoi imperii razdelennoi na gubernii s pokazaniem glavnykh pochtovykh dorog. 1808. St Petersburg: Imperatorskoe Depo kart.

Karpeev, E. P. 2003. *Bol'shoi Gottorpskii globus*. St Petersburg: Muzei antropologii i etnografii (Kunstkamera).

Keenan, P. 2015. 'A space between two worlds: St Petersburg in the early eighteenth century'. In *The Uses of Space in Early Modern History*, edited by P. Stock, 97–124. Basingstoke: Palgrave Macmillan.

Kennedy, D. (ed.). 2014. *Reinterpreting Exploration: The West in the world*. Oxford: Oxford University Press.

Kimble, G. H. T. 1938. *Geography in the Middle Ages*. London: Methuen.

Kirilov, I. K. 1831. *Tsvetushchee sostoyanie Vserossiiskogo gosudarstva*. Moscow: Universitetskaya tipografiya.

Kirilov, I. K. 1977. *Tsvetushchee sostoyanie Vserossiiskogo gosudarstva*. Moscow: Nauka.

Kivelson, V. 2006. *Cartographies of Tsardom*. Ithaca, NY: Cornell University Press.

Kivelson, V. 2008. '"Between all parts of the universe": Russian cosmographies and imperial strategies in early modern Siberia and Ukraine', *Imago Mundi* 60/2: 166–81.

Kizel', A. and Solov'ev, V. 1960a. 'Vvedenie: Nikolai Milesku Spafarii (1636–1708)'. In *Nikolai Milesku Spafarii: Sibir' i Kitai*, 3–18. Kishinev: Gosudarstvennoe izdatel'stvo 'Karta Mondovenyasku'.

Kizel', A. and Solov'ev, V. 1960b. *Nikolai Milesku Spafarii: Sibir' i Kitai*. Kishinev: Gosudarstvennoe izdatel'stvo 'Karta Mondovenyasku'.

Knight, D. M. 2014. *Voyaging in Strange Seas: The great revolution in science*. New Haven, CT: Yale University Press.

Kochin, G. 1936. 'Pistsovye knigi v burzhuaznoi istoriografii', *Problemy istochnikovedeniya* 2: 145–86.

Kohn, H. (ed.). 1962. *The Mind of Modern Russia: Historical and political thought of Russia's great age*. New York: Harper & Row.
Kokkonen, P. 1992. 'Map printing in early eighteenth-century Russia', *Fennia* 170/1: 1–24.
Kolchinskii, E. I. (ed.). 2009. *Stelleriana v Rossii*. St Petersburg: Nestor-Istoriya.
Konvitz, J. W. 1987. *Cartography in France, 1660–1848: Science, engineering and statecraft*. Chicago: University of Chicago Press.
Kopelev, D. N. 2021. *Ot mysa Golovnina k Zemle Aleksandra I: rossiiskie krugosvetnye ekspeditsii v pervoi polovine XIX veke*. Moscow: ROSSPEN.
Kopelevich, Yu. Kh. 1977. *Osnovanie Peterburgskoi Akademii nauk*. Leningrad: Nauka.
Kosmografiya 1670 g. Kniga glagolemaya Kosmografiya sirech', opisanie vsego sveta zemel' i gosudarstv velikikh (1878–81). St Petersburg, tip. V. S. Balasheva.
Kotilaine, J. and Poe, M. (eds.). 2004. *Modernizing Muscovy: Reform and social change in seventeenth-century Russia*. London: Routledge.
Krasheninnikov, S. P. 1755. *Opisanie zemli Kamchatki*. St Petersburg: Imperatorskaya Akademiya nauk.
Krasheninnikov, S. P. 1764. *The History of Kamtschatka and the Kurilski Islands with the Countries Adjacent*, translated by James Grieve, MD. Gloucester: R. Raikes.
Krasheninnikov, S. P. 1973. *The History of Kamtschatka*. Richmond (London): Richmond Publishing.
Krusenstern, A. J. von. 1813a. *Voyage around the World, in the Years 1803, 1804, 1805, and 1806, by order of His Imperial Majesty Alexander the First, on Board the Ships Nadeshda and Neva*. Translated from the original German by R. B. Hoppner, 2 vols. London: J. Murray.
Krusenstern, A. J. von [Kruzenshtern, I, F.]. 1813b. *Atlas k puteshestviyu vokrug sveta kapitana Krusenshterna*. St Petersburg: Morskaya tipografiya.
Krusenstern, A. J. von [Kruzenshtern, I. F]. 1823–6. *Atlas Yuzhnogo morya, sochinennyi flota kapitan-komandirom Kruzenshternom; sobranie sochinenii sluzhashchikh razborom i iz'yasneniem Atlasa Yuzhnogo morya*. St Petersburg: Morskaya tipografiya.
Kuentzel-Witt, K. 2018. 'Peter the Great's intermezzo with G. W. Leibniz and G. Delisle: the development of geographical knowledge in Russia', *Quaestio Rossica* 6/1: 63–78.
Kuentzel-Witt, K. 2019. 'Georg Wilhelm Steller and Carl Heinrich Merck: German scientists in Russian service as explorers in the North Pacific in the eighteenth century'. In *Explorations and Entanglements: Germans in Pacific Worlds from the Early Modern Period to World War One*, edited by H. Berghoff, F. Biess and U. Strasser, 103–26. New York: Berghahn.
Kusov, V. S. 1993. *Chertezhi zemli russkoi XVI–XVIIi- vv*. Moscow: 'Russkii mir'.
Latour, B. 1987. *Science in Action: How to follow scientists and engineers through society*. Cambridge, MA: Harvard University Press.
Lebedev, D. M. 1949. *Geografiya v Rossii v XVII veke (dopetrovskoi epokhi)*. Moscow & Leningrad: Izdatel'stvo Akademii nauk SSSR.
Lebedev, D. M. 1950. *Geografiya v Rossii petrovskogo vremeni*. Moscow & Leningrad: Izdatel'stvo Akademii nauk SSSR.
Lebedev, D. M. 1956. *Ocherki po istorii geografii v Rossii v XV i XVI vv*. Moscow: Izdatel'stvo Akademii nauk SSSR.
Lebedev, D. M. 1957. *Ocherki po istorii geografii v Rossii XVIII v. (1725–1800 gg.)*. Moscow: Izdatel'stvo Akademii nauk SSSR.
Leckey, C. 2011. *Patrons of Enlightenment: The Free Economic Society in eighteenth-century Russia*. Newark: University of Delaware Press.
Leckey, C. 2017. 'Envisioning imperial space: P. I. Rychkov's Narratives of Orenburg, 1730s–70s', *REGION: Regional Studies of Russia, Eastern Europe and Central Asia* 6/2, 175–99.
Leckey, C. 2022. 'Birth of the thick journal: Gerhard Müller and *Monthly Compositions*', *Vivliofika: E-Journal of Eighteenth-Century Russian Studies* 10: 177–83.
Lehning, J. R. 2013. *European Colonialism since 1700*. Cambridge: Cambridge University Press.
Lepekhin, I. I. 1771–1805. *Dnevnye zapiski puteshestviya doktora Akademii nauk ad'yunkta Ivana Lepekhina po raznym provintsiyam Rossiiskogo gosudarstva v 1768–1772 gg.*, 4 vols. St Petersburg: Imperatorskaya Akademiya nauk.
Livingstone, D. N. 1992. *The Geographical Tradition: Episodes in the history of a contested enterprise*. Oxford: Blackwell.
Livingstone, D. N. 2003. *Putting Science in its Place: Geographies of scientific knowledge*. Chicago: University of Chicago Press.

Lukina, T. A. 1965. *Ivan Ivanovich Lepekhin*. Moscow & Leningrad: Nauka.
Luppov, S. P. 1973. *Kniga v Rossii v pervoi chetverti XVIII veke*. Leningrad: Nauka.
MacKenzie, D. 1988. 'The conquest and administration of Turkestan, 1860–85'. In *Russian Colonial Expansion to 1917*, edited by M. Rywkin, 208–34. London: Mansell.
Madariaga, I. de. 1981. *Russia in the Age of Catherine the Great*, London: Weidenfeld and Nicolson.
Maksimovich, L. M. 1788–9. *Novyi i polnyi geograficheskii slovar' Rossiiskogo gosudarstva*. Moscow: Imperatorskii Moskovskii universitet.
Marker, G. 1985. *Printing, Publishing and the Origins of Intellectual Life in Russia, 1700–1800*, Princeton: Princeton University Press.
Martin, J. 1986. *Treasure of the Land of Darkness: The fur trade and its significance for medieval Russia*. Cambridge: Cambridge University Press.
Martin, J. 1995. *Medieval Russia, 980–1584*. Cambridge: Cambridge University Press.
Materialy dlya istorii Imperatorskoi Akademii nauk, vol. 1. 1885. St Petersburg: Tipografiya Imperatorskoi Akademii nauk.
Materialy dlya istorii Voronezhskoi i sosednikh gubernii: Voronezhskie pistsovye knigi. 1891. Voronezh: Voronezhskii gubernskii statisticheskii komitet.
Mayhew, R. J. 2001. 'The effacement of early modern geography (c. 1600–1850): A historiographical essay', *Progress in Human Geography* 25/3: 383–401.
Mayhew, R. J. 2007. 'From hackwork to classic: The English editing of the *Geographia Generalis*'. In *Bernhard Varenius, 1622–1650*, edited by M. Schuchard, 239–57. Leiden: Brill.
Mel'nikova, E. A. 1998. *Obraz mira: geograficheskie predstavleniya v zapadnoi i severnoi Evrope, V–XIV vv*. Moscow: Yanus-K.
Merzon, A. Ts. 1956. *Pistsovye i perepisnye knigi XV–XVII vekov*. Moscow: Moskovskii Gosudarstvennyi istoriko-arkhivnyi institut.
Messerschmidt, D. G. 1962, 1964. *Forschungsreise durch Sibirien, 1720–1727*, parts 1–2. Berlin: Akademie Verlag.
Mil'kov, F. N. 1953. *P. I. Rychkov*. Moscow: Geografgiz.
Milov, L. V. 1965. *Issledovanie ob 'Ekononomicheskikh primechaniyakh' k general'nomu mezhevaniyu*. Moscow: Izdatel'stvo Moskovskogo universiteta.
Moon, D. 2010. 'The Russian Academy of Sciences expeditions to the steppes in the late eighteenth century', *Slavonic and East European Review*, 88/1–2: 204–36.
Moon, D. 2013. *The Plough that Broke the Steppes: Agriculture and environment on Russia's grasslands, 1700–1914*. Oxford: Oxford University Press.
Morrison, A. 2017. 'Russian settler colonialism'. In *The Routledge Handbook of the History of Settler Colonialism*, 313–26. New York: Routledge.
Morrison, A. 2020. *The Russian Conquest of Central Asia: A study in imperial expansion, 1814–1914*. Cambridge: Cambridge University Press.
Morse, J. 1789. *The American Geography, or a View of the Present Situation of the United States of America*, Elizabethtown, NJ: Shepard Kollock, for the Author.
Muetzell, A. A. 1821–5. *Neues topographisch-statistisch-geographisches Wörterbuch des Preussischen Staats*. Halle: Karl August Kümmel.
Novlyanskaya, M. G. 1966. *Filipp Iogann Stralenberg : Ego raboty po issledovaniyu Sibiri*. Moscow & Leningrad: Akademiya nauk SSSR.
Novlyanskaya, M. G. 1970. *Daniil Gotlib Messershmidt i ego raboty po issledovaniyu Sibiri*. Leningrad: Izdatel'stvo 'Nauka', Leningradskoe otdelenie.
Ogborn, M. 1998. *Spaces of Modernity: London's geographies, 1680–1780*. New York: Guilford Press.
Okenfuss, M. J. 1973. 'Russian students in Europe in the age of Peter the Great'. In *The Eighteenth Century in Russia*, edited by J. G. Garrard, 133–45. Oxford: Clarendon Press.
Okenfuss, M. J. 1995. *The Rise and Fall of Latin Humanism in Early Modern Russia: Pagan authors, Ukrainians and the resilience of Muscovy*. Leiden: Brill.
Oldfield, J. D. and Shaw, D. J. B. 2016. *The Development of Russian Environmental Thought: Scientific and geographical perspectives on the natural environment*. London: Routledge.
Opisanie Tobol'skogo namestnichestva 1982. Novosibirsk: Izdatel'stvo 'Nauka', Sibirskoe otdelenie.
Osipov, V. I. 1995. *Peterburgskaya Akademiya nauk i russko-nemetskie nauchnye svyazi v poslednei treti XVIII veka*. St Petersburg: PFA RAN.
Pagden, A. 1993. *European Encounters with the New World: from the Renaissance to Romanticism*. New Haven, CT: Yale University Press.

Pallas, P. S. 1771–6. *Reise durch verschiedene Provinzen des Russischen Reichs*, parts 1–3. St Petersburg: Imperatorskaya Akademiya nauk.
Pallas, P. S. 1784–8. *Flora Rossica*, 2 vols. St Petersburg: Imperatorskaya tipografiya.
Pallas, P. S. 1795. *Kratkoe fizicheskoe i topograficheskoe opisanie Tavricheskoi oblasti* . St Petersburg: Imperatorskaya tipografiya.
Pallas, P. S. 1801. *Bemerkungen auf einer Reise in die südlichen Statthalterschaften des russischen Reichs in den Jahren 1793 und 1794*. Leipzig: Gottfried Martini.
Pallas, P. S. 1811–31. *Zoogeographia Rosso-Asiatica*, 3 vols. St Petersburg: Imperatorskaya Akademiya nauk.
Parry, J. H. 1981. *The Age of Reconnaissance: Discovery, exploration and settlement, 1450–1650*. Berkeley: University of California Press.
Pearson, K. 1978. *The History of Statistics in the Seventeenth and Eighteenth Centuries*. London: Griffin.
Pekarskii, P. P. 1862. *Nauka i literatura v Rossii pri Petre Velikom*, vol. 1. St Petersburg: Tovarishchestvo 'Obshchestvennaya pol'za'.
Pennington, D. H. 1989. *Europe in the Seventeenth Century*, 2nd edition. London: Longman.
Perry, J. 1967. *An Account of Russia, Particularly of those remarkable Things done by the present Czar*. In *The State of Russia*. London: Frank Cass.
Pertsik, E. N. 1996. 'Konstantin Ivanovich Arsen'ev (1789–1865)'. In *Tvortsy otechestvennoi nauki: geografiya*, 103–14. Moscow: AGAR.
Petrov, V. A. 1950. 'Geograficheskie spravochniki XVII v.', *Istoricheskii istochnik* 5: 74–165.
Pickstone, J. V. 2000. *Ways of Knowing: A new history of science, technology and medicine*. Manchester: Manchester University Press.
Pleshcheev, S. I. 1790. *Pleshcheeva obozrenie Rossiiskoi imperii v nyneshnem ee novoustroennom sostoyanii, izdanie tret'e protivu pervykh dvukh umnozhennoe*. St Petersburg: Imperatorskaya Akademaya nauk.
Pleshcheev, S. I. 1792. *Survey of the Russian Empire: According to its present newly regulated state, divided into different governments ... translated from the Russian, with considerable additions, by James Smirnove*. London: J. Debrett.
Podrobnaya karta Rossiiskoi imperii i blizlezhashchikh zagranichnykh vladenii. 1805. St Petersburg: Imperatorskoe Depo kart.
Polevoi, B. P. 1994. 'Predislovie'. In *Opisanie zemli Kamchatki v dvukh tomakh*, by S. P. Krasheninnikov, 3–29. St Petersburg: Nauka.
Polunin, F. A. 1773. *Geograficheskii leksikon Rossiiskogo gosudarstva*. Moscow: Imperatorskii Moskovskii universitet.
Porter, R., (ed.). 2003. *The Cambridge History of Science*, vol. 4: *Eighteenth-Century Science*. Cambridge: Cambridge University Press.
Postnikov, A. V. 1989. *Razvitie krupnomasshtabnoi kartografii v Rossii*. Moscow: Nauka.
Postnikov, A. V. 1996. *Russia in Maps: A history of the geographical study and cartography of the country*. Moscow: Nash Dom/l'Age d'Homme.
Prokof'ev, N. I. 1988. 'Vvedenie'. In *Zapiski russkikh puteshestvennikov XVI–XVII vekov*, 5–20. Moscow: Sovetskaya Rossiya.
Ptukha, M. 1945. *Ocherki po istorii statistiki XVI–XVIII vekov*. Moscow: OGIZ.
Pushkarev, L. N. 1984. *Yurii Krizhanich: ocherk zhizni i tvorchestva*. Moscow: Nauka.
Raeff, M. 1983. *The Well-Ordered Police State: Social and institutional change through law in the Germanies and Russia*. New Haven, CT: Yale University Press.
Riasanovsky, N. V. 1969. *A History of Russia*, 2nd edition. Oxford: Oxford University Press.
Rossiiskii atlas, iz soroka chetyrekh kart sostoyashchii. 1792. St Petersburg: Gornoye uchilishche.
Rousseau, G. S. and Porter, R. (eds.). 1980. *The Ferment of Knowledge: Studies in the historiography of eighteenth-century science*. Cambridge: Cambridge University Press.
Rubinshtein, N. L. 1953. 'Topograficheskie opisaniya namestnichestv i gubernii XVIII v.: Pamyatniki ekonomicheskogo i geograficheskogo izucheniya Rossii', *Voprosy geografii* 31: 39–89, 106–10.
Rüegg, W. (ed.). 1992–2011. *A History of the University in Europe*, 4 vols. Cambridge: Cambridge University Press.
Rupke, N. 2011. 'Afterword: putting the geography of science in its place'. In *Geographies of Nineteenth-Century Science*, edited by D. N. Livingstone and C. W. J. Withers, 439–54. Chicago: University of Chicago Press.

Ryan, W. F. 1991. 'Navigation and the modernization of Petrine Russia: teachers, textbooks, terminology'. In *Russia in the Age of the Enlightenment: Essays for Isabel de Madariaga*, edited by R. Bartlett and J. M. Hartley, 75–105. London: Macmillan.
Ryan, W. F. 1999. *The Bathhouse at Midnight: An historical survey of magic and divination in Russia*. Stroud: Sutton Publishing.
Rybakov, B. A. 1974. *Russkie karty XV-nachala XVI veka*. Moscow: Nauka.
Rychkov, P. I. 1762. *Topografiya Orenburgskaya, to est' obstoyatel'noe opisanie Orenburgskoi gubernii*. St Petersburg: Imperatorskaya Akademaya nauk.
Rychkov, P. I. 1999. *Topografiya Orenburgskoi gubernii*. Ufa: Kitap.
Salmon, T. 1746. *The Modern Gazetteer: Or a short view of the several nations of the world*, London: The Author.
Sarazin, J-Y. 2015. 'Geografiya epokhi Prosveshcheniya: opyt proshlogo i novye gorizonty'. In *Vek Prosveshcheniya*, vol. 5: *Geografiya epokhi Prosveshcheniya: mezhdu voobrazheniem i real'nost'yu*, edited by S. Ya. Karp, 5–14. Moscow: Nauka.
Schuchard, M. (ed.). 2007a. *Bernhard Varenius, 1622–1650*. Leiden: Brill.
Schuchard, M. 2007b. 'Notes on *Geographia Generalis* and its Introduction to England and North America'. In *Bernhard Varenius, 1622–1650*, edited by M. Schuchard, 227–37. Leiden: Brill.
Schulze, L. 1985. 'The Russification of the St Petersburg Academy of Arts and Sciences in the eighteenth century', *British Journal for the History of Science* 18: 305–35.
Seegel, S. 2012. *Mapping Europe's Borderlands: Russian cartography in the age of empire*. Chicago: University of Chicago Press.
Serbina, K. N. 1950. *Kniga bol'shomu chertezhu*. Moscow & Leningrad: Izdatel'stvo Akademii nauk.
Shapin, S. 1996. *The Scientific Revolution*. Chicago: University of Chicago Press.
Shapin, S. 1998. 'Placing the view from nowhere: Historical and sociological problems in the location of knowledge', *Transactions of the Institute of British Geographers* (New Series) 23/1: 5–12.
Shaw, D. J. B. 1983. 'Southern frontiers of Muscovy, 1550–1700'. In *Studies in Russian Historical Geography*, edited by J. H. Bater and R. A. French, vol. 1: 118–42. London: Academic Press.
Shaw, D. J. B. 1989. 'The settlement of European Russia during the Romanov period (1613–1917)', *Soviet Geography* 30/3: 207–28.
Shaw, D. J. B. 1990a. 'The Odnodvortsy'. In *Landscape and Settlement in Romanov Russia*, edited by J. Pallot, J. and D. J. B. Shaw, 33–54. Oxford: Clarendon Press.
Shaw, D. J. B. 1990b. 'The province of Voronezh under Catherine the Great'. In *Landscape and Settlement in Romanov Russia*, edited by J. Pallot, J. and D. J. B. Shaw, 55–78. Oxford: Clarendon Press.
Shaw, D. J. B. 1990c. 'Landholding and commune origins among the Odnodvortsy'. In *Land Commune and Peasant Community in Russia*, edited by R. Bartlett, 106–19. London: Macmillan.
Shaw, D. J. B. 1991. 'Settlement and landholding on Russia's southern frontier in the early seventeenth century', *Slavonic and East European Review* 69/2: 232–56.
Shaw, D. J. B. 1996. 'Geographical practice and its significance in Peter the Great's Russia', *Journal of Historical Geography* 22: 160–76.
Shaw, D. J. B. 1999a. *Russia in the Modern World: A new geography*. Oxford: Blackwell.
Shaw, D. J. B. 1999b. '"A strong and prosperous condition": The geography of state building and social reform in Peter the Great's Russia', *Political Geography* 18: 991–1015.
Shaw, D. J. B. 2005. 'Mapmaking, science and state building in Russia before Peter the Great', *Journal of Historical Geography* 31: 409–29.
Shaw, D. J. B. 2007a. '2 November 1716: publishing geographies for Tsar Peter'. In *Days from the Reigns of Eighteenth-Century Russian Rulers* (Proceedings of a workshop dedicated to the memory of Professor Lindsey Hughes), edited by A. Cross, part 1: 61–9. Cambridge: Study Group on Eighteenth-Century Russia.
Shaw, D. J. B. 2007b. 'Bernhard Varenius' *Geographia Generalis* and the rise of modern geographical studies in Russia'. In *Bernhard Varenius, 1622–1650*, edited by M. Schuchard, 271–87. Leiden: Brill.
Shaw, D. J. B. 2010. 'Utility in natural history: Some eighteenth-century Russian perceptions of the living environment', *Istoriko-Biologicheskie Issledovaniya* [Studies in the History of Biology] 2/4: 35–50.
Shaw, D. J. B. 2021. 'The transition to "Enlightenment exploration": Russian expeditions to Siberia and the Far East in the late seventeenth and early eighteenth centuries'. In *Magic, Texts and*

Travel: Homage to a scholar, Will Ryan, edited by J. M. Hartley and D. J. B. Shaw, 227–44. London: Study Group on Eighteenth-Century Russia.

Shaw, D. J. B. 2023. 'Empire, settlement and environment: the Russian Empire and Donald Meinig's "macrogeography of Western imperialism"'. In *Thinking Russia's History Environmentally*, edited by C. Evtuhov, J. Lajus and D. Moon, 253–76. Oxford: Berghahn.

Shaw, D. J. B. and Oldfield, J. D. 2015. 'Soviet geographers and the Great Patriotic War, 1941–1945: Lev Berg and Andrei Grigor'ev', *Journal of Historical Geography* 47: 40–9.

Shchekatov, A. M. 1801–09. *Geograficheskii slovar' Rossiiskogo gosudarstva, sochinenyi v nastoyashchem odnogo vide*, 9 vols. Moscow: Universitetskaya tipografiya.

Shmurlo, E. F. 1888a. *Bibliograficheskii spisok literaturnykh trudov Kievskogo Mitropolita Evgeniya Bolkhovitinova*, part 1. St Petersburg: Tipografiya Iu. Zh. Frank.

Shmurlo, E. F. 1888b. *Mitropolit Evgenii kak uchenyi. Rannie gody zhizni, 1767–1804*. St Petersburg: Tipografiya V. S. Balasheva.

Sinclair, Sir J. 1973–83. *The Statistical Account of Scotland, 1791–1799*, edited by Sir John Sinclair, 20 vols. Wakefield: EP Publishing.

'Skaski Vladimira Atlasova o puteshestvii na Kamchatku'. 1988. In *Zapiski russkikh puteshestvennikov XVI–XVII vekov*, 415–28, 506–9. Moscow: Sovetskaya Rossiya.

Skelton, R. A. 1967. *The Military Survey of Scotland, 1747–1755*. Edinburgh: The Royal Scottish Geographical Society, Special Publication No. 1.

Smith, R. E. F. 1968. *The Enserfment of the Russian Peasantry*. Cambridge: Cambridge University Press.

Smith-Peter, S. 2007. 'Defining the Russian people: Konstantin Arsen'ev and Russian statistics before 1861', *History of Science* 45: 47–64.

Sobolevskii, A. I. 1903. *Perevodnaya literatura Moskovskoi Rusi*. St Petersburg: Imperatorskaya Akademiya nauk.

Solov'ev, A. I. 1955. 'Geografiya v Moskovskom universitete v dorevolyutsionnogo vremya'. In *Geografiya v Moskovskom universitete za 200 let, 1755–1955*, edited by K. K. Markov and Yu. G. Saushkin, 23–45. Moscow: Izdanie Moskovskogo universiteta.

Sorrenson, R. 1996. 'The ship as a scientific instrument in the eighteenth century', *Osiris* (2nd Series) 11: 221–36.

Spafarii, N.G. 1882. *Puteshestvie chrez Sibir' ot Tobol'ska do Nerchinska i granits Kitaya, russkogo poslannika Nikolaya Spafariya v 1675g*, edited by Yu. V. Arsen'eva ('Zapiski IRGO po otdeleniyu etnografii', vol. 10/1). St Petersburg: Imperatorskogo Russkogo geograficheskogo obshchestva.

Staffhorst, U. 2007. 'Miszellen zur *Geographia Generalis* des Bernhard Varenius'. In *Bernhard Varenius, 1622–1650*, edited by M. Schuchard, 215–25. Leiden, Brill.

Steller, G. W. 1751. 'De bestii marinis', *Novi Commentarii Academiae Scientiarum Imperialis Petropolitanae* 2: 289–398.

Steller, G. W. 1774. *Beschreibung von dem Land Kamtschatka, dessen Einwohnern, deren Sitten, Nahmen, Lebensart und verschiedenen Gewohnheiten*: Frankfurt & Leipzig: Johann Georg Fleischer.

Steller, G. W. 1988. *Journal of a Voyage with Bering, 1741–1742*, edited by O. W. Frost, translated by M. A. Engel and O. W. Frost. Stanford: Stanford University Press.

Steller, G. W. [Steller, G. V.]. 2011. *Opisanie zemli Kamchatki*. Petropavlovsk-Kamchatskii: Novaya kniga.

Steller, G. W. 2020. *Eastbound through Siberia: Observations from the Great Northern Expedition by Georg Wilhelm Steller*, translated and annotated by M. A. Engel and K. E. Willmore. Bloomington: Indiana University Press.

Stock, P. (ed.). 2015. *The Uses of Space in Early Modern History*. Basingstoke: Palgrave Macmillan.

Stock, P. 2019. *Europe and the British Geographical Imagination, 1760–1830*. Oxford: Oxford University Press.

Stout, F. J. 2015. *Exploring Russia in the Elizabethan Commonwealth: The Muscovy Company and Giles Fletcher the Elder, 1546–1611*. Manchester: Manchester University Press.

Strahlenberg, P. J. von. 1730. *Das Nord- und Östliche Theil von Europa und Asia*. Stockholm: The Author.

Strahlenberg, P. J. von. 1738. *An Historico-Geographical Description of the Northern and Eastern Parts of Europe and Asia; But more particularly of Russia, Siberia and Great Tartary*. London: W. Innys and R. Manby.

Strahlenberg, P. J. von [Stralenberg, F. I.]. 1797. *Istoricheskoe i geograficheskoe opisanie polunochno-vostochnoi chasti Evropy i Azii*, St Petersburg.
Sunderland, W. 2004. *Taming the Wild Field: Colonization and empire on the Russian steppe*. Ithaca, NY: Cornell University Press.
Sunderland, W. 2007. 'Imperial space: territorial thought and practice in the eighteenth century'. In *Russian Empire: Space, people, power, 1700–1930*, edited by J. Burbank, M. von Hagen and A. Remnev, 33–66. Bloomington: Indiana University Press.
Sytin, A. K. 2014. *Botanik Petr Simon Pallas*. Moscow: Tovarishchestvo nauchnykh izdanii.
Taagepera, R. 1988. 'An overview of the growth of the Russian empire'. In *Russian Colonial Expansion to 1917*, edited by M. Rywkin, M., 1–7. London: Mansell.
Tammiksaar, E. 2016. 'The Russian Antarctic Expedition under the command of Fabian Gottlieb von Bellingshausen and its reception in Russia and the world', *Polar Record* 52/2: 578–600.
Tammiksaar, E. and Kiik, T. 2013. 'Origins of the Russian Antarctic Expedition, 1819–21', *Polar Record* 49/2: 180–92.
Tatishchev, V. N. 1793. *Leksikon rossiiskoi istoricheskoi, geograficheskoi, politicheskoi i grazhdanskoi*. St Petersburg: Tipografiya gornogo uchilishcha.
Tatishchev, V. N. 1950. *Izbrannye trudy po geografii Rossii*. Moscow: Gosudarstvennoe izdatel'stvo geograficheskoi literatury.
Thrower, N. J. W. 1966. *Original Survey and Land Subdivision: A comparative study of the form and effect of contrasting cadastral surveys*. Chicago: Rand McNally.
Titov, A. A. 1890. *Sibir' v XVII veke: sbornik starinnykh russkikh statei o Sibiri i prilezhashchikh k nei zemlyakh*. Moscow: Tipografiya L. & A. Snegirevykh.
Topograficheskoe opisanie Kaluzhskogo namestnichestva. 1785. St Petersburg: Imperatorskaya Akademaya nauk.
Tsvetkov, M. A. 1953. 'Kartograficheskie materialy general'nogo mezhevaniya', *Voprosy geografii* 31: 90–110.
Turoma, S. and Waldstein, M. 2013. 'Introduction. Empire and space: Russia and the Soviet Union in focus'. In *Empire De/Centred: New Spatial Histories of Russia and the Soviet Union*, edited by S. Turoma and M. Waldstein, 1–28. Farnham: Ashgate.
Urness, C. 2003. 'The First Kamchatka Expedition in focus'. In *Under Vitus Bering's Command: New perspectives on the Russian Kamchatka Expeditions*, edited by P. U. Møller and N. O. Lind, 17–31. Aarhus: Aarhus University Press.
Varenius, B. 1718. *Geografiya general'naya; nebesnyi i zemnovodnyi krugi*, Moscow: Sinodal'naya tipografiya.
Varenius, B. 1733. *A Compleate System of General Geography ... Originally Written in Latin by Bernhard Varenius, M. D. Since Improved and Illustrated by Sir Isaac Newton and Dr. Jurin. And now Translated into English, with additional Notes ... by Mr. Dugdale. The Whole Revised and Corrected by Peter Shaw M. D*. 2 vols. London: Stephen Austen.
Vtoraya Kamchatskaya ekspeditsiya, part 1: *Dokumenty 1730–1733*. 2001. Moscow: Pamyatniki istoricheskoi mysli.
Vtoraya Kamchatskaya ekspeditsiya, part 2: *Dokumenty 1734–1736*. 2009. Moscow: Pamyatniki istoricheskoi mysli.
Vucinich, A. 1963. *Science in Russian Culture: A history to 1860*. Stanford: Stanford University Press.
Vulpius, R. 2016. 'Räumliches, Ordnen und Gewaltmobilisierung: Festungslinien an der südlichen russländischen Frontier im 18. Jahrhundert'. In *Umkämpfte Räume: Raumbilder, Ordnungswillen und Gewaltmobilisierung*, edited by U. Jureit, 139–57. Göttingen: Wallstein Verlag.
Wakefield, A. 2009. *The Disordered Police State: German cameralism as science and practice*. Chicago: University of Chicago Press.
White, R. C. 1968. 'Early geographical dictionaries', *Geographical Review* 58/4: 652–9.
Wilson, D. 2017. *Superstition and Science: Mystics, sceptics, truth-seekers and charlatans*. London: Robinson.
Winter, E. 1953. *Halle als Ausgangspunkt der deutschen Russlandkunde im 18. Jahrhundert* (Veröffentlichungen des Instituts für Slawistik, 2). Berlin: Akademie-Verlag.
Winter, E. [Vinter, E.]. 1971. *Nauchnoe issledovanie Sibiri v petrovskoe vremya. Semiletnyaya nauchnaya ekspeditsiya D. G. Messershmidta v Sibir' (1720–1727)*. Moscow: Nauka.

Winter, E. and Figurovskii, N. A. 1962. 'Einleitung'. In *D. G. Messerschmidt, Forschungsreise durch Sibirien, 1720–1727*, edited by E. Winter and N. A. Figurovskii, part 1: 1–20. Berlin: Akademie Verlag.

Withers, C. W. J. 2006. 'Eighteenth-century geography: Texts, practices, sites', *Progress in Human Geography* 30/6: 711–29.

Withers, C. W. J. 2007. *Placing the Enlightenment: Thinking geographically about the age of reason*. Chicago: University of Chicago Press.

Withers, C. W. J. and Mayhew, R. J. 2002. 'Rethinking "disciplinary" history: Geography in British universities, c. 1580–1887', *Transactions of the Institute of British Geographers* 27/1: 11–29.

Wood, A. 2011. *Russia's Frozen Frontier: A history of Siberia and the Russian far east, 1581–1991*. London: Bloomsbury Academic.

Woolf, S. 1989. 'Statistics and the modern state', *Comparative Studies in Society and History* 31/3: 588–604.

Yeo, R. 2001. *Encyclopedic Visions: Scientific dictionaries and Enlightenment culture*. Cambridge: Cambridge University Press.

Yeo, R. 2003. 'Classifying the sciences'. In *The Cambridge History of Science*, vol. 4: *Eighteenth-Century Science*, edited by R. Porter, 241–66. Cambridge: Cambridge University Press.

Zagorovskii, V. P. 1969. *Belgorodskaya cherta*. Voronezh: Izdatel'stvo Voronezhskogo universiteta.

Zapiski russkikh puteshestvennikov XVI–XVII vv. 1988. Moscow: Sovetskaya Rossiya.

Zyablovskii, E. F. 1842. *Rossiiskaya statistika*, part 1, 2nd edition. St Petersburg: Tipografiya Il'i Glazunova.

Index

References to figures appear in *italic* type; those in **bold** type refer to text boxes. References to chapter notes show both the page number and the note number (26n1).

Académie des sciences (France) 32, 76, 85, 89
'Academy Atlas' (*Atlas Russicus*) 91–3
Academy of Sciences
   archives and collections 83, 83–4, 91, 103
   expeditions 7, 94–5, 103, 130–6, 136, 143, 168–9
   founding and charter 65, 88, 148
   funding 147–8
   Geography Department 92, 150, 151
   mapping activities 149, 150
   members and office holders 61, 89, 90, 97, 102, 152, 156, 161
   publications 91–2, 102, 103, 110–14, 133, 137, 149–50
   questionnaire surveys 126, 127
Admiralty 73, 94
Afonin, M. A. 137
agriculture 14, 42–5, 131, 158–60, 162–3
Alaska 11, 78, 95–6, 168, 173
Aleksandrovskaya, Olga A. xi–xii, 65, 74–5, 84, 126, 137, 138, 143, 157
Alexander I, Tsar (r. 1801–25) 147–8, 168, 173–4
Alexander II, Tsar (r. 1855–81) 161
Alexis, Tsar (r. 1645–76) 56n2
ambassadorial journeys and reports 49–50
Amu Darya (Oxus) river 76, 77
Amur, River 51, 169–71, 173, 174n13
Anderson, M. S. 61

Andreev, Aleksandr Ignatievich 107
Anna, Tsarina (r. 1730–40) 84, 94
Antarctica 174n14
anthropology 82, 94, 96, 96–7, 101, 104, 105–6
Apothecaries' Chancellery 82, 83–4
Aral Sea 76, 117
Arkhangel'sk 48, 90, 135–6
Arsen'ev, Konstantin Ivanovich 157, 160–3
   Kratkaya vseobshchaya geografiya ('Short General Geography') 161
   Nachertanie statistiki rossiiskogo gosudarstva ('Outline of the Statistics of the Russian State') 161–3
   Statisticheskie ocherki Rossii ('Statistical Notes on Russia') 163
Asiatic Museum 148
Astrakhan' 11, 74, 75
Astrakhan' expedition (1768–72) 130–2
astronomy 30, 56n2, 92, 94–5
atamans 43, 56n18, 183
Atlas Novus (Blaeu) 29, 31, 32, 53
Atlas of the Counties of England and Wales (Saxton) 31
Atlas Rossiiskoi Imperii ('Atlas of the Russian Empire') 89
Atlas Russicus ('Academy Atlas') 91–3
Atlasov, Vladimir 51–2, 53
Aubrey, John, *Natural History of Wiltshire* 128
Azov, Sea of 41, 62, 140

Bacmeister, Hartwig Ludwig Christian, *Topograficheskie izvestiya* ('Topographical Information') 126
badger 113
Baikal, Lake 50–1, 79, 130, 140, 159
Baltic provinces 23, 62, 176
Baltic Sea 62
Bashkiria 13
Batu Khan 8
Beauplan, Guillaume de 35
Bekasova, Alexandra 172–3
Beketov, Petr 51
Bekovich-Cherkasskii, Aleksandr 76
Belarus 47–8, 133
Bellingshausen, Fabian von 174n14
Bering, Vitus 84, 93–6, 98, 102, 103
Bielski, Marcin 35, 54
Billings, Joseph 95, 136
Black Sea 62, 117
Blome, Richard 68
Blumentrost, Johann Deodat 82
Bolkhovitinov, Evgenii 152–5
Bol'shoi chertezh ('Great Map') 35–7
'Book of the Great Map' (*Kniga Bol'shomu Chertezhu*) 35–7, 46–7
Boris Godunov, Tsar (r. 1598–1605) 35, 37
Brinkin, Dr Theodor (Fedor) 169
Bruce, James (Bryus, Yakov) 62, *63*, 66, 66–7, 90, 125
Bugge, Professor Thomas 169
Bukhara 13
Büsching, Anton Friedrich 156
    Neue Erdbeschreibung ('New Earth Description') 156
Byzantine tradition 18, 19, 32

cadastral surveys
    fifteenth century 40
    sixteenth and seventeenth centuries 40–5, 55
    under Peter the Great 7, 72–4
    post-Petrine 120
    under Catherine the Great 120–5
    purpose of 39, 45, 71–2
Cambridge History of Science 4

cameralism 131, 137–8, 155–64
Caspian Sea 62, 75–6, 85
Cassini survey of France 32, 89–90
Catherine I, Tsarina (r. 1725–27) 83, 87
Catherine the Great (Catherine II) 87, 117, 119, 130, 145n12, 147
Catherine the Great: reign (1762–96)
    overview 117–19
    administrative reforms 149
    cadastral survey 120–5
    Charter to the Towns 174n3
    expeditionary activity 130–7
    geographical publications 138–44
    higher education 137–8
    mapping 121–5, 149–50
    questionnaire surveys 125–6, 127
    secularization of Church land 145n6
    topographical descriptions 126–30
Catholic Church 18, 19, 23
Caucasus 13
censuses 40, 72
Central Asia 14, 74–7
Chaadaev, Petr 1–2
Charykov, Nikolai 53–5
Chebotarev, Kh. A. 137
Chelyuskin, Semen 95
Cherepanov, N. E. 137
China 49–50, 78–9, 94
Chirikov, Aleksei 93, 96
church land 124, 145n6
Chusovaya river 80
class structure 21–3, 41–2
classical culture 18–19, 32
clergy 18–19, 21, 22
climate 14, 98, 106, 109, 111, 132
climates (*strany*) 70
Cook, James 95, 170, 172
Copernicus, Nicholas 31
Cosmas Indicopleustes, *Christian Topography* 18, 54
cosmographies 53–5
Cossacks 11, 43, 56n18, 183
Cracraft 71

Cracraft, James 70
Crimea 37, 56n14, 117, 130, 136, 159
Cromwell, Oliver 29
Cross, Anthony 26n1
Cruys, Cornelius 62

De l'Isle de la Croyère, Louis 94–5, 97
Delisle, Claude 90
Delisle, Guillaume 61, 64, 89, 90
Delisle, Joseph-Nicolas 61, 65, 89, 90, 91, 92, 94
Denbei (Japanese captive) 78
Dezhnev, Semen 51, 78
dictionaries *see* geographical dictionaries
Dixon, Simon 19–20, 22
Don, River 41, 43, 61–2, 131, 154, 178
Donnelly, Alton S. 75

early modern, use of term 26n2
Eaton, H. L. 40–1
economic geography 72, 121–5, 126, 152, 157–9, 162–3
Economic peasants 124
education 21–2, 64–5, 137–8, 148
Elizabeth, Tsarina (r. 1741–62) 119, 120
Elsevier, Louis 68
Engel, Margritt 103
engraving 56n4
Enisei, River 95, 128, 140
Ermak 11
etching 56n4
ethnography 82, 94, 96, 96–7, 104, 105–6, 133–6, 171–2
Euler, Leonhard 92
Evreinov, Ivan 77, 78
expeditions
    sixteenth and seventeenth centuries 50–2
    under Peter the Great 74–84, 93
    post-Petrine 93–7
    under Catherine the Great 130–7
    early nineteenth century 166–73

Falck, Johann Peter 130–1
farming 14, 42–5, 131, 158–60, 162–3
Farquharson, Henry 64–5, 66
Fedorov, Ivan 95
Fedyukin, Igor 86n4
food and diet 98–9
foreign language translation 35
forest surveys 42–3, 72, 73–4, 122–5
Fox, Adam 125
Fradkin, N. G. 131, 134, 135
Fraser, Antonia 29
Free Economic Society 119, 126, 147–8, 160
Frost, Orcutt W. 96

General Survey 120–5
geodesists 64, 64–5, 77, 89, 90–1, 121
geographical dictionaries 108, 109–10, 138, 142–4, 164–6, *165*
Georgi, Johann 138
Gerritsz, Hessel 35
Giddens, Anthony 71
Glete, Jan 5–6
Gmelin, Johann Georg 87, 94, 96, 96–7, 97, 102, 103, 112
Gmelin, Samuel 154
Gmelin, Samuel Gottlieb 131
Golden Horde 8–10
Gordon, Patrick 58
Gottorp globe 29–30
Grand Embassy (Peter the Great) 58, 62, 66
Grice, Richard 64
Grieve, James 98, 101
Güldenstädt, Johann Anton 131, 139
Guthrie, William, *New Geographical, Historical and Commercial Grammar* 141, 142
Gvozdev, Mikhail 95
Gwyn, Stephen 64–5

Harvey, P. D. A. 34
Heesen, Anke te 83

Heim, Johann 138
Hereford *mappa mundi* 4
Hermann, Carl Theodor von 161
Hintzsche, Wieland 102
Horner, Dr Jean Gaspard 169, 172
Hübner, Johann, *Kurtze Fragen* 66–7, 69
Huttenbach, Henry R. 175
Huygens, Christiaan, *Cosmotheoros* 66
hydrographic studies 95, 170

Ides, Evert Ysbrants 79–81
illnesses and treatments 98–9, 127, 131
India 74, 75, 76
Ingermanland 120, 176
Inokhodtsev, Petr Borisovich 149
Irkutsk 90–1
Islen'ev, Ivan Ivanovich 149
itineraries 46–8
Ivan the Terrible (r. 1533–84) 11, 32, 35, 166
Ivanov, Kurbat 51

James I and VI, King 31
Japan 77, 78, 94, 168, 170, 171
John of Damascus 18
Jurin, James 68

Kabuzan, V. M. 127
Kaluga province 121, 125, 128
Kamchatka 51–2, 77, 93–6, 97, 97–106
Kamchatka Expeditions, First and Second 84, 92, 93–6, 102, 143
Karimov, Aleksei E. 45, 73, 74, 120
Kazakhstan 13
Kazan' 11, 90–1, 166
Khabarov, Erofei 51
Khiva 13, 76
Kievan Russia 8
Kiprianov, V. O. 66
Kireevskii, Grigorii 41

Kirilov, Ivan Kirilovich 64, 89, 90, 91, 110–11
Tsvetushchee sostoyanie Vserossiiskogo gosudarstva ('Flourishing Condition of the All-Russian State') 106–7, 125–6
Kivelson, Valerie 33–5, 39
Kniga Bol'shomu Chertezhu ('Book of the Great Map') 35–7, 46–7
Kokand 13
Kokkonen, Pellervo 93
Kolyma, River 51, 95, 136
Kosmografiya 1670g ('Cosmography of 1670') 53–5
Kotzebue, Otto von 172–3
Krasheninnikov, Stepan 95, 96–7, 102
  'Description of the Land of Kamchatka' 97–101
Krasil'nikov, Andrei Dmitrievich 111
Krizhanich, Yurii 53, 56n18
Krusenstern, Adam Johann von 166–73
  Atlas k puteshestviyu vokrug sveta ('Atlas of the Voyage around the World') 172
  Atlas Yuzhnogo Morya ('Atlas of the Southern Sea') 172
Krusenstern, Adam von 147
Kunstkammer ('Cabinet of Curiosities') 83, 97, 132, 166
Kusov, Vladimir Svyatoslavovich 34

land ownership 124, 145n1
  see also state service
land surveys *see* cadastral surveys
Langsdorff, Dr Georg von 169
Laptev, Dmitrii 95
Laptev, Khariton 95
Latin and Greek 18–19, 32
Lebedev, Dmitrii M. xi–xii, 49, 52, 54, 74, 78, 80–1, 81
Lefort, Franz 58
Leibniz, Gottfried Wilhelm 64, 65, 83, 94
Lena, River 95, 100, 102, 104, 136
Lepekhin, Ivan Ivanovich 130, 132–6
  'Daily Notes' 133–4

Lisyanskii, Yurii Fedorovich 169–70, 173
local studies (*kraevedenie*) 152–5
Lomonosov, Mikhail Vasilievich 126
Luppov, S. P. 61
Luzhin, Fedor 77, 78
Lykov, Bogdan 54

Magnitskii, Leontii 66
Makowski, Tomasz 35
Maksimovich, Lev 144, 164
  Novyi i polnyi geograficheskii slovar' ('New and Full Geographical Dictionary') 143–4
mapping
  sixteenth and seventeenth centuries 31–9, 55
  under Peter the Great 61–4, 75–6, 77
  post-Petrine 89–93, 95, 96
  under Catherine the Great 121–5, 149–50
  late-eighteenth and early-nineteenth centuries 149–51, 169
maps, role and importance of 6–7
Marquesas Islands 170, 171–2
Massa, Isaac, map *10*, 35
mathematical approaches 33, 69–70, 89–90, 150, 151
  see also statistical approaches
Mayhew, Robert J. 27n7
medicines 98–9, 127, 131
Meier, Captain (German cartographer) 75–6
Meinig, Donald W. 14, 16, *17*
Mengden, Yu. A. 62, *63*, 66
Menshikov, Prince Aleksandr 87
Mercator, Gerardus 31, 32, 54, 92
Messerschmidt, Daniel Gottlieb 81–4, 94, 102, 110
military maps 149–50, 151, 176–7
military service *see* state service
Mil'kov, F. N. 112
Milov, L. V. 121, 125
mineral resources 72, 131, 135

Mineralogical Society 148
Mongol-Tatar conquest 8–10
Mordvinov, Admiral Nikolai 168
Morse, Jedediah, *The American Geography* 141
Moscow 8, 67, 121, 126
Moscow School of Mathematics and Navigation 64–5
Moscow University 3, 119, 137–8, 144, 148
Moskvitin, Ivan 51
Müller, Gerhard Friedrich 84, 92, 94, 96, 96–7, 97, 102, 103, 112, 137, 143, 156
Muscovy Company 20

Nagasaki 170, 171
natural history 82–4, 94–5, 96–105, 111–14, 129, 131–6
Nauwkeurige afbeelding vande Rivier Don ('Atlas of the Don') 62
navigation 170
Neva, River 77, 164
'New Monthly Compositions' (Academy of Sciences) 133, 137
Newton, Isaac 68
Nicholas I, Tsar (r. 1825–55) 161, 174n6
nobility 22–3, 124
North Pacific 94–6, 167–9, 172
Novgorod 10–11, 40, 73–4, 126
Novikov, Nikolai Ivanovich 37, 79, 138
Novlyanskaya, M. G. 81
Nukahiwa 171–2

Ob', River 11, 80, 95, 136, 140, 160
oceanography 169
Okhotsk 11
Olearius, Adam 29, 30
Opisanie rasstoyaniyu stolits narochitykh gradov slavnykh gosudarstv zemel' – grada Moskvy ('Description of the Distance from Moscow to the Most Important Cities of Foreign States') 46, 47–8, **48**

Opisanie Tobol'skogo namestnichestva ('Description of Tobol'sk Province') 127–8
Orenburg 111–14
Orenburg Expedition (1734–44) 90–1, 110–11
Orenburg expedition (1768–74) 130–6
Ortelius, Abraham 31, 32
Ovtsyn, Dmitrii 95
Ozeretskovskii, Nikolai Yakovlevich 132, 133, 136

Pallas, Peter Simon 130, 134, 136–7, 138, 138–9
Paul I, Tsar (r. 1796–1801) 147–8, 149, 173
Pavlovsk 154
Peace of Andrusovo 47–8
peasantry 21–2, 23, 124
Perry, John 57, 60
Persia 13, 74, 75
Peter the Great
　attitude to nature 77
　character and influences 29–30, 57, 58, 60–1
　correspondence with Leibnitz 64, 65, 82, 94
　death and succession 87
　intellectual curiosity 60–1
　library 61
Peter the Great: reign (1682–1725)
　educational and scientific initiatives 64–5
　geographical endeavour
　　cadastral surveys 72–4
　　embrace of science 85–6
　　European character 85
　　expeditionary activity 74–84, 93
　　mapping 61–4, 75–6, 77
　　other surveys and data collection 72
　　printing and publishing 66–71, 85
　reforms
　　context to 58–9
　　cultural changes 60
　　economic changes and taxation 7, 59–60, 72
　　government administration 59, 62
　　modernization not Westernization 20, 60
　　state service 7, 22, 60, 73
　　town planning 63–4
Petlin, Ivan 49
Petropavlovsk 96
Petrov, V. A. 46–8
Pickstone, John V. 81
Pleshcheev, Sergei Ivanovich 139
　Obozrenie Rossiiskoi imperii ('Survey of the Russian Empire') 139–41
Podovskii, Il'ya Kirilovich 124
Podrobnaya karta Rossiiskoi imperii ('100-page Atlas') 150
Poland 23, 176
Polikarpov, Fedor 68, 70–1
Polish-Lithuanian Commonwealth 176
Polotskii, Simeon 32
Polunin, Fedor 143, 164
　Geograficheskii leksikon ('Geographical Lexicon') 138
　Geograficheskii leksikon Rossiiskogo gosudarstva ('Geographical Lexicon of the Russian State') 143
Polynesia 171–2
Popov, Petr 78
Porter, Roy 4, 27n5
postal services 46, 47, 48
Postnikov, A. V. 91, 149, 151
Potemkin, Prince Grigorii 145n12
Poyarkov, Vasilii 51
printing and publishing
　sixteenth and seventeenth centuries 20, 32
　under Peter the Great 66–8
　post-Petrine 97–101, 103, 106–14
　under Catherine the Great 138–44
　late-eighteenth and early-nineteenth centuries 152–5, 156–66
Prokof'ev, N. I. 49

Prokopovich, Archbishop Feofan 84
Pronchishchev, V. M. 95
property maps (pre-Petrine) 34–5
Protestant Church 23
Ptolemy, Claudius 3–4, 18
publishing *see* printing and publishing

questionnaire surveys 106–7, 108, 125–6, 127, 128–9

Raeff, Marc 71–2, 156
regional maps 35, 37–9, 111–14
Reichel, Johann Gottfried 137
Remezov, Semen Ul'yanovich 38–9, 50, 53
Rezanov, Nikolai 168, 169, 170
rose pelican 113
Rossiiskii atlas, iz soroka chetyrekh kart sostoyashchii ('Russian Atlas Consisting of 44 Maps') 150
Rowley, Alexander 29
Roy, William 6
Rubinshtein, N. L. 126–7, 152
Rumyantsev, Count Nikolai 168, 172
Russian empire
  climate 14
  development of 8–13
  education 21–2
  intellectual isolation 18–19
  maps *9, 10, 12, 15, 17*
  modernization 19–22, 30, 60
  natural environment 14, *15*
  religion 18–19, 21, 22, 23
  settlement by ethnic Russians 14–16
  Western influences 20, 60
Russian Geographical Society 7, 50, 148, 161, 173
Russian Orthodox Church 18–19, 21, 22
Russian State Archive of Ancient Acts (RGADA) 145n2
Russian-American Company 168, 174n10
Ryan, Will 18, 19
Rychkov, Petr Ivanovich 110–11

Topografiya Orenburgskaya ('Topography of Orenburg Province') 110, 111–14, 126

St Petersburg 59–60, 67, 73–4
St Petersburg Naval Academy 65
Sakhalin 170–1, 174n13
Samoyeds 81
Sarazin, Jean-Yves 32
Sarychev, Gavriil Andreevich 136
Savich, D. V. 137
Schlözer, August Ludwig von 156–7
  Neuverändertes Russland 157
Schmidt, Jakob Friedrich 149, 150
Schoonebeek, Adriaan 66
Schubert, Friedrich von 150
Schumacher, Johann Daniel von 76
Senate 59, 89, 91–2, 121, 124–5, 125, 127, 150
Serbina, Kseniya Nikolaevna 35
serfdom 21–2, 23, 43–5, 161, 162–3
Service Lands Chancellery 34, 34–5, 40
servitors 22, 41–5
  see also state service
Shafirov, Petr Pavlovich 65, 83
Shchekatov, Afanasii Mikhailovich 164
  Geograficheskii slovar' ('Geographical Dictionary') 164–6, *165*
shipbuilding 61, 61–2
Siberia 11, 38, 39, 50, 51–2, 53, 77–84, 90–1, 92, 94, 98, 104–5, 107–8, 127, 135–6, 140–1, 159–60
Sibir' Khanate 11
Sinclair, Sir John, *Statistical Account of Scotland* 128–9
Skjelkrup (Danish cartographer) 75
Smith-Peter, Susan 155
social strata 21–3, 41–5
Society of Naturalists 148
Soimonov, Petr Aleksandrovich 128
sokha (unit of assessment) 40, 184
Sontsov, A. B. 153
Spafarii, Nikolai Milesku 49–50, 53
Spangberg, Martin 93, 94

Stadukhin, Mikhail 51
state service 7, 22, 39, 41–5, 73
statistical approaches 125, 155–64
    see also cameralism
Steller, Georg Wilhelm 97, 98, 99, 101–4
    'De bestiis marinis' 103
    Description of the Land of Kamchatka 105–6
Strabo 4
Strahlenberg, Philipp Johann von (aka Tabbert), 82, 84, 108–9
    Das Nord- und Ostliche Teil von Europa und Asia ('The Northern and Eastern Part of Europe and Asia') 108–10
Strakhov, P. I. 137
Stroganov (merchant family) 11
surveying *see* mapping
Sweden 59, 62, 72, 176

Table of Ranks 22, 60
Tatarchukovo, Mariya Fedorovna 122
Tatishchev, Vasilii Nikitich 84, 90–1, 92, 107–8, 109, 111, 125–6, 138
    Izbrannye trudy ('Selected Works') 107–8
    Leksikon rossiiskoi ('Russian Lexicon') 108, 142–3
taxation 7, 39, 40, 41, 59–60, 72–3
Tenner, Carl Friedrich 151
Tessing, Jan 62, 66
Theatre of the Empire of Great Britain (Speed) 31
Tilesius von Tilenau, Dr Wilhelm Gottlieb 169, 172
Titov, A. A. 53
Tobol'sk 80, 82, 127–8, 129, 160
topographical surveys and descriptions 110, 111–14, 126–30
Tournefort, Joseph Pitton de 82–3
trading links 20, 49, 49–50, 167
translations of foreign literature 67–71
Treaty of Nerchinsk (1689) 11

triangulation 89–90, 150, 151
tribute (*yasak*) 51
Truscott, John 149, 150
Tsaritsyn 131, 136
Turanian tiger 113

Ukraine 23, 47–8, 117, *118*, 145n5
universities 3, 119, 137–8, 148
Urals 79–80, 90–1, 102, 110–14, 139–40, 182
Urness, Carol 94

Varenius, Bernhardus 68
    Geographia Generalis 61, 66, 67–71
Veniaminov, P. D. 137
'Verst-Book' (*Poverstnaya kniga*) 46, 47, **47**
Vinius, Andrei A. 46
Volga, River 8, 11, 48, 74-5, 117, 130–1, 133–6, 140, 164, 166
Voltaire 117
Voronezh 41–5, *44*, 62, 73, 122–4, *123*, 152–5
Vucinich, Alexander 18, 29, 87

war 59, 61–2, 62, 176–7
    see also military maps
weather 83, 106, 107, 111, 132
White Sea 54, 134, 136
Wilbrecht, Alexander (A. M. Vil'brekht) 150
wildlife 80
Willmore, Karen 103
Witsen, Nicolaes 35, 61
Wolff, Christian 65
woodcuts 56n4
Woolf, Stuart 155
Wrangel, Ferdinand von 95

Zapiski russkikh puteshestvennikov ('Notes of Russian Travellers') 53
Zuev, Vasilii 136
Zyablovskii, Evdokim Filippovich 157
    Rossiiskaya statistika ('Russian Statistics') 157–60

Milton Keynes UK
Ingram Content Group UK Ltd.
UKHW020022290924
448954UK00016B/397